D1084326

JUSTICE

Views from the Social Sciences

CRITICAL ISSUES IN SOCIAL JUSTICE

Series Editor: **MELVIN J. LERNER**
University of Waterloo
Waterloo, Ontario, Canada

A Continuation Order Plan is available for this series. A continuation order will bring
delivery of each new volume immediately upon publication. Volumes are billed only
upon actual shipment. For further information please contact the publisher.

JUSTICE

Views from the Social Sciences

Edited by
Ronald L. Cohen
Bennington College
Bennington, Vermont

PLENUM PRESS • NEW YORK AND LONDON

Library of Congress Cataloging in Publication Data

Justice: views from the social sciences.

(Critical issues in social justice)
Includes bibliographies and index.
1. Justice. 2. Social justice. 3. Distributive justice. I. Cohen, Ronald L. (Ronald Lee),
1944–   . II. Series.
JC578.J89 1986   320′.01′1   86-20503
ISBN 0-306-42256-5

© 1986 Plenum Press, New York
A Division of Plenum Publishing Corporation
233 Spring Street, New York, N.Y. 10013

Printed in the United States of America

Contributors

Allen Buchanan
Department of Philosophy
University of Arizona
Tucson, Arizona

Ronald L. Cohen
Social Science Division
Bennington College
Bennington, Vermont

Arthur DiQuattro
Department of Political Science
Texas A & M University
College Station, Texas

Lita Furby
Eugene Research Institute
474 Willamette St.
Eugene, Oregon

Deborah Mathieu
Department of Political Science
University of Arizona
Tucson, Arizona

Laura Nader
Department of Anthropology
University of California
Berkeley, California

Steve Rytina
Department of Sociology
Harvard University
Cambridge, Massachusetts

Karol Soltan
Department of Government and Politics
University of Maryland
College Park, Maryland

Andrée Sursock
Department of Anthropology
University of California
Berkeley, California

Stephen T. Worland
Department of Economics
University of Notre Dame
Notre Dame, Indiana

Acknowledgments

In bringing this project to its somewhat belated conclusion, I have had the advice, encouragement, and help of many people and several organizations. I am pleased to take this opportunity to thank them.

Some of the early work on this project was undertaken while I held a National Endowment for the Humanities Fellowship for College Teachers, for which I am grateful. Some of the work was completed while I was a visitor at the Research Center for Group Dynamics at the Institute for Social Research; I would like to thank all those associated with the center, especially Eugene Burnstein and Robert Zajonc. I would also like to thank Bennington College for providing me many of the resources for completing this work.

There are many specific individuals who helped in many different ways: Lita Furby, Jerald Greenberg, Kenneth Kensinger, Joanna Kirkpatrick, Michael McPherson, Andrew Pienkos, and Joanne Schultz—thanks. Eliot Werner and Melvin Lerner also provided encouragement and help for which I am grateful.

Becky, Jessie, and Hannah Cohen have taught me much about justice, but they will also be among the first to say that I have a lot more to learn. Judy Cohen continues to provide the most important criticism, advice, encouragement, and help. She has also taught me much about justice and compassion.

Contents

4

Political Studies and Justice 85

Arthur DiQuattro

5

Sociology and Justice 117

Steve Rytina

CHAPTER 1

Introduction

Ronald L. Cohen

Justice is a central moral standard in social life. It is invoked in judging individual persons and in judging the basic structure of societies. It has been described as akin to a "human hunger or thirst" (Pascal, *Pensées*, cited in Hirschman, 1982, p. 91), "more powerful than any physical hunger, and endlessly resilient" (Pitkin, 1981, p. 349). The most prominent contemporary theory of justice proceeds from the claim that justice is "the first virtue of social institutions, as truth is systems of thought" (Rawls, 1971, p. 3).

However, as the following chapters demonstrate, justice has a complex and controversial history. If, as has been claimed, justice is a central category of human thought and a central aspect of human motivation, can it also be the case that to invoke justice is no more than "banging on the table: an emotional expression which turns one's demand into an absolute postulate" (Ross, 1959, p. 274)? If justice is the first virtue of social institutions, can the concept of social or economic justice at the same time be "entirely empty and meaningless" so that any attempt to employ it is "either thoughtless or fraudulent" (Hayek, 1976, pp. xi–xii)?

In a formal sense, justice concerns ensuring that each person receives what she or he is due. But what is each due; in virtue of what condition, conduct, or characteristic is this to be established, and how? Controversy over these questions appears throughout the histories of different societies, in varying forms across human cultures, and in a wide variety of contemporary settings. It appears in informal social gatherings and private lives, in settings structured for public discourse on matters of public debate and policymaking

RONALD L. COHEN • Social Science Division, Bennington College, Bennington, Vermont 05201.

1

(e.g., town meetings, parliaments, legislatures) and in settings structured explicitly to develop theory and research relevant to the controversy (universities and scholarly communities).

Controversy over the meaning and interpretation of justice is closely related to the shifting tides of conflict and cooperation that characterize social life. Different interpretations of justice and disagreements over the existence of injustice and what it demands have transformed individual lives, relationships, policies, and entire societies, and there is every reason to expect this to continue.

These controversies exist, and they reappear, because theories of justice have cutting or dulling edges. In the assumptions they make about persons and their social relations, theories of justice suggest the limits within which human social life must operate. In suggesting these limits, of course, these theories also identify arenas of individual and collective choice among alternative forms of conduct and social and institutional structures. In discussing what people are due and why, and in fashioning explanations for the production and reproduction of structured access to scarce and valuable resources, theories of justice suggest either the inevitability of certain social arrangements or their susceptibility to change. Theories of justice also identify the facilitative or disruptive effects that structured inequalities have on other characteristic features of human conduct. In this, they lend themselves to, and are sometimes designed to support, calls for social action or cautions against such action.

Even those who disagree vehemently about the meaning and interpretation of justice agree about the central role it has had in social theory and social action. Thus, Hayek, even while arguing that the concept of social justice is meaningless, nevertheless believes that it is rarely questioned as "the standard which ought to guide political action" (1976, p. 65). And a recent statement by a committee of U.S. Roman Catholic bishops suggests that justice provides precisely the kind of central moral standard needed to ensure "minimal levels of participation by all persons in the life of the human community" ("Catholic Social Teaching," 1984, p. 351).

These statements and the calls for or cautions on action that they represent are part of an extensive literature on justice that has emerged over the past 15 years. This literature should be seen, at least in part, as a response to the tumultuous political movements and events of the 1960s. The emergence of newly independent states, conflicts over the boundaries of already established states, interventions by the superpowers, and the growth of various liberation movements based on gender, nationality, ethnicity, and age all called attention to issues of justice, to predominant strains of work in social science, and to the relationship between the two.

The scholarly attention is probably best illustrated by the appearance of Rawls's A Theory of Justice in 1971 and by the critical literature it has since stimulated in philosophy (e.g., Ackerman, 1980; Barry, 1973; Buchanan, 1982; Cohen, Nagel, & Scanlon, 1980; Daniels, n.d.; Kamenka & Tay, 1979; Nozick, 1974; Paul, 1981; Sandel, 1982; Wolff, 1977). But the work by Rawls, the historical and sociopolitical situation, or some complex interaction among these and other factors also have contributed to a resurgence of interest outside of philosophy—in the social sciences more generally. There is now an extensive and sprawling literature in psychology and sociology (e.g., Bierhoff, Cohen, & Greenberg, 1986; Deutsch, 1985; Folger, 1984; Greenberg & Cohen, 1982; Lerner, 1980; Lerner & Lerner, 1981; Messick & Cook, 1983; Mikula, 1980; Moore, 1978; Sampson, 1983). And the concept of justice and the critical issues to which it is addressed are also receiving increased attention in other disciplines in the social sciences as well: in economics (e.g., Arthur & Shaw, 1978; Phelps, 1973; Schaffer & Lamb, 1981; Sen, 1973, 1982; Skurski, 1983; Thurow, 1980); in public policy (e.g., Hochschild, 1981; Rainwater, 1974); and in political theory (e.g., Miller, 1976; Walzer, 1983).

These developments are encouraging, but much more remains to be done. In a discussion of the relationship between work on justice by philosophers and by other social scientists, Brian Barry (1981) identifies what he calls a form of "cultural lag in academia," where "practitioners in one discipline tak[e] over the theories from other disciplines only when they are thoroughly discredited in the original discipline" (p. 107). Given the societal and institutional pressures for specialization, this type of dogged ignorance or cross-disciplinary reliance on discredited ideas may be widespread and becoming increasingly so. But Rawls's (1971) work itself and the enormous response it has evoked in scholars working in philosophy and across the social sciences suggest there are counterforces at work as well.

Whatever its initial (and perhaps, disciplinary) foundation, an understanding of justice and injustice will require attention to concerns that are psychological, economic, sociological, and philosophical. Failure to recognize this may lead those working in the area to substitute unacknowledged, and therefore unexamined, assumptions based on their ignorance of work in related disciplines. It may also lead to reliance on ideas with no knowledge of the critical history in which they developed.

Even when the inter- or transdisciplinary nature of the issues of justice is recognized, relevant work in related disciplines is often unavailable or inaccessible. One of the primary purposes of this volume is to provide a solid foundation for future work on justice that not only makes a perfunctory bow toward perspectives beyond the narrow confines of its own base but also employs a critical understanding of the work undertaken from other perspectives.

This book also has a second major purpose. Justice is a central moral standard against which social conduct, practices, and institutions are evaluated, and this is as it should be. A systematic organization of previous attempts to understand justice might well provide (or help to provide) the grounds for identifying and then reducing current levels of injustice and human suffering. To imagine that the present volume could provide such an effect directly would be naive. But if the real human suffering caused by currently existing structures of power and existing distributions of the benefits and burdens of social life is to be reduced, it will require close and careful examination of those structures and distributions and their intellectual supports in theories of justice.

It will require much more. Justice is a complex idea with a long and continuing history. This is the case because, despite the various definitions it has been given throughout that history, the issues it addresses are fundamental to social life. The question is not whether social life produces, and is in part constituted by, collective burdens and benefits but rather how those burdens and benefits are allocated among individuals, families, gender-, racial-, and class-based aggregates, and nation states and how we understand what benefits and burdens they are due. And because social life has a history and (may have) a future, present allocations and understandings are outgrowths of the past that pave the way for the allocations and understandings of the future. Barring the extinction of social life altogether, barring the elimination of scarcity or substantially enough change in current understandings of scarcity, and barring the emergence of forms of social organization that permit and encourage the preeminence of human generosity and caring, questions of justice are likely to confront us for some time to come.

In hopes of providing a groundwork for the thinking and acting that will be necessary, the authors of each of the next seven chapters have considered how the discipline in which their own work is primarily located has confronted issues of justice. They have organized their discussions around the following four questions:

1. How have the concepts of justice and injustice emerged in the theoretical and practical history of the discipline?
2. What are the major controversies that have emerged from this history and that characterize current discussions of justice in the discipline?
3. What are the crucial issues one might propose as an agenda for work in the discipline in the immediate future?
4. What specific aspects of this agenda would require work conducted primarily from the perspective of other disciplines in the social sciences, and how would such work contribute to advancing the understanding of issues on that agenda?

Each of the chapters addresses these questions in different ways.

Justice is a central personal and a central social standard of morality. A major theme that appears in all the chapters that follow concerns the interdependence of a theory of justice and a conception of human personhood. Buchanan and Mathieu (Chapter 2) put the matter clearly: "Different views of what human traits must be taken into account—including a conception of which are fundamental and which are secondary—will lead to different conceptions of justice." The predominant conception of the person invoked in current work on justice stresses the supposedly separate individual whose self-understanding requires separation from others and whose motivation is narrowly self-interested.

In part, this is a consequence of the dominant Western conception of the person as a "bounded, unique, more or less integrated motivational and cognitive universe, a dynamic center of awareness, emotion, judgment and action organized into a distinctive whole and set contrastively against a social and natural background" (Geertz, 1979, p. 229). Nader and Sursock (Chapter 7) suggest that in holistic societies less affected by the Western conception of the person, the individual is more likely to be seen as "a social being, a member of a group, be it a family, a clan, a religious sect, or a caste."

In part, it is also the result of the characteristics of the liberalism of current psychological and social theory. The liberal theory of justice, that theory most prevalent in contemporary work, "begins and ends with individuals and their interests, makes no sense without their consideration, owes its political strategies to its egalitarian conception of individuals, and radically distinguishes itself from competing (utilitarian, communitarian) theories because of that conception" (DiQuattro, Chapter 4).

MacPherson (1962) suggests that classical liberalism takes infinite desire, competitive motivation, and indefatigable power-seeking as fundamental human characteristics and that even the newer liberalism that stresses the right of each person to exert and develop his or her uniquely human capacities is tied to the institution of the market, which prevents the development of those uniquely human capacities. Does reliance on the market as a society's primary distributive mechanism necessarily prevent the development of justice? Does "the market, as a distributive device, force a self-interested rationality geared to the competitive struggle for existence" (as Di-Quattro suggests in his chapter)? Does the neoclassical perspective in economics terminate in the paradox suggested by Worland (Chapter 3): that the rules of justice appropriate to a market society cannot be implemented because such a society "generates psychological processes that preclude their implementation"? Liberal institutions such as the market may "require" individuals with precisely the characteristics that preclude justice.

The most prominent contemporary liberal theory of justice, that of Rawls (1971), draws explicitly on Kohlberg's theory of moral judgment. As Furby (Chapter 6) demonstrates, these theories have been subject to similar criticisms, one of the most important of which focuses on their concept of the person. Both Gilligan (1982, for example, with respect to Kohlberg) and Sandel (1982, for example, with respect to Rawls) argue that their concept of the person is unimaginably or unimaginatively asocial, that they conceive the individual only in terms of a set of relations that strip him or her of the inevitably social aspects of identity. This criticism leads Gilligan to suggest that Kohlberg has limited his conception of the person to one whose morality denies the importance of empathy and care, and it leads Sandel to a similar conclusion about the extent to which the individual of Rawlsian liberalism lacks human sociality.

Recent work in other disciplines also addresses this kind of issue. Rytina (Chapter 5) discusses recent sociological work on collective responses to injustice that appears to overcome the nature of Olson's free-rider dilemma that "rational self-interest" restrains an "individual's" contribution to a collective good. Although some of these remain within the more narrowly defined conception of "rational individual self-interest" (such as Axelrod, 1984; Hardin, 1982; and Margolis, 1982), others begin to question the boundaries of that conception by stressing the impact of community structures that provide ample selective incentives or by reinterpreting rebellion as a "self-affirming act of moral witness that can be an end in itself." And in his chapter on public policy, Soltan (Chapter 8) suggests four different types of moral evaluations that differ in the extent to which the evaluation is (in the present terms "narrowly") self-interested or impartial and the extent to which the conduct or institution being evaluated is seen as an end in itself or a means to some recognized end. Soltan hypothesizes a universal second-order preference (a preference among different preference orderings) for the position that is impartial and treats actions and institutions as ends in themselves, that is, a deontological morality.

If a more complete understanding of justice is to be achieved, it will be the result of work that is truly interdisciplinary. That work will need to address such central themes as the interdependence of justice and a conception of human personhood discussed here, the nature of moral inquiry in the social sciences (cf. Haan, Bellah, Rabinow, & Sullivan, 1983), and the relationship of justice to other moral standards. It will also need to address the different issues that have emerged from the history of each discipline's attempt to understand justice. The ultimate value of this book will depend on how well it contributes to future attempts to address these central themes and issues and how much it contributes to future action on matters of justice.

References

Ackerman, B. (1980). *Social justice and the liberal state*. New Haven: Yale University Press.

Arthur, J., & Shaw, W. H. (Eds.). (1978). *Justice and economic distribution*. Englewood Cliffs, NJ: Prentice-Hall.

Axelrod, R. (1984). *The evolution of cooperation*. New York: Basic Books.

Barry, B. (1973). *The liberal theory of justice*. Oxford: Clarendon Press.

Barry, B. (1981). Social science and distributive justice. In R. A. Solo & C. W. Anderson (Eds.), *Value judgement and income distribution*. New York: Praeger.

Bierhoff, H. W., Cohen, R. L., & Greenberg, J. (Eds.). (1986). *Justice in social relations*. New York: Plenum Press.

Buchanan, A. E. (1982). *Marx and justice: The radical critique of liberalism*. Totowa, NJ: Rowman & Littlefield.

Catholic social teaching and the U.S. economy. (1984, November 15). *Origins: NC Documentary Service, 14*(22–23), 337–383.

Cohen, M., Nagel, T., & Scanlon, T. (Eds.). (1980). *Marx, justice, and history*. Princeton: Princeton University Press.

Daniels, N. (Ed.). (n.d.). *Reading Rawls: Critical studies in "A Theory of Justice."* New York: Basic Books.

Deutsch, M. (1985). *The social psychology of justice*. New Haven: Yale University Press.

Folger, R. (Ed.). (1984). *The sense of injustice*. New York: Plenum Press.

Geertz, C. (1979). From the native's point of view: On the nature of anthropological understanding. In P. Rabinow & W. M. Sullivan (Eds.), *Interpretive social science* (pp. 225–241). Berkeley: University of California Press.

Gilligan, C. (1982). *In a different voice: Psychological theory and women's development*. Cambridge: Harvard University Press.

Greenberg, J., & Cohen, R. L. (Eds.). (1982). *Equity and justice in social behavior*. New York: Academic Press.

Haan, N., Bellah, R. N., Rabinow, P., & Sullivan, W. M. (Eds.). (1983). *Social science as moral inquiry*. New York: Columbia University Press.

Hardin, R. (1982). *Collective action*. Baltimore: Johns Hopkins University Press.

Hayek, F. A. (1976). *Law, legislation, and liberty: Vol. 2. The mirage of social justice*. Chicago: University of Chicago Press.

Hirschman, A. O. (1982). *Shifting involvements: Private interest and public action*. Princeton: Princeton University Press.

Hochschild, J. (1981). *What's fair? American beliefs about distributive justice*. Cambridge: Harvard University Press.

Kamenka, E., & Tay, E. S. (Eds.). (1979). *Justice*. London: Edward Arnold.

Kohlberg, L. (1976). Moral stages and moralization: The cognitive–developmental approach. In T. Lickona (Ed.), *Moral development and behavior* (pp. 31–53). New York: Holt, Rinehart & Winston.

Lerner, M. J. (1980). *The belief in a just world*. New York: Plenum Press.

Lerner, M. J., & Lerner, S. C. (Eds.). (1981). *The justice motive in social behavior: Adapting to times of scarcity and change*. New York: Plenum Press.

Macpherson, C. B. (1962). *The political theory of possessive individualism*. Oxford: Oxford University Press.

Margolis, H. (1982). *Selfishness, altruism, and rationality*. Chicago: University of Chicago Press.

Messick, D., & Cook, K. S. (Eds.). (1983). *Equity theory: Sociological and psychological perspectives*. New York: Praeger.

Mikula, G. (Ed.). (1980). *Justice and social interaction*. New York: Springer-Verlag.

Miller, D. (1976). *Social justice*. Oxford: Clarendon Press.

Moore, B., Jr. (1978). *Injustice: The social bases of obedience and revolt*. White Plains, NY: M. E. Sharpe.

Nozick, R. (1974). *Anarchy, state, and utopia*. New York: Basic Books.

Paul, J. (Ed.). (1981). *Reading Nozick: Essays on "Anarchy, State and Utopia."* Totowa, NJ: Rowman & Littlefield.

Phelps, E. S. (Ed.). (1973). *Economic justice*. Baltimore: Penguin.

Pitkin, H. F. (1981). Justice: On relating public and private. *Political Theory, 9(3)*, 327–352.

Rainwater, L. (1974). *What money buys: Inequality and the social meanings of income*. New York: Basic Books.

Rawls, J. (1971). *A theory of justice*. Cambridge: Harvard University Press.

Ross, A. (1959). *On law and justice*. Berkeley: University of California Press.

Sampson, E. E. (1983). *Justice and the critique of pure psychology*. New York: Plenum Press.

Sandel, M. J. (1982). *Liberalism and the limits of justice*. Cambridge: Cambridge University Press.

Schaffer, B., & Lamb, G. (1981). *Can equity be organized?* Paris: UNESCO.

Sen, A. K. (1973). *On economic inequality*. Oxford: Clarendon Press.

Sen, A. K. (1982). *Poverty and famines: An essay on entitlement and deprivation*. Oxford: Oxford University Press.

Skurski, R. (Ed.). (1983). *New directions in economic justice*. Notre Dame: University of Notre Dame Press.

Thurow, L. C. (1980). *The zero-sum society*. New York: Basic Books.

Walzer, M. (1983). *Spheres of justice: A defense of pluralism and equality*. New York: Basic Books.

Wolff, R. P. (1977). *Understanding Rawls: A reconstruction and critique of "A Theory of Justice."* Princeton: Princeton University Press.

CHAPTER 2

Philosophy and Justice

Allen Buchanan and Deborah Mathieu

Justice is usually said to exist when a person receives that to which he or she is entitled, namely, exactly those benefits and burdens that are due the individual because of his or her particular characteristics and circumstances. If someone states that a certain person or act is good or moral or virtuous, he or she does not necessarily mean that that person or act is just. Mary may believe, for example, that Tom's lending her his coat when she was cold was good or generous—but it was an act of beneficence, not of justice. Similarly, if someone states that a certain person or act is immoral or wrong, he or she does not necessarily mean that it is unjust. Tom may be deliberately rude to his employees, and he may show callous disregard for the suffering of a poor man whom he could easily help—but although he acts immorally in both instances, he may perhaps ease his conscience by reminding himself that at least he did not act unjustly. The point here is simply that justice is not the whole of morality, it is only one part of it. Thus justice is one characteristic among many of a good society. As William Frankena (1962, p. ix) states, "Societies can be loving, efficient, prosperous, or good, as well as just, but they may be just without being notably benevolent, efficient, prosperous, or good."[1]

This essay provides a philosophical exploration of features of the concept of justice, construed as one important aspect of morality.

[1]This conception of justice as only one aspect of morality is shared by most theorists of justice: David Hume, John Stuart Mill, John Rawls, and Robert Nozick, to name a few. However, justice has at times been more broadly construed by some philoso-

ALLEN BUCHANAN • Department of Philosophy, University of Arizona, Tucson, Arizona 85721. DEBORAH MATHIEU • Department of Political Science, University of Arizona, Tucson, Arizona 85721.

Although this concept is not applicable to all moral dilemmas, it usually is claimed to be appropriately applied to the problem of distributing benefits and burdens within society. This will be the focus of our examination. It should be noted, however, that the claim that the concept of justice is always meaningfully applicable to the distribution of benefits and burdens in a society is not an entirely uncontroversial one. Karl Marx, for instance, held that the very need for principles of justice is conclusive evidence of defects in the productive processes that form a society's core and that the superiority of communism is that it makes the whole issue of justice otiose (Buchanan, 1982).

Philosophical approaches to justice have been concerned primarily with answering two types of questions about justice: *metaethical* questions (i.e., questions regarding the meaning of terms used in moral discourse as well as the rules of reasoning and/or methods of knowing by which moral beliefs can be shown to be true or false) and *normative* questions (i.e., questions that concern what people *ought* to do, in contrast with what they do in fact do). The chief metaethical questions concerning justice are these: (a) What is the distinctive function in moral discourse of terms such as *just* and *right*? (b) Can judgments about the justice or injustice of institutions or actions or relationships be rationally justified? The chief normative ethical questions are these: (a) How ought we to act in order to be just? (b) How ought social institutions be structured so as to achieve justice?

The chapter is divided into three parts. The first explores the major elements of the concept of justice. The second describes and critically examines the leading contemporary attempts to go beyond an analysis of the concept of justice to provide systematic theories about one important type of justice—distributive justice. The third part argues for the dependency of philosophical theories of distributive justice—as well as radical critiques of those theories—upon work in the other social sciences.

---

phers to include all of morality, and so to mean something closer to "good" or "right." Plato (circa 427–347 B.C.), for instance, held that a just man is one whose various capacities are well-integrated and harmoniously governed by reason. Similarly, he held that a just society is one in which the various classes of men—each performing their appropriate function—are harmoniously governed by the most rational members of society (1945, translation). For further discussion of the relationship of justice to other moral values, see Frankena (1973), Feinberg (1973), Feinberg and Gross (1980).

Basic Categories of Justice

There are four main types of conceptions of justice: (a) principles of justice may be retributive or distributive; (b) they may be comparative or noncomparative; (c) they may vary according to the status assigned to the actions and/or the characteristics of individuals; and (d) they may differ in their methods of relating just procedures to just outcomes. Each shall be explained in turn.

Justice May be Retributive or Distributive

Understood as a basic division between types of justice, the traditional distinction between retributive and distributive justice is somewhat misleading. Retributivism is only one type of theory of criminal justice. Criminal justice consists of the proper procedures and principles for ascertaining guilt or innocence and for determining punishment of the guilty and restitution or compensation for victims of crimes. In its most simple form, a retributivist theory of criminal justice maintains that the guilty are to be punished, not in order to deter others from committing similar offenses nor to satisfy the desire for revenge or otherwise contribute to social utility, but simply because wrongdoing as such ought to be punished, regardless of the consequences of doing so. A more moderate and plausible version of retributivism holds that punishment is needed to correct an imbalance in the distribution of burdens of restraint that the law imposes and the benefits that the law bestows. According to this view, the criminal takes unfair advantage of the law-abiding populace by refusing to bear the burden of restraint that must be borne if we are all to reap the benefits of a system of law and order. Therefore a special burden—some form of punishment—must be inflicted on the criminal to right the balance of burdens and benefits. In non-retributive theories of criminal justice, including utilitarian theories, the proper goal of punishment—or at least one legitimate goal—is deterrence (Feinberg & Gross, 1975; Gross, 1979; Hart, 1968; Murphy, 1973).

Our principal concern in this chapter is not with criminal justice but with those principles of justice that are designed to regulate social and economic inequalities—that is, principles of distributive justice. David Hume (1775/1975) contended that the need for principles of distributive justice presupposes competing claims and con-

flicts of interest due not only to the scarcity of goods but to the
limitations of human benevolence as well.

> Let us suppose that nature has bestowed on the human race such profuse
> abundance of all external conveniences that, without any uncertainty in
> the event, without any care or industry on our part, every human finds
> himself fully provided with whatever his most voracious appetites can
> want. . . . It seems evident that, in such a happy state, every other social
> virtue would flourish . . . but the cautious, jealous virtue of justice
> would never once have been dreamed of. For what purpose make a
> partition of goods, where every one has already more than enough? Why
> give rise to property, where there cannot possibly be any injury? . . .
> Again, suppose, that, though the necessities of the human race continue
> the same as at present, yet the mind is so enlarged, and so replete with
> friendship and generosity, that every man has the utmost tenderness for
> every man, and feels no more concern for his own interests than for that
> of his fellows; it seems evident that the use of justice would, in this case,
> be suspended by such an extensive benevolence, nor would the divi-
> sions and barriers of property and obligations have ever been thought of.
> (pp. 184–185)

As we shall see, different theorists of justice make varying assumptions about the limits of benevolence and the causes of scarcity.

Justice May Be Comparative or Noncomparative

If justice pertains to each person's receiving that which is his or
her due, then what is due to each person may be determined on a
comparative or a noncomparative basis. That is, what a person is
owed may be relative to other persons' entitlements, or it may be
based on an objective standard to which the situations of other people are irrelevant.

If each person is entitled to a fair trial, for example, then Able's
right to a fair trial does not depend on what happened during Baker's
trial (assuming, of course, that the verdict in Baker's case does not
set a precedent), nor does it depend on the number and kinds of
other cases waiting to be scheduled for hearings. Rather, Able is to
receive a fair trial because he is entitled to one, and the fairness of
the trial will be determined according to specific notions of what
procedures constitute fair trials (this issue will be addressed later).
This is a case of noncomparative justice; Able's entitlements alone
determine what is due him.

But often the determination of what is owed to one person depends on what is owed to another—and so the two claims must be
compared in order to ascertain what would be just treatment of them
both. This might be the case, for example, when there are several

individuals with the same entitlements vying for limited quantities of goods. In these instances, some sort of balance must be arranged among their competing claims, and this requires a comparison among them. A mundane example would be the distribution of the cake at a birthday party. Everyone at the party has a claim to a piece of cake; if there are eight people present, then a just allocation might be for each person to receive one-eighth of the cake. But if two more guests arrive, then each person's share automatically reduces to one-tenth of the cake. Although each person has an equal entitlement to the good (here, the cake), the amount that each will receive depends on the number of people pressing their claims and the size of the good to be divided. Thus an acknowledgment of entitlements is not always sufficient to determine how an individual should be treated; sometimes justice requires an interpersonal comparison.

The most fundamental element of comparative justice is its *formal principle*, which is usually attributed to Aristotle: Equals should be treated equally and unequals unequally—but in proportion to their relevant similarities and differences. If Able and Baker are both rational adults, yet Able was allowed to vote in the last presidential election and Baker was not, then Baker seems to be the victim of an injustice because she was not treated the same as Able. But this is too hasty. Inequality of treatment is not in itself unjust; what is unjust is unequal treatment for irrelevant reasons. In this instance, there may have been good reasons—based on relevant differentiating factors—to treat Able and Baker differently. Perhaps, for instance, Baker was not allowed to vote because she was not a citizen (and Able was). If this were the case, then Baker was not a victim of injustice after all because the difference in her treatment was based on a relevant differentiating characteristic. But if Able was allowed to vote and Baker was not because Able is male and Baker is not, then Baker is a victim of an injustice because she was treated unequally based on a difference that is not relevant to the ability to vote.

Thus the formal principle of comparative justice does not eschew the idea of unequal treatment but rather prohibits arbitrary treatment.[2] Hence it allows for just inequalities. An inequality is just

---

[2]This does not mean that all arbitrary treatment is unjust. As John Stuart Mill (1801/1961, p. 454) points out, I may be "bound to practice charity or beneficience, but not towards any definite person, not at any prescribed time." Thus there may be instances when it is not unjust to treat equals unequally. If, for instance, I give one dollar to a beggar and nothing to another, I have not necessarily treated them unjustly. That is because I was free to give them any amount of money—or no money at all—according to my whims or desires. Justice does not turn a voluntary act into an obligatory one, nor does it cover all aspects of morality.

if and only if it is based on relevant factors; the principle is silent, however, as to what characteristics are relevant to specific distributions. This specification of relevant characteristics is the function of the *material principles* of justice (which will be discussed in the next section). The role of the formal principle is to ensure that, in determining the appropriate treatment of an individual, only those characteristics that are relevant to the issue at hand may be taken into account.

Say, for instance, that it has been determined that the distribution of wages to workers in a box factory should be based solely on productivity. If Able is responsible for calculating Baker's wages, then he must consider only the number of boxes Baker produced. That Baker made them with a smile, that she needs more money in order to feed her family, that she worked faster than her co-workers, that she is a relative of Able—all of these factors are irrelevant to the allocation of wages under this distributive principle, and Able would be acting unjustly if he took any of them into account.

Thus a fundamental element of the formal principle of comparative justice is the notion of impartiality. Justice demands that each person be judged according to—and only according to—those characteristics that have relevant bearing on the issue at hand. Each person, then, has a right to be given the same consideration in making the distributive determination, a right to be judged according to the relevant factors.

Some philosophers have taken this aspect of comparative justice as its defining feature. William Frankena (1962, p. 5), for instance, states that "all men are to be treated equally, and that inequalities must be justified. . . . The demand for equality is built into the very concept of justice." Similarily, S. I. Benn and R. S. Peters (1965) claim that

> to act justly . . . is to treat all men alike except where there are relevant differences between them. This is not a formula from which anyone can deduce in particular cases, how he ought to act, or make decisions. . . . At the most we have arrived at a rule of procedure for taking decisions: Presume equality until there is reason to presume otherwise. (p. 128)

Isaiah Berlin (1956) describes the results of this identification of justice with equality:

> The assumption is that equality needs no reasons, only inequality does so; that uniformity, regularity, similarity, symmetry, the functional correlation of certain characteristics with corresponding rights . . . need not be specifically accounted for, whereas differences, unsystematic behavior, change in conduct, need explanation and, as a rule, justification. (p. 305)

However, as Berlin realizes, it is a mistake to assume that the formal principle of justice itself entails a presumption in favor of equal treatment in this sense. Frankena, Benn, and Peters have mistakenly identified the material principle of equality with the formal principle of justice.

One difficulty with their presumption for equality is that it is not the only presumption that is consistent with the formal principle of justice. One could also presume that justice requires treating people differently—because no one is identical to anyone else—until certain similarities that some people share are shown to be relevant. Aristotle, for instance, believed that men are not naturally equal; he held an aristocratic, nondemocratic world view. If one agreed with him, one might tend to hold a presumption in favor of unequal treatment until relevant similarities are shown to exist. But actually, neither of these presumptions is appropriate because they each emphasize only one aspect of a complex concept. The formal principle of comparative justice is: Treat equals equally and unequals unequally—in proportion to their relevant similarities and differences. One cannot simply hack off a particular section and hold it up as equivalent to the whole concept. Thus the presumption for equality fails because it does not presume enough. But it also fails because it presumes too much. The formal principle of justice does not tell us what to do when we do not know whether the relevant characteristics of the individuals involved are similarities or differences. If we presume (without knowing) that the individuals involved are equal in the relevant respects, then there is a good chance that we will treat them justly if we treat them equally. But this is merely a chance; if it turns out that they were unequal in the relevant respects, then we will have treated them unjustly by treating them equally.[3] The formal principle of comparative justice does not tell us how to play the odds or what probabilities to assume. Rather, it tells us that, when people are equal, they should be treated equally; and when people are unequal, they should be treated unequally.

[3]Joel Feinberg (1973, pp. 100–102) concludes that one must not confuse the edict to "treat all men alike *except* where there are relevant differences between them"— which he calls an "exceptive principle"—with the edict to "treat all men alike *until it can be shown* that there are relevant differences between them"—which he calls a "presumptive principle." The exceptive principle is purely formal, allowing us to presume neither equal treatment nor unequal treatment when we do not know whether the relevent characteristics of the individuals involved are similarities or differences. The presumptive principle, on the other hand, "has us presume equal treatment even in this case, and that would be to make a presumption in favor of *unequal* treatment in the absence of knowledge of the persons involved" (p. 102).

The point of this brief discussion on the presumption for equality is that the formal principle of comparative justice is *purely* formal; by itself it yields no positive prescriptions. The formal principle does not involve a presumption for equality, nor does it demand that distributions be made equally or that they be made in order to provide for equality. The only function of the concept of equality within the principle is to set a constraining condition on distributions that are made on the basis of other values and standards (one of which may or may not be equality). These other standards will be addressed later in the chapter, when we discuss material principles of justice and theories of distributive justice.

There is another basic element of the formal principle of comparative justice—the appeal to consistency. This appeal is made on two levels. The first is on the level of the choice of distributive principles. If it is determined, for example, that need is the only factor relevant to the distribution of free lunches to second graders, then it would be inconsistent, and therefore unjust, to judge that ability to pay and not need is the relevant criterion for sixth graders (unless some morally relevant difference between the situations of second and sixth graders can be cited). The other appeal to consistency is made on the level of the distribution. If it is determined, for example, that lollipops are to be equally distributed to all children attending Noble Grammar School, then it would be inconsistent—and unjust—to exclude the third graders.

Justice, then, demands a certain consistency or uniformity. At every level, it prohibits arbitrary treatment. But this consistency must be tempered by a proportionality. Trophies, for example, typically are awarded according to merit. If Able wins the race, and Baker comes in third, then they both may equally merit a trophy. But if the trophy Able receives is made of bronze, whereas Baker's is made of the more precious gold, then Able could well claim that the distribution of trophies was unjust because it was not performed in proportion to the merits of the recipients. It is not enough, then, to treat equals as equals; people should be treated as equals *in the proportion to which they are equals.* This applies also, of course, to the treatment of unequals; people should be treated as unequals only to the extent that they are unequal. If Able and Baker again finish the race first and third, respectively, but this time Able receives a gold medal and Baker receives a dunking, Baker could legitimately complain that she was treated unjustly because the differences between her success and Able's, although relevant, were not great enough to warrant the discrepancy in treatment. A relevant difference will not justify any degree of discrimination, only a reasonable degree.

Thus the formal principle of comparative justice is a complex principle that includes the concepts of impartiality, consistency, and proportionality. These elements retain the formal nature of the fundamental principle; they add no material, substantive components. The formal principle of comparative justice presupposes other values and standards according to which claims are regulated and justified. These standards identify the benefits and burdens to be distributed, the relevant properties on the basis of which they are to be distributed, and the relative weights the properties have. The role of these standards in fleshing out the formal principle of comparative justice is the next topic for discussion.

Material Principles of Justice

The formal principle of justice provides the basic outlines of justice; it does not tell us how to apply them. We are told, for instance, that we should not discriminate between persons who are alike in all relevant respects. But what are the relevant respects? As Feinberg (1973, p. 102) suggests, "Which respects are relevant depends upon the occasion for justice, on our purposes and objectives, and on the internal rules of the 'game' we are playing."

Take the following case. Able is the director of a summer camp, and he is responsible for the just distribution (among other things) of archery trophies and Band-Aids. The purpose of allocating the trophies is to honor excellent performances in archery. In determining a just allocation, Able would take into account which children participated in that sport, which children excelled in it, and which particular aspects of the sport were mastered by which particular children. He would then distribute the trophy for the highest overall average to the child who had achieved it; he would give the trophy for the most bull's-eyes to the child who had achieved that, and so on. The purpose of distributing Band-Aids, on the other hand, is to help people in need. Therefore, not only is it not important which children participated in which activities, but it is not even important which children are registered at the camp; a young girl visiting her brother on Family Day is likely to have as much need for a Band-Aid—and thus as much of an entitlement to one—as her brother, the champion archer.

The formal principle of comparative justice cannot tell us how to distribute trophies and Band-Aids; it is useless without an identification of the relevant properties on the basis of which goods are to be distributed. And it is obvious from our examples that what counts as relevant in one instance (athletic prowess) is irrelevant in another (need for health care). Thus, the concept of justice has, in H. L. A. Hart's (1961) words,

> a shifting or varying criterion used in determining when, for any given purpose, cases are alike or different. In this respect justice is like the notions of what is genuine, or tall, or warm, which contain an implicit reference to a standard which varies with the classification of the thing to which they are applied. (p. 156)

These varying standards constitute the *material principles* of justice.

Rescher (1972) suggests that there are seven common material principles of distributive justice recognized today: equality, need, ability, effort, productivity, public utility, and supply and demand. Societies employ these criteria in different ways, depending on the context. The United States, for instance (at least attempts to) distribute votes on the basis of equality, welfare payments on the basis of need, jobs on the basis of ability, income on the basis of effort and productivity, luxury items on the basis of supply and demand, and tax burdens (at least partly) on the basis of social utility. Other material principles have been employed, of course. Historically, benefits and burdens often were distributed according to family status, skin color, sex—attributes we consider irrelevant today.

The existence of a wide assortment of conflicting material principles of justice makes it difficult to decide which one should be applied in a given instance. The problem is somewhat mitigated by an appeal to the formal principle of comparative justice. In the preceding section, it was noted that justice eschews arbitrary treatment; it prohibits taking irrelevant factors into account as well as ignoring relevant factors. This prohibition exists on two levels: (a) the application of the material principles and (b) the initial choice of the material principles. Thus there are two sources of formal injustice. One might accept a specific material principle as relevant to a certain distribution, yet complain that it is being arbitrarily applied. Or one might reject the material principle itself as irrelevant to the issue at hand and thus condemn the resulting distribution as arbitrary. The first kind of injustice is relatively easy to recognize and to correct. The other is more problematic and rests on the *justification* for the material principle.

Material principles of justice can be related in various ways to conceptions of human needs and capacities, ideals of a good society, and determinations of goals and ends. One cannot ascertain which properties must be taken into account for the application of justice without assuming a certain scale of values, a determination of what is important and what is not. Different views of what the fundamental burdens and benefits of life are, how they are to be weighed, and which ones can be dealt with by social arrangements will lead to different conceptions of distributive justice. And different views of what human traits must be taken into account—including a conception of which are fundamental and which are secondary—will lead to different conceptions of justice. These decisions will be shaped by determinations of the appropriate goals of the distribution as well as the appropriate goals of a good society.

Relation of Just Procedures to Just Outcomes

The relation of just procedures to just outcomes varies with the limitations we meet. Sometimes it is possible to determine an independent standard for deciding what outcome is just and to devise a procedure for guaranteeing that outcome, but this is rare. More frequently we can do one or the other but not both. For instance, we may agree on what a just outcome would be but have no procedure that will guarantee that outcome. Or we may have no independent criterion of a just outcome, and yet we have a fair procedure that, when followed, gives a just outcome.

That felicitous situation in which we are able to develop both a criterion of a just outcome and a fair procedure for ensuring the outcome is an instance of "perfect procedural justice." As John Rawls (1971) explains:

> A number of men are to divide a cake: assuming that the fair division is an equal one, which procedure, if any, will give this outcome? Technicalities aside, the obvious solution is to have one man divide the cake and get the last piece, the others being allowed their pick before him. He will divide the cake equally, since in this way he assures for himself the largest share possible. This example illustrates the two characteristic features of perfect procedural justice. First, there is an independent criterion for what is a fair division, a criterion defined separately from and prior to the procedure which is to be followed. And second, it is possible to devise a procedure that is sure to give the desired outcome. (p. 85)

But frequently, it is not possible to devise a procedure that will ensure the desired outcome; this is an instance of "imperfect procedural justice." Rawls (1971) points out that a criminal trial is an instance of this.

> The desired outcome is that the defendant should be declared guilty if and only if he has committed the offense with which he is charged. The trial procedure is framed to search for and to establish the truth in this

> regard. But it seems impossible to design the legal rules so that they
> always lead to the correct result. . . . Even though the law is carefully
> followed, and the proceedings fairly and properly conducted, it may
> reach the wrong outcome. (pp. 85–86)

And often we can reach no agreement on what would be a just
outcome. In this case, we tend to rely on "pure procedural justice"—
agreeing that whatever results from following a fair procedure will
be fair. Rawls (1971) illustrates this situation with the case of
gambling:

> If a number of persons engage in a series of fair bets, the distribution of
> cash after the last bet is fair, or at least not unfair, whatever this distribu-
> tion is. . . . A distinctive feature of pure procedural justice is that the
> procedure for determining the just result must actually be carried out; for
> in these cases there is no independent criterion by reference to which a
> definite outcome can be known to be just. (p. 86)

As we shall see in the next section, both Rawls and Robert Nozick
treat the issue of distributive shares as a matter of pure procedural
justice—but in doing so they develop very different conceptions of
just outcomes.

Theories of Distributive Justice

An awareness that seemingly plausible material principles of
distributive justice can conflict and a recognition of the need to
relate material principles in a coherent structure of values have led
contemporary philosophers to develop systematic theories of distributive justice. This part of the chapter examines three of the most
important contemporary theories of distributive justice: utilitarianism, Rawls's theory of justice as fairness, and Nozick's libertarian
theory.

Utilitarianism is the most influential version of a *teleological*
moral theory. A moral theory is teleological if and only if it defines
the good independently of the right and defines the right as that
which maximizes the good. Utilitarianism defines the good as happiness (satisfaction or pleasure) independently of any account of
what is morally right, and then defines the morally right as that
which maximizes the good (either in the particular case or at the
institutional level). A moral theory is *deontological* if and only if it is
not a teleological theory; that is, if and only if it either does not

define the good independently of the right or does not define the right as that which maximizes the good. Both Rawls's and Nozick's theories of justice are deontological theories.

Utilitarianism

Utilitarianism purports to be a comprehensive moral theory, of which a utilitarian theory of justice is only one part. There are two main types of comprehensive theory: act and rule utilitarianism. Act utilitarianism defines "rightness" with respect to particular acts: An act is right if and only if it maximizes utility. Rule utilitarianism defines "right" with respect to rules of action and makes the rightness of particular acts depend upon the rules under which those acts fall. A rule is right if and only if general compliance with that rule (or with a set of rules of which it is an element) maximizes utility, and a particular action is right if and only if it falls under such a rule.

Both act and rule utilitarianism may be versions of either classic or average utilitarianism. Classic utilitarianism defines the rightness of acts or rules as maximization of *aggregate* utility: The aggregate utility produced by an act or by general compliance with a rule is the sum of the utility produced for each individual affected. Average utilitarianism, on the other hand, defines rightness as maximization of utility per capita; this is the aggregate utility divided by the number of individuals affected. *Utility* is defined as pleasure, satisfaction, happiness, or as the realization of preferences, as the latter are revealed through individuals' choices.

The distinction between act and rule utilitarianism is important for a utilitarian theory of justice because the latter must include an account of when institutions are just. Thus institutional rules may maximize utility even though those rules do not direct individuals as individuals or as occupants of institutional positions to maximize utility in a case-by-case fashion. For example, it may be that a judicial system that maximizes utility will do so by including rules that prohibit judges from deciding a case according to their estimates of what would maximize utility in that particular case. Thus the utilitarian justification of a particular action or decision may not be that it maximizes utility but rather that it falls under some rule of an institution or set of institutions that maximizes utility.

Some utilitarians, such as John Stuart Mill (1861/1961), hold that principles of justice are the most basic moral principles because the utility of adherence to them is especially great. According to this view, utilitarian principles of justice are those utilitarian moral principles that are of such importance that they may be enforced, if necessary. Some utilitarians, including Mill perhaps, also hold that among the utilitarian principles of justice are principles specifying individual rights, where the latter are thought of as enforceable claims that take precedence over appeals to what would maximize utility in the particular case.[4]

A utilitarian moral theory, then, can include rights principles that themselves prohibit appeals to utility maximization, so long as the justification of those principles is that they are part of an institutional system that maximizes utility.[5] In cases where two or more rights principles conflict, considerations of utility may be invoked to determine which rights principles are to be given priority. For example, utility might best be served by generally recognizing both a right to free speech and a right to a fair trial. However, if, in a particular case, these rights conflicted so that respecting one required violating the other, then the utilitarian would determine which right to respect by asking whether respecting one right rather than another would maximize overall utility.

Utilitarianism has been criticized on technical, epistemic, and moral grounds (Smart & Williams, 1973). The most serious technical objection stems from the fact that utilitarianism requires us to make interpersonal utility comparisons. The problem is that it appears that such comparisons cannot be made because there is no nonarbitrary way of selecting a common zero point or baseline from which different individuals' utilities could all be measured and no nonarbitrary way of determining a common unit of measurement. So even if a utility scale can be constructed for each individual by recording the choices he or she makes among various goods or options, observation of different individuals' revealed preferences provides no

---

[4]Rights founded ultimately on considerations of utility may be called *derivative* to distinguish them from rights in the *strict* sense. Some contemporary rights theorists, such as Ronald Dworkin (1977), define a (justified) right claim as one that takes precedence over mere appeals to what would maximize utility.

   For an explicit statement of a thesis that is widely assumed but usually not argued for—namely that acting justly always involves respecting rights and injustice is always a matter of violating rights, see Foot (1977). For a variety of issues concerning rights, see Lyons (1979).

[5]Utilitarianism is incompatible with rights only if rights exclude appeals to utility maximization at all levels of justification, including the most basic institutional level.

basis for relating their respective utility scales to one another (Brock, 1973; Sartorius, 1975).[6]

The second major objection to utilitarianism is epistemic. Critics argue that even if the technical problem of making interpersonal utility comparisons could be overcome, the amount of information needed for even minimally accurate utilitarian calculations for matters of broad social significance would be unmanageably large. In determining, for example, whether society should invest heavily in nuclear power, it would be necessary to list all of the alternatives and then calculate the resulting utilities and disutilities for everyone who will be affected by each option. The magnitude of the task becomes apparent once it is acknowledged that it would be a mistake to limit the calculations to effects on the present generation and that it would also be wrong to include only the utilities and disutilities of human beings because other animals are capable of utility and disutility as well (if only in the form of simple pleasures and pains).

A third basic objection to utilitarianism is moral and would remain even if the first two objections were successfully rebutted. At the common sense level, this objection is based on the charge that utilitarianism is inadequate as a moral theory in general and as theory of justice in particular for two reasons: (a) it fails to take seriously the value of fairness; and (b) it does not provide an adequate foundation for equal civil and political liberties. For the utilitarian, there is

---

[6]The prominent view among economists is that interpersonal utility comparisons cannot be made. For this reason, economists more frequently employ the Pareto optimality (or efficiency) principle, rather than the principle of utility, as a criterion for assessing distributional states. A distribution of goods is Pareto optimal if and only if there is no way of redistributing the goods that would make at least one individual better off without making someone worse off. The Pareto optimality principle requires only intrapersonal, not interpersonal, utility comparisons because it is only necessary to compare an individual's own utility under two different distributions. A move from one distributional state to another is a Pareto "improvement" if and only if that move makes at least one individual better off without worsening anyone else's condition. Utilitarians can argue that even if interpersonal utility comparisons are impossible, we can rely upon the Pareto improvement (or Pareto superiority) principle to guide our efforts to maximize utility. For even if making a Pareto improvement does not guarantee that we have maximized utility, it at least ensures that we have made some gain in utility, even if we cannot determine the magnitude of the gain. Critics of the Pareto principles point out, however, that they are of little practical use in making important social policy decisions because in the latter there will typically be some losers no matter which option is taken. The Pareto principles only apply to those felicitous situations in which there are only winners and no losers. For further discussion of the Pareto principles, see Buchanan (1985).

only one feature of a distribution that is relevant to judging it just or unjust: Does it maximize overall utility? If it happened to be the case that distributing almost all of the goods to a minority and leaving the majority to do without maximized overall utility, then this grossly inegalitarian distribution would be required by utilitarianism. Similarly, it is at least possible that maximizing overall utility might permit or even require that members of one segment of society lead lives of impoverished slaves, lacking even the most basic civil and political liberties. According to the utilitarian, such an arrangement would be just, so long as the contribution their servitude made to the utility of their masters exceeded the slaves' own disutility.

Rawls (1971) has deepened these familiar objections to utilitarianism. He notes that even if the utilitarian could show that *as a matter of fact* utility would not be maximized by such unfair distributions or unacceptable infringements on basic liberties, there is something fundamentally wrong with a moral theory that makes such important matters depend upon contingent facts about what will create the most happiness. Rawls goes a step further by explaining the source of this deficiency in utilitarianism as its failure to take seriously the distinctness of persons. According to Rawls, utilitarianism draws no fundamental distinctions between a person and his or her desires. Instead of treating persons as equals, then, utilitarianism treats desires as equals. Thus the utilitarian slogan "each is to count as one" is really elliptical for "each desire is to count as one." Rawls believes that what ultimately counts morally is persons and that a person is distinct from whatever desires he or she happens to have at any particular time. For Rawls (1974, 1975), a person is a being that stands in a critical relationship to his or her desires—he or she is a critical chooser of ends, an agent who can exercise judgment about which desires are to be fulfilled and which are to be inhibited or modified. This concept of the person will be explained further in the following section.

John Rawls's Theory of Justice as Fairness

The Principles of Justice

In *A Theory of Justice*, Rawls (1971) pursues two main goals. The first is to set out a small but powerful set of principles of justice that underlie and explain the considered moral judgments we make about particular actions, policies, laws, and institutions. The second

is to offer a theory of justice superior to utilitarianism.[7] The principles of justice Rawls offers are as follows:

1. The principle of greatest equal liberty: Each person is to have
an equal right to the most extensive system of equal basic liberties
compatible with a similar system of liberty for all.

2. The principle of equality of fair opportunity:[8] Offices and
positions are to be open to all under conditions of equality of fair
opportunity—persons with similar abilities and skills are to have
equal access to offices and positions.

3. The difference principle: Social and economic institutions are
to be arranged so as to benefit maximally the worst off.[9]

The basic liberties referred to in the principle of greatest equal
liberty include freedom of speech, freedom of conscience, freedom
from arbitrary arrest, the right to hold personal property, and freedom of political participation (the right to vote, to run for office,
etc.).

Because the demands of these principles may conflict, some
way of ordering them is needed. According to Rawls, (1) is *lexically*
prior to (2), and (2) is lexically prior to (3). This means that we are
first to satisfy all the requirements of (1) before going on to satisfy the
requirements of (2), and all the requirements of (2) before going on to
(3). Lexical priority allows no trade-offs between the demands of
conflicting principles: The lexically prior principle takes absolute
priority.

Rawls (1971, p. 7) notes that "many kinds of things are said to be
just or unjust: not only laws, institutions, and social systems, but
also particular actions . . . decisions, judgments and imputations."
But he insists that the primary subject of justice is the *basic structure*
of society because it exerts a pervasive and profound influence on
individuals' life prospects. The basic structure is the entire set of
major political, legal, economic, and social institutions. In our society, the basic structure includes the Constitution, private ownership
of the means of production, competitive markets, and the monog-
amous family. The basic structure plays a large role in distributing

[7]These two goals are intimately related for Rawls because he believes that the theory
that does a better job of supporting and accounting for our considered judgments is
the better theory, other things being equal.

[8]Rawls sometimes refers to the "principle of equality of fair opportunity" and sometimes to the "principle of fair equality of opportunity." For convenience, the former
label will be utilized here.

[9]The phrase *worst off* refers to those who are worst off with respect to prospects of the
social primary goods regulated by the difference principle.

the burdens and benefits of cooperation among the members of society.

If the primary subject of justice is the basic structure, then the primary problem of justice is to formulate and justify a set of principles that a just basic structure must satisfy. These principles will specify how the basic structure is to distribute prospects of what Rawls calls "primary goods." These include the basic liberties (listed before) as well as powers, authority, opportunities, income, and wealth. Rawls (1971) says that primary goods are things that every rational person is presumed to want because they normally have a use, whatever a person's rational plan of life. The principle of greatest equal liberty (Principle 1) regulates the distribution of prospects of basic liberties; the principle of equality of fair opportunity (Principle 2) regulates the distribution of prospects of powers and authority, so far as these are attached to institutional offices and positions; and the difference principle (Principle 3) regulates the distribution of prospects of the other primary goods, including wealth and income. Although the first and second principles require equality, the difference principle allows inequalities so long as the total system of institutions of which they are a part maximizes the prospects of the worst off to the primary goods in question.

Justifications for the Principles

Rawls advances three distinct types of justification for his principles of justice. Two appeal to our considered judgments; the third is based on what he calls the Kantian interpretation of his theory.

The first type of justification rests on the idea that if a set of principles provides the best account of our considered judgments about what is just or unjust, then that is a reason for accepting those principles. A set of principles accounts for our judgments only if those judgments can be derived from the principles, granted the relevant facts for their application.

Rawls's second type of justification maintains that if a set of principles would be chosen under conditions that, according to our considered judgments, are appropriate conditions for choosing principles of justice, then this is a reason for accepting those principles. This justification includes three tasks: (a) a set of conditions for choosing principles of justice—which Rawls labels the *original position*—must be specified; (b) it must be shown that the conditions specified are (according to our considered judgments) the appropriate conditions of choice; and (c) it must be shown that Rawls's principles are indeed the principles that would be chosen under those conditions.

Rawls (1971, p. 11) construes the choice of principles of justice as an ideal social contract:

> The principles of justice for the basic structure of society are the principles that free and rational persons . . . would accept in an initial situation of equality as defining the fundamental terms of their association.

The idea of a social contract has several advantages. First, it allows us to view principles of justice as the object of a rational collective choice. Second, the idea of contractual obligation is used to emphasize that the choice expresses a basic commitment and that the principles agreed on may rightly be enforced. Third, the idea of a contract as a voluntary agreement that sets terms for mutual advantage suggests that the principles of justice should be "such as to draw forth the willing cooperation" of all members of society, including those who are worse off.

The most important elements of the original position for our purposes are (a) the characterization of the parties to the contract as individuals who desire to pursue their own life plans effectively and who "have a highest order interest in how . . . their interests . . . are shaped and regulated by social institutions"; (b) the "veil of ignorance," which is a constraint on the information the parties are able to utilize in choosing principles of justice; and (c) the requirement that the principles are to be chosen on the assumption that they will be complied with by all (the universalizability condition) (Rawls, 1971, pp. 132–142; 1974, p. 641).

The parties are characterized as desiring to maximize their shares of primary goods because these goods enable one to implement the widest range of life plans effectively and because at least some of them, such as freedom of speech and of conscience, facilitate one's freedom to choose and revise one's life plan or conception of the good. The parties are to choose "from behind a veil of ignorance" so that information about their own particular characteristics or social positions will not lead to bias in the choice of principles. Thus they are described as not knowing their race, sex, socioeconomic or political status, or even the nature of their particular conceptions of the good. The informational restriction also helps to insure that the principles chosen will not place avoidable restrictions on the individual's freedom to choose and revise his or her life plan.

Although Rawls offers several arguments to show that his principles would be chosen in the original position, the most striking is the *maximin argument*. According to this argument, the rational strategy in the original position is to choose that set of principles whose implementation will maximize the minimum share of prospects of primary goods that one can receive as a member of society, and Principles 1, 2, and 3 will insure the greatest minimal share. Rawls's claim is that because these principles protect one's basic liberties and opportunities and insure an adequate minimum of goods such as wealth and income (even if one should turn out to be among the worst off), the rational thing is to choose them, rather than to gamble with one's life prospects by opting for alternative principles. In particular, Rawls contends that it would be irrational to reject his principles and allow one's life prospects to be determined by what would maximize utility because utility maximization might allow severe deprivation or even slavery for some, so long as this contributed sufficiently to the welfare of others.

Rawls (1971) raises an important question about this second mode of justification when he notes that this original position is purely hypothetical. Granted that the agreement is never actually entered into, why should we regard the principles as binding? The answer, according to Rawls (p. 21), is that "the conditions embodied in the description of the original position are ones that we do in fact accept. Or, if we do not, then perhaps we can be persuaded to do so by philosophical reflection." This qualification introduces Rawls's third type of justification for the conditions that make up the original position—a justification based on Immanuel Kant's conception of the autonomous agent.

For Kant (1785/1959), an autonomous agent's will is determined by rational principles—principles that can serve as principles for all rational beings (not just this or that individual, depending upon whether or not the individual has some particular desire that other rational beings may not have). Rawls (1971) invites us to think of the original position as the perspective from which autonomous agents see the world. The original position provides a "procedural interpretation" of Kant's idea of a "realm of ends" or community of "free and equal rational beings." We express our nature as autonomous agents when we act from principles that would be chosen in conditions that reflect that nature.

Rawls concludes that, when people like us accept those principles that would be chosen in the original position, we express our nature as autonomous agents, that is, we act autonomously. There are three main grounds for this thesis, corresponding to the three features of the original position. First, because the veil of ignorance excludes information about any particular desire that a rational agent may or may not have, the choice of principles is not determined by any particular desire. Second, because the parties strive to maximize their share of prospects of primary goods—and because primary goods are attractive to them because they facilitate freedom in choosing and revising life plans and because they are flexible means not tied to any particular ends—this is another respect in which their choice is not determined by particular desires. Third, the original position includes the requirement that the principles of justice must be universalizable, that the parties must be willing for the principles to be accepted and complied with by all. This is to insure that they will be principles for rational agents in general and not just for agents who happen to have this or that particular desire.

In the *Foundations of the Metaphysics of Morals* (1785/1959), Kant advances a moral philosophy that identifies autonomy with rationality. Hence for Kant, the question "Why should one express our nature as autonomous agents?" is answered by the thesis that rationality requires it. Thus if Rawls's third type of justification succeeds in showing that we best express our autonomy when we accept those principles in the belief that they would be chosen from the original position, and if Kant's identification of autonomy with rationality is successful, then the result will be a justification of Rawls's principles that is distinct from both the first and second modes of justification. So far as this third type of justification does not make the acceptance of Rawls's principles hinge on whether the principles themselves or the conditions from which they would be chosen match our considered judgments, it is not directly vulnerable either to the charge that Rawls has misconstrued our considered judgments or that congruence with considered judgments (like the appeal to mere consensus) has no justificatory force.

In several articles published after *A Theory of Justice*, Rawls (1981) appears to have abandoned one of the most ambitious Kantian elements of his theory: the attempt to identify autonomy with rationality and to argue that rationality requires that we adopt the perspective of the original position and accept the principles of justice that would be chosen from that vantage point. Instead, Rawls now argues that the description of the original position is drawn from a normative ideal of the person as an autonomous, critical chooser of ends and that persons who espouse this ideal will seek to accept the principles of justice that would be chosen from the original position. Rawls then concedes that there may be no rational way of persuading those who espouse a different ideal of the person to accept his principles. In other words, Rawls now appears to have embraced a basic moral relativism. In later articles, Rawls (1980, 1985) seems to carry relativism further: He suggests that his theory is not a theory for all those who aspire to be autonomous, critical choosers of ends but for those who hold this ideal of the person and seek principles of justice for a modern democratic society.

Objections and Criticisms

By abandoning the Kantian attempt to found principles of justice on rationality, Rawls leaves himself open to an obvious objection—why should we accept this particular ideal of the person (and hence everything that, according to Rawls, accompanies the ideal)? And further, what are we to conclude about the relationship between justice and democracy? Is there one theory of justice for democratic societies and another for nondemocratic societies? Or can the theory of justice tell us something about which form of political order is morally preferable?

Quite apart from these objections—which arise in response to Rawls's later writings—many criticisms have been raised against Rawls's view as presented in A Theory of Justice (Daniels, n.d.). Some have been advanced by Robert Nozick in the course of presenting his own theory of justice and will be considered in the next section. Here we will sketch a few of the more important objections to Rawls's difference principle.

According to Rawls, it is uniquely rational for the parties in the original position to follow the maximin rule, which states that one should select the alternative whose worst outcome is better than the worst outcome of any of the other alternatives. The result of this is the choice of the difference principle. However, to follow the maximin rule is to rank alternatives as if one had an infinite aversion to risk because the maximin rule tells us to attend only to worst outcomes and choose the best worst outcome, while completely ignoring the best outcomes that might be achieved under the various options. But surely it would be more rational to choose in a way that reflects both the fear of doing badly and the desire to do well.

Rawls would presumably reply that there is a very special feature of the choice to be made in the original position that makes it rational to choose so as to be assured of the best worst outcome if things should go badly and to ignore the possibility of doing better than that. According to Rawls, the choice is made not just under

uncertainty but under *radical uncertainty*. It is not simply that the
parties cannot assign probabilities to various outcomes under the list
of competing principles from which they are to choose, but that they
also do not even have enough information to construct a list of the
possible outcomes that might occur under the various principles—
and some of these outcomes might be utterly intolerable. Because of
this radical uncertainty and because the choice is so momentous,
Rawls concludes that it is rational for the parties to choose so as to
protect themselves as best they can against extremely unfortunate
results. This they can do by choosing the principle that will give
them the best worst outcome—the difference principle.

The reply, however, is not adequate. Rawls fails to consider the
possibility that instead of choosing only one distributive principle,
the difference principle, the parties might choose two or more distributive principles—each of which is to go into effect contingent
upon specified circumstances. The parties could achieve the protection Rawls desires by agreeing that distribution would be governed
by the difference principle if, when the veil of ignorance is lifted, it
turns out that only the best worst outcome would be tolerable. In
other words, they might conclude that the difference principle, because of the extreme protection it provides for the worst off, is the
appropriate principle for very hard times. Yet they also might choose
another distributive principle to be put into effect if their society
turns out to be blessed with greater resources. This second principle
would establish a "decent minimum" of income—a socially guaranteed "welfare safety net" below which no one would be allowed to
fall—but would permit market processes to distribute wealth beyond the minimum in a much more inegalitarian way than would
the difference principle. This alternative to the difference principle
would capture the view that lies at the heart of the broad consensus
that the difference principle expresses an implausibly strong aversion to risk, and that it is rational to care about the possibility of
"winning big," at least if we are already protected from intolerable
losses. Rawls seems to offer no good reason for rejecting this alternative to the difference principle, and he provides no justification
for his assumption that there is only one principle of distributive
justice rather than a set of principles, each of which is appropriate
for different contingencies, depending upon how rich or poor the
society's resource base is.

The idea that different distributive principles are appropriate
for different societies, depending upon how serious their problem of
scarcity, enables us better to understand a widespread belief that the

difference principle is too demanding of the better off to be plausible as a principle of justice, as opposed to a principle of charity or generosity. The difference principle seems overly demanding insofar as it requires us to continue (without limit) improving the prospects of the worst off, regardless of how well-off they already are and regardless of the costs (in terms of economic liberty, for example) of further improvements for them. Improving the lot of the worst off may in fact be a requirement of justice that should take precedence over the freedom of the better off to use resources as they wish, so long as the worst off fall below some "decent minimum" or "adequate level" of wealth. But it does not follow that justice requires unlimited efforts to improve the condition of the worst off, especially if marginal improvements for the worst off entail more government control and greater restrictions on people's freedom to strive for a share of wealth that exceeds this minimum. Rawls may have confused justice with generosity.

Robert Nozick's Libertarian Theory

There are many versions of libertarian theory, but their characteristic doctrine is that coercion may only be used to prevent or punish the infliction of physical harm, theft, and fraud, and to enforce contracts. Perhaps the most influential and systematic recent instance of libertarianism is presented by Robert Nozick in *Anarchy, State, and Utopia* (1974). In Nozick's theory of justice, as in libertarian theories generally, the right to private property is fundamental and determines both the legitimate role of the state and the most basic principles of individual conduct.

Nozick (1974) contends that individuals have a property right in their persons and in whatever "holdings" they come to have through actions that conform to (a) "the principle of justice in acquisition" and (b) "the principle of justice in transfer." The first principle specifies the ways in which an individual may come to own hitherto unowned things without violating anyone else's rights. Here Nozick largely follows John Locke's (1698/1967) famous account of how one makes natural objects one's own by "mixing one's labor" with them or improving them through one's labor. Although Nozick does not actually formulate a principle of justice in (initial) acquisition, he does argue that whatever the appropriate formulation is, it must include a "Lockean proviso," which places a constraint on the holdings that one may acquire through one's labor. Nozick (pp. 178–179) maintains that one may appropriate as much of an unowned item as one desires so long as (a) one's appropriation does not worsen the conditions of others in a special way, namely by creating a situation in which others are "no longer . . . able to use freely what [they] previously could"; or (b) one properly compensates those whose condition is worsened by one's appropriation in the way specified in (a). Nozick emphasizes that the proviso only picks out one way in which one's appropriation may worsen the condition of others; it does not forbid appropriation or require compensation in cases in which one's appropriation of an unowned thing worsens another's condition merely by limiting his or her opportunities to appropriate (rather than merely use) that thing (i.e., to make it his or her property).

The second principle states that one may justly transfer one's legitimate holdings to another through sale, trade, gift, or bequest and that one is entitled to whatever one receives in any of these ways, so long as the person from whom one receives it was entitled to that which that person transferred to you. The right to property that Nozick advances is the right to exclusive control over anything one can get through initial appropriation (subject to the Lockean proviso) or through voluntary gifts or exchanges with others entitled to what they transfer. Nozick (1974, p. 151) concludes that a distribution is just if and only if it arose from another just distribution by legitimate means. The principle of justice in initial acquisition specifies the legitimate "first moves," whereas the principle of justice in transfer specifies the legitimate ways of moving from one distribution to another: "Whatever arises from a just situation by just steps is itself just."

Because not all existing holdings arose through the just steps specified by the principles of justice in acquisition and transfer, there will be a need for a *principle of rectification* of past injustices. Although Nozick does not attempt to formulate such a principle, he thinks that it might well require significant redistribution of holdings.

Apart from the case of rectifying past violations of the principles of acquisition and transfer, however, Nozick's theory is strikingly antiredistributive. Nozick contends that attempts to force anyone to contribute any part of his or her legitimate holdings to the welfare of others is a violation of that person's property rights, whether it is undertaken by private individuals or the state. On this view, coercively backed taxation to raise funds for welfare programs of any kind is literally theft. Thus a large proportion of the activities now engaged in by the United States government involve gross injustices.

After stating his theory of rights, Nozick tries to show that the state is legitimate so long as it limits its activities to the enforcement of these rights and eschews redistributive functions. To do this he employs an "invisible hand explanation," which purports to show how the minimal state could arise as an unintended consequence of a series of voluntary transactions that violate no one's rights.[10] The phrase *invisible hand explanation* is chosen to stress that the process by which the minimal state could emerge fits Adam Smith's famous account of how individuals freely pursuing their own private ends in the market collectively produce benefits that are not the aim of anyone.

It is striking that Nozick does not attempt to provide any systematic justification for the Lockean rights principles he advocates. In this respect, he departs radically from Rawls. Instead, Nozick assumes the correctness of the Lockean principles and then, on the basis of that assumption, argues that the minimal state and only the minimal state is compatible with the rights those principles specify.

He does, however, offer some arguments against the more-than-minimal state that purport to be independent of that particular theory of property rights that he assumes. These arguments may provide indirect support for his principles insofar as they are designed to make alternative principles, such as Rawls's, unattractive. Perhaps the most important of these is an argument designed to show that any principle of justice that demands a certain distributive end state or pattern of holdings will require frequent and gross disruptions of individuals' lives for the sake of maintaining that end state or pattern. Nozick (1974) supports this general conclusion by a vivid example.

[10]The process by which the minimal state could arise without violating anyone's rights is said to include four main steps. First, individuals in a "state of nature" in which (libertarian) moral principles are generally respected would form a plurality of protective agencies to enforce their libertarian rights because individual efforts at enforcement would be inefficient and liable to abuse. Second, through competition for clients, a "dominant protective agency" would eventually emerge in a given geographical area. Third, such an agency would eventually become a "minimal state" by asserting a claim of monopoly over protective services in order to prevent less reliable efforts at enforcement that might endanger their clients; it would forbid "independents" from seeking other forms of enforcement. Fourth, again assuming that correct moral principles are generally followed, those belonging to the dominant protective agency would compensate the independents, presumably by providing them with free or partially subsidized protection services. With the exception of taxing its clients to provide compensation for the independents, the minimal state would act only to protect persons against physical injury, theft, fraud, and violations of contracts (Nozick, 1974, pp. 10–25). For a fundamental objection to Nozick's invisible hand explanation, see Rolf Sartorius (1975).

He asks us to suppose that the distribution of holdings prescribed by some end state or patterned principle of justice is achieved at Time T—call this Distribution D. Suppose that the famous basketball player Wilt Chamberlain signs a contract stating that he is to receive twenty-five cents of the price of each ticket to all of the home games in which he plays. Suppose that Chamberlain makes $250,000 from this arrangement. At Time T^1, when Chamberlain receives his $250,000, we no longer have Distribution D; instead, we have Distribution D^1. In assuming that Distribution D was just, we assumed that those who paid twenty-five cents to Chamberlain had a property right in the resources they possessed at T. The new distribution at T^1 arose through strictly voluntary exchanges of just holdings. Surely we must agree, Nozick says, that the new distribution at T^1 (after Chamberlain has received $250,000) cannot be unjust. Nozick concludes that in order to prevent departures from a prescribed end state or pattern of holdings it would be necessary to interfere in unwarranted ways in peoples' voluntary exchanges. He seems to think that these interferences would be not only severe and frequent but also unjust, independently of their disruptiveness.

Nozick's use of this example to defend his theory of property rights and the market system that his theory supports is open to several serious objections. First, although the example may show that maintaining rather precisely specified distributive patterns or end states, including strict equality, would require unacceptably frequent and severe disruptions of people's lives, it does not show that all distributive patterns or end states suffer from this problem. In particular, a principle requiring that everyone is to be guaranteed a decent minimum of certain basic goods such as food and shelter need not require frequent severe interferences. Long-standing, publicized laws specifying tax obligations can be and in fact are used to provide funds for providing a core of welfare goods. Such an arrangement avoids the disruption that would result from ad hoc prohibitions of particular actions or unpredictable expropriations of individuals' holdings. Consequently, as Friederich Hayek (1960, pp. 223–258) has observed, not all redistributive programs—or in Nozick's terms, not all attempts to achieve and maintain distributive patterns or end states—are incompatible with the existence of that stable framework of expectations that is the essence of the "rule of law."

In the face of this criticism, Nozick might concede that continued satisfaction of an end state or patterned principle need not require frequent and severe disruptions. Nevertheless, he could argue, the Chamberlain example shows that it is intuitively unjust to interfere, through taxation or otherwise, with the results that arise when people voluntarily exchange what they have a right to, according to some initially just distributive end state or pattern. For if people only voluntarily exchange what they have a right to, how could anyone have a right to interfere with the resulting distribution?

Although his reasoning is far from clear here, Nozick may be assuming that it is permissible to interfere with a particular action only if that action, considered in isolation, is morally wrong or otherwise defective. This assumption, however, is very implausible because it ignores something that is surely relevant from the standpoint of distributive justice in particular and the justification of interferences with liberty in general—the fact that a group of actions, none of which is criticizable in isolation, may collectively or cumulatively have unacceptable results.

To make this fundamental point more concrete, let us return to Nozick's example. Suppose that over an extended period of time, voluntary exchanges of the sort Nozick describes in the Chamberlain case have the following extremely unfortunate result: A certain individual (or small group of individuals) comes to control a very large proportion of society's wealth and is able to use this financial power to gain a disproportionate share of political power, either through legal or illegal means (Cohen, 1978).[11] Considered in isolation, none of the voluntary exchanges that collectively produced this unacceptable result was itself criticizable in any way. But even if this is so, it does not follow that it would be wrong to prevent this extremely undesirable cumulative result by interferring with such exchanges— either by prohibiting them or by taxing the wealth of those who gain the most from them. Such interferences with liberty may be necessary to prevent concentrations of wealth and hence of power that would be even more detrimental to liberty. To assume that the cumulative result of a series of just actions must itself be just is to commit the fallacy of composition (Buchanan, 1985; Paul, 1981).

The Dependence of Philosophical Theories of Justice on the Social Sciences

Although most philosophers have been slow to acknowledge it, philosophical theories of justice often rest on assumptions from within the domain of the social sciences. In the authors' opinion,

[11]This, of course, is precisely what most socialist critics claim has in fact happened in all countries in which the market is largely unrestricted.

continued progress in the development of philosophical theories of justice will depend in part upon the ability of philosophers to support their analyses with social scientific research in several areas. Although no attempt can be made in this chapter to propose a detailed interdisciplinary agenda for theorizing on justice, we shall indicate several points at which the philosophical theories of justice examined previously can be criticized for disciplinary parochialism.

First, two points can be gleaned from our discussion of utilitarian theories of justice. On one hand, technical expertise from mathematical economics is needed to resolve the dispute over whether it is possible to make coherent and accurate interpersonal utility comparisons. At present several prominent mathematical economists hold that the problem of interpersonal comparisons is not insurmountable, whereas perhaps the majority believe it is (Brock, 1973; Sartorius, 1975). On the other hand, even if we assume that the problem of interpersonal utility comparisons can be solved, utilitarian theories of justice are more heavily dependent upon expertise from the social sciences than other theories because the principle of utility itself (in any of its forms) tells us nothing concrete about how we are to act or how our institutions are to be structured, in the absence of a multitude of empirical premises to be drawn from political science, psychology, economics, and sociology. Moreover, in many cases, psychological and sociological theories are not at present sufficiently developed to provide what a utilitarian philosophical theory of justice requires.

The dependence of Rawls's theory of justice upon the social sciences can perhaps best be made clear by examining two important Marxist objections to it. The first is that Rawls's theory is utopian—in the pejorative Marxian sense—because it merely paints a picture of the just or "well-ordered" society but provides no account of how the transition from an unjust society like ours to the Rawlsian ideal will or even could be achieved (Wolff, 1977). So far as Rawls even suggests the barest elements of such an account, his approach is "idealistic"—it relies exclusively upon the individual's sense of justice, ignoring the powerful influence of material interests and, above all, of class interests. Marx's scathing criticism of the utopian socialists of his day, who naively relied upon the motivating power of moral ideals, applies with undiminished force to Rawls (McCellan, 1977).[12]

---

[12]The Marxian could argue that even if our class interests do not prevent us from performing the feat of abstraction required by the veil of ignorance and from working through the argument to Rawls's principles, there is no reason to believe that our sense of justice will be strong enough to overcome our allegience to the existing

The second Marxist objection indicates another respect in which Rawls tacitly assumes empirical generalizations that are very much in dispute in the social sciences. It is true that Rawls emphasizes that his principles of justice are themselves neutral as to whether a just society will be capitalistic (i.e., will have private ownership of the means of production) or socialistic (i.e., will have public ownership of the means of production). Nevertheless, when he presents a working model of the implementation of his principles in a society like ours, he assumes that considerable inequalities in wealth will be needed to motivate people to produce enough to maximize the prospects of the worst off. In other words, Rawls assumes what Marxist social scientists deny—that personal gain is the only incentive powerful enough to achieve sufficient productivity to provide the material resources for the good society (Buchanan, 1983a).

It is important to note that Rawls is not alone in making tacit—and inadequately supported—psychosociological assumptions. Libertarian theories of justice, like that of Robert Nozick, also share this weakness. This can be illustrated by examining the libertarian's response to the charge that libertarian theory is inhumane.

This charge arises because the libertarian theory of justice (which is equated with respecting individuals' negative rights) is compatible with a society in which large numbers of people live in misery, without even the most minimal support from others. If the

---

order, especially if we profit greatly from its injustices. The occasions on which we soberly adopt the perspective of the original position will be like those ecstatic spiritual episodes that occur when the "bourgeois" briefly becomes a "citoyen" as he or she steps into the voting booth (Easton & Guddhat, 1967). Unfortunately, as with transubstantiation, everything will still look and taste the same, in spite of an alleged miraculous inner metamorphosis. Even if we acknowledge that Rawls's principles would be chosen by beings concerned to express their nature as free and equal moral beings, the motivational structure imposed by our social position will continue to govern our conduct. Rawls provides neither a theory of moral education nor a theory of how socioeconomic transformation will produce, or at least make possible, the needed motivational shift.

It is important to note that the force of this objection does not depend upon whether one adopts a "materialist" theory of the source of social change, and in particular, of the motivation for social change. One need not require that Rawls provide an account of how changes in the "material base" produce changes in the "ideological superstructure." Instead, the objection can be formulated in terms of Rawls's broader, more cautious notion of the basic structure. Rawls's own emphasis on how our interests and even our deepest values are shaped and regulated by the basic structure demands an account of how the sense of justice can become an effective force for social change.

libertarian theory of justice were intended to capture the whole of morality, then this charge would be fatal. But the libertarian argues that the theory is in no way committed to reducing morality to justice, nor, hence, to reducing it to respect for negative rights. Libertarianism is only committed to the view that whereas the purely negative duties of justice may be enforced, duties of charity—which require us to render aid to those in need—are strictly voluntary and cannot be enforced without violating individuals' rights. Thus, the libertarian concludes, in such a society, individuals will not only respect each other's rights, they also will practice the virtue of charity toward the needy.

There are several difficulties with this defense of libertarianism. First of all, Nozick and other libertarians who rely upon voluntary acts of charity to give a more humane face to a libertarian theory of morality seem to assume, without argument, that individuals will actually be able to achieve their charitable goals by strictly voluntary association. This assumption ignores the fact that some important forms of charity are public goods and that consequently, collective action to achieve charitable goals may falter because (a) some individuals attempt to be free riders on the contributions of others; or (b) some individuals are willing to contribute only if they have assurance that others will reciprocate. Interestingly, the only examples of voluntary charity Nozick discusses are ones in which the benefit to be provided is not a public good but rather is one that can be provided by the independent effort of one individual. Whether or not important forms of charity that have the relevant features of public goods actually will be provided through strictly voluntary efforts—without reliance upon government coercion to solve the free-rider or assurance problems—depends upon two factors: (a) whether rational individuals would contribute voluntarily, and (b) the extent to which actual individuals in a given society behave in a purely rational fashion (Olson, 1965). The former question is the proper subject matter of decision theory; the latter question can only be answered by social scientific research, not by philosophical reflection.

In addition, libertarians who appeal to the virtue of charity to soften their otherwise austere theory must also appeal to findings in social psychology (as well as cultural anthropology and history) to support their assumption that a libertarian society—one in which the market plays a much greater role in human affairs than it now does even in the most capitalistic societies—would be the sort of society that would nurture concern for the welfare of others. In other words, even if the libertarian theory of justice is logically compatible with the flourishing of charity, it may not be realistically so. Instead, the desire of the classical Homo economicus to maximize his own utility might well drive out altruistic motivations, as market relations extended their sway into all aspects of human life. This issue, of course, is a matter for the social scientist to determine, not the philosopher.

Finally, it should be noted that it is easy to point to any number of philosophical theories of justice that tacitly rely on assumptions to be confirmed or discomfirmed by the social sciences. For example, Marxian theorists—from Marx and Engels themselves to contemporary social philosophers such as G. A. Cohen (1978) and Allen Wood (1981)—have made problematic assumptions and have failed to support them adequately.[13]

Marx provides what may be the most radical critique conceivable of the whole enterprise of constructing a philosophical theory of justice. Although he maintains that capitalism does not live up to its own standards of justice in several important respects, his most fundamental criticisms are designed to show that the concern about justice is itself symptomatic of more profound ills in capitalist society. Marx believes that it is the private ownership of the means of production and with it production for profit rather than for the satisfaction of human needs that guarantee that individuals will be in such serious conflict with one another that they need to rely upon principles of justice to restrain conflicts of interests to a manageable level (Buchanan, 1983a). In particular, Marx believes that there is a sense in which the scarcity of goods characteristic of capitalism, and hence the conflicts that arise from this scarcity, are unnecessary. This scarcity and scarcity-based conflict are the predictable features of the capitalist mode of production, but they can be eliminated if a new mode of production—communism—is adopted.

Marx is not only committed to the prediction that communism will be more productive than capitalism and more efficient in distributing what it produces; he is also committed to the much more ambitious prediction that the increase in productivity and efficiency will be achieved through a new mode of social organization. This new social arrangement is (a) nonexploitive; (b) democratic (in the sense that each enjoys roughly equal control over production); (c)

---

[13]Cohen and Wood both assume, without argument, that communism can achieve a high level of productivity through democratic control over the means of production and that it can do so without reliance upon the division of labor as we know it in capitalistic economies. For a critique of their positions, see Buchanan (1983b).

noncoercive (inasmuch as there will be no role for the state as a coercive apparatus, such as command economies of the Soviet type); and (d) free from reliance on a division of labor into relatively fixed specialized occupations.

Whether a society can achieve greater productivity and efficiency than capitalism while at the same time satisfying the other ambitious constraints Marx imposes on communism cannot be decided through philosophical analysis alone. In particular, what is needed is a theory powerful enough to show how an entire economy can be managed democratically without unacceptable losses in efficiency due to the well-known time costs and information costs of democratic decision procedures (Buchanan, 1983a; Mueller, 1979). Further, the Marxian social philosopher must also appeal to the social sciences to substantiate Marx's sweeping hypothesis that the sorts of conflicts that make reliance upon principles of justice necessary are all results of egoism and class conflicts and will disappear with the abolition of private property in the means of production.

Conclusions

In the past two decades, the sharp division between metaethical and normative enquiries has become blurred in philosophical theorizing about justice. Instead of assuming that there is one shared concept of justice, whose content can be clearly determined by analysis of our use of the term *justice* in ordinary language, many philosophers have come to believe that answering both the normative ethical questions and the metaethical questions requires the development and comparative evaluation of normative theories of justice. These theories of justice go beyond an analysis of the formal elements of justice to offer systematically related material principles—principles that in turn are embedded in a broad theoretical structure that includes an account of human good and/or an ideal of the person.

The most detailed and influential examples of recent philosophical theorizing about justice have concentrated on the systematic articulation and justification of principles of distributive justice. Each of the three main approaches to distributive justice we have examined—utilitarianism, Rawls's contract theory, and Nozick's libertarianism—has considerable strength and intuitive appeal. But as we have seen, each is also subject to serious objections. This is hardly surprising because systematic theorizing about justice is, in a sense, in its infancy. However, it would be a mistake to assume that progress toward a convergence of belief about what is the most reasonable philosophical theory of justice can be achieved simply by refinements in philosophical thinking. On the contrary, it is becoming increasingly clear that philosophical disputes about justice cannot be resolved without significant contributions from the social sciences. Similarly, as we hope this chapter makes clear, philosophy has its own distinctive role in examining the most fundamental conceptual and normative issues in the study of justice.

References

Aristotle. (1953). *Nichomachean ethics* (J. A. K. Thompson, Trans.). London: George Allen & Unwin.

Benn, S., & Peters, R. S. (1965). *The principles of political thought*. New York: Free Press.

Berlin, I. (1956). Equality. *Proceedings of the Aristotelian Society*, LVI, 301–326.

Brock, D. W. (1973). Recent work in utilitarianism. *American Philosophical Quarterly, 10*, 245–249.

Buchanan, A. E. (1982). *Marx and justice: The radical critique of liberalism*. Totowa, NJ: Rowman & Allanheld.

Buchanan, A. E. (1983a). Marx on democracy and the obsolescence of rights. *South African Journal of Philosophy, 2*, 130–135.

Buchanan, A. E. (1983b). Review: Wood's *Karl Marx*. *The Journal of Philosophy, LXXX*, 424–434.

Buchanan, A. E. (1985). *Ethics, efficiency, and the market*. Totowa, NJ: Rowman & Allanheld.

Cohen, G. A. (1978). *Karl Marx's theory of history: A defense*. Oxford: Routledge & Kegan Paul.

Cohen, G. A. (1981). Robert Nozick and Wilt Chamberlain: How patterns preserve liberty. In J. Arthur & W. H. Shaw (Eds.), *Justice and economic distribution* (pp. 246–262). Englewood Cliffs, NJ: Prentice-Hall.

Daniels, N. (Ed.). (n.d.). *Reading Rawls: Critical studies of A Theory of Justice*. New York: Basic Books.

Dworkin, Ronald. (1977). *Taking Rights Seriously*. Cambridge: Harvard University Press.

Easton, L. D., & Guddhat, K. H. (1967). *Writings of the young Marx on philosophy and society*. Garden City, NY: Doubleday.

Feinberg, J. (1973). *Social philosophy*. Englewood Cliffs, NJ: Prentice-Hall.

Feinberg, J., & Gross, H. (Eds.). (1975). *Punishment: Selected readings*. Belmont, CA: Dickenson Publishing.

Feinberg, J., & Gross, H. (Eds.). (1980). *Philosophy of law* (2nd ed.). Belmont, CA: Wadsworth.

Foot, P. (1977). Euthanasia. *Philosophy and Public Affairs, 6*, 85–112.

Frankena, W. (1962). The concept of social justice. In R. B. Brandt (Ed.), *Social justice* (pp. 1–29). Englewood Cliffs, NJ: Prentice-Hall.

Frankena, W. (1973). *Ethics* (2nd ed.). Englewood Cliffs, NJ: Prentice-Hall.

Gross, H. (1979). *A theory of criminal justice*. New York: Oxford University Press.

Hart, H. L. A. (1961). *The concept of law*. Oxford: Clarendon Press.

Hart, H. L. A. (1968). *Punishment and responsibility*. Oxford: Clarendon Press.

Hayek, F. (1960). *The constitution of liberty*. Chicago: University of Chicago Press.

Hume, D. (1975). An enquiry concerning the principles of morals. In L. A. Selby-Bigge (Ed.), *Enquiries concerning human understanding and concerning the principles of morals*. Oxford: Clarendon Press. (Originally published 1775)

Kant, I. (1959). *Foundations of the metaphysics of morals* (L. W. Beck, Trans.) New York: Bobbs-Merrill. (Originally published 1785)

Locke, J. (1967). *Two treatises of government* (2nd ed.). P. Laslett (Ed.). Cambridge: Cambridge University Press. (Originally published 1698)

Lyons, D. (Ed.). (1979). *Rights*. Belmont, CA: Wadsworth.

McLellan, D. (1977). *Karl Marx: Selected writings*. Oxford: Oxford University Press.

Mill, J. S. (1961). *Utilitarianism*. Garden City, NY: Doubleday. (Originally published 1861)

Mueller, D. (1979). *Public choice*. Cambridge: Cambridge University Press.

Murphy, J. G. (Ed.). (1973). *Punishment and rehabilitation*. Belmont, CA: Wadsworth.

Nozick, R. (1974). *Anarchy, state, and utopia*. New York: Basic Books.

Olson, M. (1965). *The logic of collective action*. Cambridge: Harvard University Press.

Paul, J. (Ed.). (1981). *Reading Nozick*. Totowa, NJ: Rowman & Littlefield.

Plato. (1945). *The republic* (F. M. Cornford, Trans.). Oxford: Oxford University Press.

Rawls, J. (1971). *A theory of justice*. Cambridge: Harvard University Press.

Rawls, J. (1974). Reply to Alexander and Musgrave. *Quarterly Journal of Economics, 88*(4), 633–655.

Rawls, J. (1975). Fairness to goodness. *Philosophical Review, 84*, 536–554.

Rawls, J. (1980). Kantian construction in moral theory. *The Journal of Philosophy, 77*, 515–571.

Rawls, J. (1981, April 10). *The basic liberties and their priority: The Tanner Lectures on Human Values*. Delivered at the University of Michigan, Ann Arbor.

Rawls, J. (1985). Justice as fairness: Political not metaphysical. *Philosophy and Public Affairs, 14*, 223–251.

Rescher, N. (1972). *Welfare: The social issue in philosophical perspective*. Pittsburgh: University of Pittsburgh Press.

Sartorius, R. E. (1975). *Individual conduct and social norms*. Encino, CA: Dickenson.

Smart, J. C. C., & Williams, B. (1973). *Utilitarianism: For and against*. London: Cambridge University Press.

Wolff, R. P. (1977). *Understanding Rawls*. Princeton: Princeton University Press.

Wood, A. W. (1981). *Karl Marx*. Boston: Routledge & Kegan Paul.

CHAPTER 3

Economics and Justice

Stephen T. Worland

Aristotle: Raising the Fundamental Questions

In the Western European cultural tradition, the attempt to define and clarify justice as a social and moral concept received its classic formulation in Book V of Aristotle's *Nichomachean Ethics*. According to some authorities, most notably Joseph A. Schumpeter (1954, pp. 60–62), Book V is also the *locus classicus* for an early but not notably felicitous effort to understand the connection between the demands of justice as a moral virtue and the ethical problems encountered by a society that relies on market relationships for the organization and coordination of economic activity. Though he may not have succeeded in answering them, Aristotle does indeed bequeath a series of basic moral questions to those successors of Adam Smith in the tradition of mainstream economics who have tried to articulate the justice imperative as it relates to a private-property, market economy.

Artistotle's treatment of justice involves an effort to differentiate three kinds of social obligations, those relating to (a) distributive justice, which has to do with the division of offices, honors, money, or other goods among participants in a common enterprise; (b) rectificatory justice, which takes account of injuries done one private individual by another; and (c) exchange, or cummutative, justice, which provides norms for the regulation of voluntary transactions between private individuals.

Thus, the first question that Aristotle's analysis raises has to do with justice in exchange. As one commentary (Cohen & Greenberg,

STEPHEN T. WORLAND • Department of Economics, University of Notre Dame, Notre Dame, Indiana 46556.

1982, p. 4) puts it, his conception of justice presupposes that there is a "going rate of exchange" and that just contracts of purchase and sale will comply with such a rate. But this leaves open both the problem of how the going rate itself is established and the further question of whether such a rate conforms with a more fundamental "fair" exchange ratio between commodities.

Distributive justice requires that common goods be allocated among members of the community in a "geometric" proportion that matches their relative social standing or "merit." Commutative justice, on the other hand, requires that commodities exchange in a ratio that is fair, or in the case of monetary exchange, that the price reflect the fair value of the product. Aristotle's own conception of the relationship between these two kinds of justice is quite obscure, probably confused, so Lowry (1969) finds, by his difficulty in bringing mathematical distinctions to bear on the problem of exchange. But at least in the work of his medieval successors, it becomes clear that the reference to *two* different kinds of justice and *two* different rules or proportions poses a crucial dilemma. If commodities sell at their fair price—or at a price that reflects the "fair" rate of exchange—then how can society guarantee that exchange at such prices will also provide society's participants with an income proportionate to their relative "merit" or standing in the community? How is the rule requiring distribution of common goods in proportion to "merit" to be reconciled with the rule requiring "reciprocal proportionate equality" in the contractual, private exchange of commodities?

Though he himself might not have identified the problem as a "moral" one (see Buchanan & Mathieu, Chapter 2, this volume), Karl Marx with his labor theory of value suggests one solution for this ethical dilemma—a revolutionary solution that demands abolition of private property and of the market system. But as indicated in the discussion that follows, Adam Smith and his successors in what economists refer to as the "mainstream" or "neoclassical" tradition, provide an alternative, non-Marxian solution for this moral problem.

Mainstream—that is, neoclassical—economics provides a well-elaborated conceptualization of market relationships and a rigorous analysis of the "efficiency" properties of resource allocation and distribution mediated through the market. In so doing, neoclassical economics also provides a frame of reference from which one could specify the set of moral and political properties required for a market system to achieve both commutative and distributive justice.

A further critical question in economic justice emerges from

Aristotle's theory of property. Rejecting communism as proposed by Plato, he argues (*Politics*, II) that there should be private, individual ownership on the grounds that such an arrangement, by stimulating the natural play of "love of self," will contribute to efficiency and order in the use of resources. Insisting as he does on individual ownership, however, Aristotle is equally insistent that goods privately owned must be utilized so as to serve the community at large. It is one of the functions of the lawmaker to set up the institutional arrangements that will bring about the required coincidence between incentive-stimulating private ownership and communal benefit from the use of property (*Politics*, II, 5). With this line of argument, Aristotle poses yet another fundamental difficulty for a theory of economic justice: What are the rules that must be discerned and implemented in order to guarantee that the private ownership and management of productive resources will contribute to the general welfare of all society?

Consideration of Aristotle's classic treatment of the problem thus reveals three fundamental questions for those contemporary philosophers and social scientists concerned with the concept of justice and its place in a market society:

1. What are the rules of justice that a market society must establish in order to achieve the "proportionate equality" that commutative justice requires in private, contractual exchange of commodities?
2. Would such rules of justice allow a market society both to achieve the incentive advantages of private ownership, yet guarantee that private property be employed so as to serve the common good of society at large?
3. And finally, given that commutative justice obtains, what further rules are required to guarantee that market institutions will satisfy the requirements for *distributive justice*?

Adam Smith: Justice in the Disembedded Economy

"What are the rules," asks Adam Smith in the opening book for the *Wealth of Nations* (1776/1937) which "men naturally observe" in exchanging commodities and services with one another? In his answer to this classic moral question, Smith gives the problem the sharp reformulation required to take account of a momentous change in the structure of the social system. Unlike his classical or medieval predecessors, Smith writes for a society that has reached the stage of development where the production, distribution, and exchange of commodities have come to be carried out in specialized institutions—business firms and markets. In their systematic interaction, these institutions make up an economic system differentiated from, though connected with, the rest of the social organism. By the time of Smith's writing, the economy—to use Polanyi's classic phrase (1957, p. 68)—had come to be *disembedded* from the rest of the social system. Given that economic activity has been so differentiated, Smith asks, what are the special moral imperatives that men will articulate, internalize, and allow to govern their conduct in the production, distribution, and exchange of commodities?

Having perceived the need to reformulate the age-old moral question of justice, Smith tries to provide an answer for it by developing a scientific explanation of how a market economy functions. The rules of justice he discerns as applicable to private conduct and public institutions are not, as might be the case for a latter-day logical positivist, grafted arbitrarily onto a set of morally neutral statements of cause and effect. Rather, believing that an understanding of nature leads to an understanding of moral law, he tries to formulate an explanatory model that would both elucidate the true nature of economic institutions and, in the process, lead to an understanding of the relationships necessary to constitute a "right," "good," and "just" economic system.

The connection between scientific explanation and elucidation of moral principle appears most clearly in Smith's classic formulation—*Wealth of Nations* (1776/1937), Book I, Chapter 7—of the law of supply and demand. Drawing a distinction that parallels the difference between "going" and "fair rate of exchange" as noted in contemporary social psychology (Cohen & Greenberg, 1982), Smith differentiates between the "market" and "natural" price of a commodity. The first is established by the relation between supply and demand, whereas the second is determined by the amount of wages, profit, and rent that must be paid for the resources required to produce a commodity. Moreover, the natural price seems to be understood as an underlying, basic standard of fairness. For if market price exceeds the natural price, movement of resources into the market will expand supply until the two are equal; outward resource migration and decreased supply will eliminate the difference if market price is less than natural price. The latter is thus the "center of repose" toward which market prices "gravitate" (Smith, 1776/1937,

p. 58) and, when sold for its natural price, Smith notes in a phrase that echoes medieval moral theology, a commodity sells "for precisely what it is worth" (p. 55).

At a first reading, Smith's explanation of supply and demand seems to provide a clear explanation of how the first of Aristotle's three questions might be answered for a market society. The shift of resources in response to supply and demand ensures compliance with commutative justice by bringing the "going rate of exchange" into equality with the underlying "fair or "natural" rate. The latter, in turn, determines the "proportionate equality" that Aristotle identifies as necessary for exchange justice. Such equality obtains when the price paid for a commodity is equal to the value of the resources required to produce it or proportionate to the normal reward for productive effort. Such a reading of Smith seems plausible, and such an interpretation, no doubt, has served as a standard component of arguments purporting to demonstrate the moral legitimacy of market capitalism. Nevertheless, such a facile understanding of the market process in fact obscures a basic ambiguity.

A fundamental question that Smith leaves unanswered concerns the manner in which the basic fair standard—the natural price—is itself determined and given moral justification. Natural price equates with normal producer reward for the required factors of production. But Smith provides no satisfactory explanation of how such factor rewards are themselves determined and, what is more fundamental for a theory of justice, no demonstration that producers are morally entitled to receive such rewards. Factor prices might be determined by arbitrary convention or—as a Marxian critic of capitalism would argue—by a power struggle between opposing social classes. If such is indeed the case, then natural price in fact has no fundamental basis and cannot serve as a morally justified standard of fairness or justice in exchange. As indicated in the discussion that follows, one of the major accomplishments of Smith's successors in the neoclassical tradition is to provide rectification for this oversight in his analysis.

Understood in terms of political philosophy, the moral basis for Smith's vindication of the market mechanism can be found in the conception of natural right. Thus, according to Lewis (1977), individuals have a natural right to self-determination, and the opening up of market opportunities, especially for the working class, serves to protect them from arbitrary authority; the market constitutes a "device for achieving recognition . . . of natural right" (p. 38). Or to use a somewhat similar political conception, the free market might be understood as an institution designed to protect the "negative liberty"—that is, freedom from possible coercion—of the market participants (Berlin, 1969) or as a "bulwark against political interference with individual liberty" (DiQuattro, Chapter 4, this volume). Such complementarity between natural rights theory and the moral justification for market institutions is, of course, quite significant for an understanding of the concept of economic justice. From an economist's perspective, however, it is also important to note that though Smith did not formally espouse utilitarianism as a moral theory, his classic analysis of the market process does rest in part on a utilitarian base.

Postulating that the basic purpose of economic activity is to "provide a plentiful revenue of subsistence for the people" (Smith, 1776/1937, p. 397) and assuming that the ability to provide such subsistence varies directly with the level of net national product, Smith points out that the profit derived from investment in a particular sector of the economy is proportionate to the value added to raw materials or to net value produced by the production process. This being the case, the profit motive will naturally induce an investor to employ resources "in support of that industry of which the produce is likely to be of greatest value." But because the "annual revenue of every society is always precisely equal to the exchangeable value of the whole annual produce of its industry," it naturally follows that profit-motivated shifts in the use of resources will expand the level of society's net product. Thus, so the famous passage reads, the investor, is "led by an invisible hand to promote an end which is no part of his intention" (p. 423)—the end being an expansion of the level of aggregate output and, by implication, an increase in the level of consumer living standards.

This passage indicates that, although his theoretical analysis was too primitive to allow him to make his point conclusively, Adam Smith in fact discerns a relationship that eventually came to be recognized as a basic principle of neoclassical welfare economics—both by those interested in perfecting the market system (Pigou, 1932) and those advocating economic planning to replace it (Lerner, 1946). For Smith has perceived that cross-sector equalization of resource productivity is a necessary condition for maximization of net national product. In less technical terms, he has discerned that the shift of resources from low productivity to high productivity sectors will raise the amount of real social income generated from the community's resource base and, further, that the free play of competitive supply and demand is the mechanism whereby such income-expanding adjustments can be achieved in a market society. His basic insight, though requiring clarification by his successors, provides a basic principle for the legitimation of market relationships and a key factor for understanding the concept of economic justice.

In this regard, one should note how neatly Smith's analysis provides an answer to the second fundamental question that Aristotle poses for a market society. Aristotle requires that ownership of goods be left in private hands (for incentive reasons) but that the use of such goods must also be "common" or contribute to the well-being of the community at large. Smith's explanation of the impact of profit-motivated resource reallocation on the level of net product indicates that the free play of supply and demand constitutes the decision-making procedure whereby a market society achieves the required reconciliation of private ownership with communal use. When resources shift to higher productivity uses (in response to profit differentials), society at large benefits from the consequent expansion of net product. Thus Smith provides an arresting moral justification for market institutions: (a) by showing how the play of supply and demand protects natural rights and thus ensures compliance with commutative justice; and further (b) by demonstrating that such a process induces property owners to invest their resources in that employment where they can make their optimal contribution to net product and society's common good.

Smith: Social and Political Constraints

Two additional factors in Smith's development of the concept of economic justice call for special emphasis. For one thing, there is strong complementarity between his economics and his sociology. In the *Theory of Moral Sentiments* (1759/1976) Smith sets out to show how a set of system-stabilizing moral norms emerges from the social interaction of a community's members. As an individual grows to maturity within a social system, the individual learns to evaluate his or her own conduct in terms of the hypothetical decision of an "impartial spectator." Judging one's conduct in such a manner, a person comes to internalize as moral imperatives the customary behavioral standards prevailing in his society. Furthermore, such a social process is dialectical and progressive. The rules change in content as successive generations come to maturity within the social system, with the given and provisional "norms of performance" gradually being transformed into objective, more nearly absolute "ideals of performance" (Worland, 1983). Internalized by the individual, such communal standards "are of great use in correcting the misrepresentation of self-love" (Smith, 1759/1976, p. 266).

Social interaction thus generates rules of justice that provide a moral restraint for the individual pursuit of self-interest. In Smith's model of the economy, the operation of such an ethical constraint is explicitly stated as a necessary condition for the operation of the market system. According to his conception of the free market, the individual is to be left free to pursue his own interest in his own way but only so long as he observes a crucial moral proviso—that is, "as long as he does not violate the laws of justice" (Smith, 1776/1937, p. 651). Seeking a middle ground between cynical egoism on the one hand and unrealistic altruism on the other (Danner, 1976), Smith thus tries to show how a market society relies on economic self-interest as a motivating force, and how such a social system generates the moral norms required to direct such a force into socially beneficial channels.

Norms of justice emerging from social interaction are not the only form of constraint imposed on the pursuit of economic self-interest. Anticipating by 200 years the procedure adopted by Rawls (1971), Smith conceives of the social system as operating through a multistage sequence with economic institutions functioning within a set of procedures established at a prior, more fundamental level of social decision making. Basic ground rules are to be adopted at an initial state-of-nature stage (the counterpart of Rawls's "original position"), and further, social interaction is to take place within the framework established by such ground rules. In Smith's model of a market society, the supply-and-demand mechanism operates within a system of property rights and contract law established by public policy anterior to the working of market procedures. Rules of justice thus restrict economic activity and self-interest in two complementary but different ways—as moral imperatives internalized by private individuals and as extramarket legal norms established through the public sector (Worland, 1983).

Adam Smith thus makes a threefold contribution to an understanding of how the moral concept of justice applies to a market society. He tries to show how such a society generates rules of justice that function as moral imperatives. He demonstrates how compliance with such rules in a free market produces a set of equilibrium "natural" prices that reflect that "proportionate equality" in exchange required by Aristotle's conception of commutative justice. Finally, his explanation of the resource allocation mechanism shows how self-interest as constrained by such rules of justice leads individuals to employ their productive resources in a manner conducive to society's communal well-being.

However, with respect to distributive justice, Smith's analysis turns out to be quite inadequate. In this regard, the best he can offer is a primitive version of Rawls's difference principle (1971). Drawing a striking contrast between a progressive and stationary society, he identifies continued economic growth as the mechanism that, by raising wages through increased demand for labor, causes the benefits of economic progress and expanding net product "to diffuse itself through the lower ranks of society" (Smith, 1776/1937, p. 11). But he does not develop a conception of distributive justice that would allow the market system to acquire true moral legitimacy. The attempt to correct this defect provides a major point of focus for Smith's successors in the development of neoclassical economics. What they accomplish can best be understood by noting how their analysis of market relationships differs from its best known ideological alternative—the Marxian labor theory of value.

Justice and the Marxian Labor Theory of Value

Adam Smith himself employs a provisional form of the labor theory of value. In a precapitalist state of nature, the rules of contractual justice dictate that the exchange ratio between two commodities—as in the famous beaver and deer illustration (Smith, 1776/1937, p. 47)—be determined by the relative quantity of labor required to produce them. It is also the case, so Smith holds, that in the state of nature "the whole produce of labor belongs to the laborer." In other words, the natural law governing economic relationships in precapitalist society determines that the amount of wealth generated in the production of a commodity is proportioned to the labor required to produce it and by natural right belongs to the laborer himself.

The transition to capitalism, however, introduces a fundamental change in the structure of economic and social relationships. The market value of a commodity is henceforth determined by cost of production that includes profit on capital and rent on land in addition to the money wage. What is more basic, the emergence of capitalism involves a differentiation between social classes. After the rise of market relationships, members of one social class—the capitalists who own the means of production—will find themselves in a position where they can extract from the laborers a portion of what the latter produce. The capitalists, by providing the laborers with raw materials and setting them to work, can "make a profit . . . by what their labor adds to the value of the materials (Smith, 1776/1937, p. 48). After the transition to capitalism, the value of a commodity will include the elements of rent and profit, but the source of these latter two factor payments is value that is produced by the workers but captured by the capitalist.

So far as economic justice is concerned, Marx's main contribution can be understood as a systematic effort to generalize Smith's explanation of how profits emerge as the economy makes the transition from the premarket state of nature to capitalism. Analysis of the exchange process and of the relationship between use value and exchange value leads Marx to the basic principle of his model: "The value of one commodity is related to the value of another . . . as the working time necessary for the production of the one is to that necessary for the production of the other" (Marx, 1887/1967, p. 397). Generalizing this premise, he then proceeds to demonstrate that in a market system where labor itself is bought and sold through contractual agreement, the value of labor power, like that of any other commodity, is determined by the labor time necessary for the production of this "special article." The production of labor power reduces to the production of the commodities consumed by the worker, so that the value of labor resolves into that of the subsistence items used up by the worker in the process of production (p. 171f.).

The Marxian indictment of capitalism then follows with apodictic certainty. Because (a) the value of a *commodity* is determined by the number of hours required for its production and because (b) the value of the *labor* employed to produce a commodity reduces to the number of hours required to produce the worker's subsistence, it follows (c) that the excess of (a) over (b)—a quantity identified by Marx as *surplus value*—is the real source of capitalists' profit and of all nonwage income. Profits emerge because the market system allows the capitalist class to exploit the workers by forcing them to work longer hours than would be required to produce their own subsistence.

Led by his theory of knowledge to the notion that each mode of production generates its own relevant concept of justice (Cohen & Greenberg, 1982, p. 5), Marx would not identify exploitation as occurring under capitalism as an "injustice." However, such a practice clearly violates the kind of "proportionate equality" that Aristotle identifies as essential for justice. And Marx claims to have demonstrated that such a violation is the natural consequence of the working of capitalist institutions. If Marx is right, it is impossible for a market society that has advanced beyond the state of nature to the capitalist stage to fulfill the moral imperatives laid down in Aristotle's conception of justice. Thus, the most fundamental and important contribution the discipline of economics can contribute to an understanding of the concept of justice has to do with the validity of Marxian analysis. If such analysis is sound, capitalism can never acquire authentic moral legitimacy.

Marxian analysis of capitalism is purportedly "scientific"—that is, it claims to be based on an accurate understanding of the "laws of motion" of the capitalist system. This being the case, if the Marxian conception of such laws could be replaced with a more accurate alternative, moral condemnation of capitalist institutions based on Marx would be deprived of its logical basis. The so-called "marginal revolution" in economic thought claims to provide such an alternative, one that would provide grounds for rejecting both (a) Marx's causal analysis of market relationships and (b) any ethical indictment of capitalism based on such causal analysis.

What orthodox, mainstream economics contributes to an understanding of the concept of justice thus can be understood by observing the way neoclassical marginal economics tries to refute the Marxian labor theory of value and, by implication, the conception of exploitation derived therefrom.

The Marginalist Alternative to Marx

The first simple step in the revolution involves a new approach to the explanation of relative exchange values. Borrowing from physics the key notion that a systematic relationship between variables is to be found by differentiating the underlying function, marginal economics postulates that the exchange ratio between commodities is determined by the ratio of their respective marginal utilities. Whereas Marx could find no systematic relationship between use value and exchange value—and thus proposed to explain the latter by reference to the relative quantity of labor required to produce a commodity—marginal analysis uses differential calculus to distinguish between total utility and the variation in total utility associated with an incremental variation in the amount of a commodity consumed. Having done so, marginal economics then concludes that relative exchange values as observed in the market can be understood as determined by the relative marginal utility of the commodities in question.

Proceeding on the assumption that a systematic connection between utility and exchange value had thus been established, the new theory then led to a reformulation of the connection between the factors of production and the value of commodities. Commodities have value because of their utility, and factors of production have value because of their effectiveness in the production of commodities. Thus, the explanatory connection runs from the value of commodities to the value of productive factors and not, as in the labor theory of value, in the opposite direction. Furthermore, as in the relationship between utility and exchange value, the concept of marginal variation is here again crucial. The causal connection between commodity output and factor input is to be determined, not by the crude process of dividing the former by the latter, but by varying the latter and estimating the concommitant variation in the former. Thus, it is the marginal product of labor—that is, not output per man-hour but the partial derivative of output with respect to labor—that indicates the connection between the two variables and measures the laborer's contribution to production. Furthermore, so the marginal economists argued, it is the function of the capitalist labor market to guarantee that the worker in fact receives a wage proportionate to his or her marginal productive contribution.

In a market economy, labor is hired by profit-maximizing business firms. Due to the law of diminishing returns, profit maximization will induce an employing firm to increase employment as the wage falls and decrease employment if the wage rises. Thus, it is the response of the firm to variations in the wage that underlie the firm's demand for labor, and aggregation of the demand from each firm generates the total demand for labor of a given grade in the labor market. Juxtaposition of such a demand against the corresponding supply of labor (determined by the workers' occupational choice) and allowing the market to clear determines an equilibrium wage rate for each grade of labor. Furthermore, if there are no barriers to labor mobility, normal migration of workers from low-wage to high-wage employments will eventually establish an equilibrium whereby wages for a given grade of labor are equalized across sectors.

The implications of this kind of analysis for the concept of economic justice are, of course, immensely important. According to the model, the worker makes a contribution to production—found by differentiating the production function—and receives in exchange from the employer a wage equal to the market value of such a contribution. As the principle was once explained by one of the founders of marginalism (Clark, 1902, p. 87), by a "right of creation," the worker has acquired a moral claim to a "part of the wealth that the day's industry has brought forth," that is, to the value of his or her marginal product, and the function of the labor market is to forstall the "institutional robbery" that would occur if the worker were denied a wage proportioned to what he or she has so earned. Or to illustrate how marginal analysis complements primordial moral intuition, the theory explains how the capitalist labor market ensures compliance with an apparently self-evident moral axiom: "Equal pay for equal work." For the analysis indicates that in the absence of obstructions to free job choice, wage differentials prevailing at equilibrium can have one and only one necessary underlying cause: They must reflect differentials in worker productivity.

Furthermore, the marginal productivity analysis can also be brought to bear in the explanation of nonwage income. If the worker's contribution to production is to be measured by the concomitant variation of output with respect to the labor input, then the productive contribution of capital equipment can be isolated using the same analytical technique. Differentiation of a production function with respect to the employment of capital—or estimating the variation in output associated with variation in the use of capital equipment—yields a measurement of capital's marginal contribution to production. And just as profit maximization by firms plus intersector labor mobility guarantee that labor will be paid a wage equal to the value of the worker's marginal product, so similar assumptions imply that capital equipment will earn a rent per machine-hour proportionate to the machine's marginal contribution to production. Similar analysis can be used to explain the rent paid for the use of natural resources also.

The ethical implications of marginal analysis can be clarified by noting the crucial contrast with Marx. According to his explanation of the "laws of motion" of the capitalist system, exploitation of labor is inevitable because the wage the worker receives is necessarily less than the value of the product the worker produces for his or her capitalist employer. Nonwage income emerges from the production process because surplus value produced by the workers can be extorted from them by those who own the means of production. According to the marginal explanation, workers are paid in proportion to their marginal productive contribution, and nonwage income is determined by the productivity of the other, physical and natural, factors of production. Whereas the labor theory of value in its normative form asserts that the worker is entitled to an income proportionate to one's productive contribution and then measures the latter in terms of average product—output per man-hour, marginalism as a rule of wage justice accepts the major premise, alters the minor to substitute marginal for average product, and draws a conclusion that allows for the moral legitimacy of property incomes. Furthermore, whereas Marxism condemns the capitalist worker to continuous penury by basing the wage on the level of subsistence, marginalism dispenses with such an implicit appeal to Malthus. There is no systematic connection in the marginal model between the level of wages and the income necessary to ensure the worker's biological survival.

Or to put the distinction in historical terms, according to a Marxian explanation of capitalist development—for example, as offered in Macpherson's (1962) well-known interpretation of Locke—profit emerges when class differentiation between property owners and laborers reaches the point where "profit . . . that was the reward of one man's labor" is transferred through the wage contract "into another man's pocket" (Locke, as quoted by Macpherson, p. 206). According to a marginalist interpretation, on the contrary, the profit so transferred is actually (though Locke could not perceive the fact because of his ignorance of differential calculus), a reflection not of the superior bargaining power of one class vis-à-vis-another but of the productivity of capital. Workers agree to the wage contract not because they are forced to do so, but because labor and capital, being complementary factors of production, working in conjunction with the employer's capital, enhances worker productivity and, through the labor market, raises the laborer's income.

Having thus explained how the reward for a factor of production is determined, marginal productivity theory explains an ambiguity in Adam Smith and in the process clarifies the rules a market society must adopt in order to achieve compliance with Aristotle's principles of justice. Smith had shown how the play of supply and demand brings market price (the "going rate of exchange") into equality with natural price (the underlying "fair rate of exchange") with the latter being made up of "three component parts"—wages, profit, and rent. Marginal analysis extends the explanation by showing how each of these component parts is determined, and determined by a common causal principle—the value of the relevant factor's contribution to production.

Once this is understood, it is evident how the Aristotelian requirement of "proportionate equality" is satisfied through free-market exchange. When commodities sell at their natural price, the arithmetic equality essential for commutative justice prevails on both sides of the transaction. Buyers pay a price equal to the natural price or "fair rate of exchange" that is determined by the value of the resources required to produce a commodity. Producers receive—indirectly from the consumer, directly from the employer—a reward precisely equal to the value of their respective contributions to production. Such a conclusion tends to reinforce a cardinal principle of liberal political philosophy. For the analysis indicates that the free play of competitive supply and demand—allowing market participants maximal freedom in the exercise of their natural rights—is indeed the appropriate procedure in a market society for guaranteeing compliance with the moral imperative of commutative justice.

Marginalism: Locating the Source of Exploitation

To extend the contrast with Marx, neoclassical marginal analysis offers its own distinctive explanation for the fact that "exploitation" can occur in the capitalist mode of production. For the analysis demonstrates that when the employer is a monopoly, profit maximization naturally causes the labor employed by the firm to receive a wage income systematically less than the value of the worker's marginal contribution to production. When estimating the contribution to profit derived from hiring an additional worker, the monopolistic firm must not only take into account the physical law of diminishing returns: The firm must also consider the fact that increased output can be sold only by reducing the price of the product. Taking account of both factors leads the firm to restrict production and in the process reduce the demand for labor. The final equilibrium that results, unlike that established in competitive industries, causes the worker to receive a wage that is less than the value of his or her marginal contribution to production. The worker gets less value than he or she produces—and the "institutional robbery" that Clark (1902) thought might occur does in fact take place. Furthermore, as Bronfenbrenner's (1971) exhaustive classification of market structures shows (p. 190), there are several forms of market imperfection—such as employer domination ("monopsony") in the labor market—that can give rise to such injustice in the labor market. To draw the general conclusion, marginal analysis indicates that it is not the wage–labor relationship characteristic of the capitalist mode of production that generates workers' exploitation; rather, such an evil results when there is deviation from the competitive ideal within the capitalist structure. Free enterprise and free market processes yield justice for the workers only if the market allows competitive forces to work their way to equilibrium (Thurow, 1973, p. 73).

Moreover, the monopolistic tendency of capitalist firms to restrict production or to dominate the labor market are not the only sources of worker exploitation. Free migration of workers from low- to high-wage employments is essential if the market process is to generate a wage proportionate to the worker's contribution to production. Therefore, if public authority allows high-wage employments to be closed to would-be entrants, that is, if government tolerates racial discrimination in the labor market or tries to minimize welfare costs by outlawing migration of labor from one locality to another or tolerates collective bargaining practices that exclude some workers from high-paying jobs, then unjustifiable wage differentials can continue indefinitely. Workers capable of making a contribution to output greater than their present wage would be denied the opportunity to do so and hence deprived of a wage proportionate to their skill level. To generalize the point, if a market society relying on the supply and demand mechanism to determine wage rates is to avoid exploitation of the workers, then such a society must select and implement those rules of justice needed to protect the workers' occupational choice.

When fully developed, neoclassical marginal productivity theory thus demonstrates that orthodox, mainstream economics cannot be dismissed as a Dr. Pangloss effort to prove that *tout est pour le mieux* in the best of all capitalist worlds. In fact, neoclassical analysis indicates that where the free-enterprise pursuit of profit takes the form of restricting production and manipulating prices, the attainment of economic justice will require that the state push beyond laissez-faire and establish an effective antitrust policy. When social factors inhibit labor mobility, public authority must intervene to protect workers' rights to effective job choices. The rules of justice to be institutionalized in society's extramarket legal framework are thus considerably more complicated than Adam Smith realized; they require greater reliance on government intervention and public sector initiatives than Smith or his latter-day supply side admirers might be willing to admit.

Marginalism and the "Common Use" of Property

As indicated previously, one of the problems a market society must solve, if it is to implement the moral principles laid down by Aristotle, concerns the use of property. What rules of justice does such a society need in order to preserve the incentive advantages of private ownership, yet guarantee that the use of private property shall conduce to the general benefit of the community at large? Adam Smith's explanation of the threefold relationship among (a) the play of supply and demand, (b) the allocation of productive resources among sectors, and (c) the level of society's net national product provides an intuitive answer to such a question. The shift of resources induced by divergence between market price and natural price brings the allocation of resources into the equilibrium pattern that is "most agreeable to the interest of the whole society"—that is, into a configuration that maximizes per capita net national product. Marginal economic analysis clarifies Smith's intuition and in the process leads to a further clarification of the concept of economic justice.

Differentiating clearly between the marginal and average product of a resource, neoclassical economics claims to show that an owner–investor's return from the employment of a resource is equal to the value of its marginal product (its VMP), that cross-sector equalization of VMPs is a necessary condition for maximizing net product, and therefore, that the free play of a competitive market" will tend to bring about such a distribution of resources among different uses . . . as will raise the national dividend . . . to a maximum" (Pigou, 1932, p. 143). In condensed form, the analysis is expressed in a basic principle of neoclassical welfare economics—the so-called "equi-VMP rule." Such a rule states that cross-sector equalization of a factor's VMP is a necessary condition for maximum net national product (NNP). If such a marginal equality does not hold, transfer of labor from low-VMP sectors to high VMP sectors will increase society's aggregate real income. Moreover, because the wage is determined by the worker's VMP, cross-sector differentials in VMPs translate into wage differentials, that is, into the kind of market-signal response that not only raises workers' incomes but also shifts the allocation of labor toward the equi-VMP, net-product-maximizing pattern.

Extending the analysis to nonhuman resources, differentials in VMP translate into differentials in the rent per hour (R) earned by

capital equipment of a given kind or, given the value (cost of replace-
ment) of the capital equipment—K—into differentials in the rent–
capital ratio (R–K) or percentage rate of return earned by equipment
employed in different sectors. If the capital is private property, the
owner has an income incentive to transfer the use of the capital from
the low-return to high-return sectors. As with the reallocation of
labor, such transfers will add to the level of per capita real income
for the community at large.

    With respect to the equi-VMP rule, the distinction between com-
petitive and monopolistic markets is again of crucial importance. As
indicated before, when monopolistic obstruction occurs within the
market system, the drive for maximum profits characteristic of the
capitalistic system will necessarily produce antisocial consequences. This conclusion is reinforced by the equi-VMP rule. For if
monopoly occurs in some sectors of the economy, resources (e.g.,
labor) employed in such sectors will not only be paid a wage less
than the value of their contribution to production (VMP); at equilibrium, the VMP produced by such resources in the monopolized
sector will exceed that of comparable resources employed in the
competitive sector. Thus transfer of resources from the latter sector
to the former would not only eliminate worker exploitation by the
monopolist. Such a resource reallocation would also raise the level
of society's NNP.

    As characterized by John Rawls (1971, p. 309), the allocative
inefficiency caused by monopoly leads to a situation wherein "the
whole community is exploited." Using the Aristotelian distinctions
introduced earlier, one could also say that when markets are perfectly competitive, income maximization by owners of capital normally shifts resource use into a pattern that expands NNP. In this
case, privately owned property is employed in a manner conducive
to the common good. If monopoly prevails, on the other hand, income maximization by property owners will not make such an optimal contribution to societal well-being. The analysis of markets as
a resource allocation procedure thus underscores the crucial importance of commutative justice as an ethical principle governing market transactions.

    To summarize the justification for such a rule of justice, com-
pliance with commutative justice is necessary, first of all, to protect
the natural rights of commodity buyers and sellers to exchange at
just prices. In addition, as indicated in the discussion of the wage–
VMP relationship, transgressions against commutative justice indi-

rectly lead to exploitation of workers. Finally, consideration of the equi-VMP principle shows how compliance with commutative justice in the market is essential if, as required by Aristotle's conception of property, private ownership is to be reconciled with communal use of society's productive resources.

Pareto Optimality and Economic Justice

The relationship between commutative justice as a moral imperative and the equi-VMP principle can be clarified by stating the latter in an alternative, perhaps more familiar, form. Such a principle states that cross-sector equalization of a productive factor's VMP is a necessary condition for maximizing per capita NNP and indicates that such a condition can be satisfied in a market economy by allowing each factor to earn a reward equal to its VMP. Standard neoclassical microanalysis (Bator, 1957) shows that such a condition requires that price equal marginal cost in all product markets; the latter equality further implies that marginal rates of substitution in consumption equate with producer marginal rates of product transformation for all commodities produced and exchanged in the economic system. Such a comprehensive general equilibrium suffices to guarantee that the economy has attained *Pareto optimality*—with the latter defined as a situation where further benefit for any one member of the community can be achieved only by imposing a loss on some other member. Expansion of the equi-VMP principle thus indicates that compliance with the rules of commutative justice in product and factor markets is a necessary condition for achieving Pareto optimality in the use of society's resources.

The attempt to base rules of economic justice on the concept of Pareto optimality, however, encounters a series of fundamental interpretive difficulties. Some of these difficulties can be seen by examining the positions held by two prominent neoclassical theorists. Buchanan (1977) holds that alternative "positions of society" (e.g., free trade vs. a tariff) can be evaluated only by reference to the possibility of "conceptual agreement" among society's members, with such agreement to be achieved where necessary by the payment of compensation to those adversely effected by a change in policy. Buchanan adopts the principle that unanimous agreement—"Wicksell unanimity" or Pareto optimality achieved by the use of compensation (p. 138)—provides the ultimate criterion for evaluating changes in the social system, including those shifts in the economic variables (prices and costs) that affect the allocation of productive resources and the level of society's NNP. In his model, the desires or preferences of the community at large constitute an ultimate ethical norm; his use of Pareto optimality thus implies acceptance of that methodological view characterized in political philosophy as *voluntarism* (Worland, 1963).

A similar conception of the nature and source of moral imperatives is implied in Posner's (1981) effort to adapt the explanatory schema constructed in neoclassical welfare economics to an interpretation of the common law. Proposing to develop a moral theory based on the criterion that an act (e.g., a judicial decision) or an institution is to be judged "just and good" to the extent that it contributes to maximizing society's wealth (p. 115), Posner defines social wealth as "the aggregate satisfaction of preferences . . . backed up by money"; such a principle is said to provide a "foundation for a theory of distributive and corrective justice" (pp. 61, 69). Having established wealth maximization as the appropriate ethical goal for the functioning of social institutions, Posner then uses "Pareto superiority" as the basic test for determining when a shift in the social system—an act of private contractual exchange, a court decision, an institutional reform—can be said to increase social wealth. When there are significant transactions costs or externalities (e.g., noise pollution) that affect third parties, it will be necessary to resort to judicial procedures to determine whether a given social adjustment does or does not have the required "superiority." But in the normal operation of market institutions, the observed fact that two parties voluntarily agree to a transaction is proof enough that the concommitant shift in economic variables has the desired property of Pareto superiority. Thus the standard test for determining whether a change in the allocation of resources contributes to wealth maximization or is "Pareto superior" is to show that "everyone affected by the change consented to it." "Consent" is identified as the "operational basis of Pareto superiority" (p. 89).

Posner (1981) is not a thoroughgoing utilitarian. He introduces a Kantian component into his analysis by insisting that only those shifts in the social variables that are Pareto superior—which rest on the voluntary consent of those affected and thus respect the autonomy of the individual person—are to be considered desirable (p. 89). Within the confines of such a proviso, however, his normative analysis does rely on a utilitarian conception of the good. Thus, he accepts Bentham's psychological assumption that "people are rational maximizers of their satisfactions in all areas of life" and converts such an assumption into a moral principle for the evaluation of social institutions by employing the concept of "economic efficiency" as an ethical as well as a scientific or explanatory concept (p. 13). It is a psychological fact of life that individuals seek maximum satisfaction of their desires, and as a matter of ethical principle, society should design institutions so as to facilitate such maximization. Insisting on consent as a side condition, Posner accepts the principle that he attributes to the utilitarians; society's happiness is "maximized when people . . . are able to satisfy their preferences, whatever those preferences may be, to the greatest possible extent" (p. 52).

Objections to the Neoclassical Model

Several fundamental questions have arisen as to the validity of neoclassical welfare economics and the rules of justice derived therefrom. Thus McKee (1979) describes welfare economics as a "surrogate ethics" that produces logically impressive rules of justice that are in fact devoid of real validity. The lack of validity derives in part from the implicit conception of moral good. According to McKee's analysis, the fundamental principle of neoclassical welfare economics—that movement toward Pareto optimality or implementation of the equi-VMP principle enhances social welfare—is based upon a series of dubious premises. Included in the latter is a crucial axiom specifying the nature of the good—the "economic good is what an individual wants—where each seeks his own egotistically" (McKee, 1979, p. 68).

The reference to economic good as "what a person wants" recalls one of the perennial problems encountered in neoclassical welfare economics. The actual desires registered in the market—those crucial "signals" to which workers, entrepeneurs, and investors are expected to respond—reflect only those desires that can be made effective through the expenditure of monetary purchasing power. Ever since the original alliance between neoclassical economics and utilitarian moral philosophy was forged toward the end of the last century (Marshall, 1890), it has been recognized that the economist's practice of taking market price as an empirical proxy for psychological and moral factors was shot through with conceptual difficulties. For one thing, a dollar spent by a poor person and an equal expenditure by a rich person cannot be said to "measure" an equal amount of "pleasure" or "satisfaction," though each dollar so spent would

have equal efficacy in controlling the allocation of productive resources. Failure to take account of this factor means that the economist's policy recommendations employ "a biased indicator of utility, and the bias is in favor of the wealthy" (see Soltan, Chapter 8,
this volume).

Similarly, Mill's well-known distinction between "higher" and
"lower" pleasures poses a problem for those who would use welfare
economics as a set of minor premises to connect utilitarian ethical
principles with judgments on public policy. Expenditure of a given
amount of purchasing power can measure only the "force" of consumer desire, but such measurement cannot take into account
qualitative differences between the nobler and baser kinds of pleasure (Marshall, 1890, p. 16f.). Desire for a dollar's worth of pushpin
is as worthy of satisfaction, so reliance on market signals would
indicate, as is the desire for a dollar's worth of poetry. Thus to the
extent that welfare economics relies on prices as indicators of pleasure, the discipline must perforce fall back on the cruder "Benthamite" version of utilitarianism as its source of moral principle and has
been "roundly and perennially criticized for doing so" (McPherson,
1982, p. 254).

Posner's (1981) psychological assumptions and the ethical principle derived therefrom have called forth another, related line of
objection. Making a point similar to one raised by McDaniel (1981),
Rohrlich (1984, p. 221) grants the legitimacy of assuming that man is
an economizing maximizer for "one phase of his self-realization"
but warns against the *pars-pro-toto* lapse or fallacy that inheres in
the attempt to use such an assumption to explain all human behavior, such as crime or family formation. Rohrlich's insight indicates
the kind of restricted interpretation that must be given neoclassical
welfare economics if such a discipline is to be used to determine
whether market institutions can be made to comply with Aristotle's
principles of justice.

Aristotle's conception of human goodness and perfection involves a crucial distinction between two classes of goods—those
that are both good and praiseworthy and those that are only useful
(Worland, 1984). Commodities and services produced and exchanged in the economy fall into the second category; they are useful
as contributory to other goods but do not have an instrinsic value of
their own. Or, as a contemporary writer on the philosophy of law
(Dworkin, 1980) makes the point, wealth is not "something worth
having for its own sake" and is not a "component of social welfare"
in its own right. Granting such a distinction between kinds of goods

requires a drastic restriction on utilitarianism as a source of moral principle. For if Aristotle's distinction between kinds of goods is adhered to, it would be inappropriate to treat artistic, cultural, or moral perfections as useful goods and to appraise them in terms of their contribution to pleasure or psychological happiness. This being the case, social institutions are not to be evaluated in terms of their efficiency in satisfying individual preferences or desires for such goods. The case is different, however, for those marketable commodities and services whose production and exchange generates society's net national product. These are desirable only for their usefulness, and it is consistent with Aristotle's conception of human good to evaluate economic institutions in terms of their efficiency in satisfying society's need for such goods. Therefore, the equi-VMP principle as established in neoclassical welfare economics can be said to play a crucial role in extending and articulating Aristotle's social philosophy. For such a principle shows how compliance with the rules of commutative justice in contractual exchange contributes to that common use of private property required by Aristotle's conception of the relationship between the human potential for perfection and human beings' material and biological resource bases.

The possibility of thus linking Aristotle's ethical system with welfare economics also brings a fresh insight to bear on one of the perennial problems economists encounter when trying to justify their recommendations concerning public policy. The rise of logical positivism, with its characteristic insistence on the disjunction between ought and is, value and fact, shattered the comfortable alliance between neoclassical economics and utilitarianism (Robbins, 1932). Henceforth convinced that value judgments cannot be reduced to scientific statements of fact, economists tried to respond by distinguishing carefully between questions having to do with distributional *equity* and those relating to the *efficiency* of the economic system. Granting that decisions concerning equity require an appeal to value judgments, they came to agree that their discipline, qua science, could not determine whether the distributional impact of a policy or institution is or is not desirable. Questions concerning distributive justice were therefore excised and turned over for solution to the political process.

At the same time, economists tried to salvage their right to criticize public policy through a careful formulation of the concept of economic efficiency. Defining the latter in terms of Pareto optimality—efficiency improves when a shift in the economic variable makes one person better off without causing harm to another. In

terms of the Hicks–Kaldor hypothetical compensation test (cf. Soltan, Chapter 8, this volume) by showing that improvements in overall efficiency warrant unanimous approval by the community at
large, economists tried to show that policy recommendations based
on a concern for overall efficiency were somehow value free. Finally
recognizing that the attempt to derive normative conclusions from
thoroughly non-normative premises must necessarily fail, they then
resorted to the dubious argument that the normative postulates required to take their analysis out of the indicative mood were the kind
of noncontroversial value judgment likely to be universally accepted
in a liberal, individualistic society. (The issues here are neatly summarized by Thurow, 1973, and, with citation of the relevant literature, by Sen, 1970, p. 56ff.).

As is indicated later, Aristotle's conception of excellence or no-
bility suggests criteria that a market society might employ in order to
achieve justice in the distribution of property rights and educational
opportunities. His ethical system also indicates where economists
might look in their so-far unavailing search for an adequate foundation for the crucial normative assumption that efficiency in the use
of the community's resource base is ethically good and desirable.
Such a foundation might be found in Aristotle's conception of the
"good life" and of the role of useful goods—including items of
wealth—in the achievement of such a life for society's members
(Worland, 1984).

To come finally to the third question raised in the introduction
to this chapter, marginal economic analysis may show how ex-
·change on a competitive market satisfies commutative justice and
may also demonstrate the much more esoteric point that such exchange tends to shift productive resources into their NNP-maximiz-
ing uses. But the deeper question remains: Would economy-wide
compliance with commutative justice through the play of supply
and demand also generate that division of benefits in geometric proportion to merit required by Aristotle's conception of distributive
justice?

Marginalism and Distributive Justice

Marginal productivity theory claims to demonstrate that, given
the cross-sector mobility characteristic of competitive markets, each
factor of production would earn an income proportionate to its contribution to social output. Or, in the words of one of the founding

fathers of marginalism, "Free competition tends to give to labor what labor creates, to capitalists what capital creates, and to the entrepreneur what the coordinating function creates" (Clark, 1902, p. 3). Clark's famous dictum certainly suggests that the competitive market provides society with a procedure for implementing Aristotle's conception of distributive justice. For if the moral claim to income is understood as based upon contribution to production, then it is indeed the case that the market process that brings market price to equality with natural price (commutative justice) also distributes the benefits of productive effort in proportion to merit. Those differing in productive capability would receive unequal shares; those equally productive would receive equal shares. One and the same institutional procedure—the free play of supply and demand in a fair and open market—simultaneously provides compliance with both kinds of justice, commutative and distributive.

Nevertheless, plausible as such a line of argument may seem, as several commentators point out (Bronfenbrenner, 1971; Clark & Gintis, 1978; Harris, 1978), the attempts to deduce a full-fledged, adequate principle of distributive justice from the marginal productivity theory of factor pricing must necessarily fail. The failure becomes evident when careful attention is paid to the distinction between labor and other factor incomes. Labor perhaps can be said to earn an income through productive effort, with the amount of income determined by the value of the marginal contribution to society's net product and hence geometrically proportioned to the relative productive "merit" of the worker (Thurow, 1973, p. 70 ff.).

Is there any sense in which property income can also be earned and hence be morally justified as the reward for productive effort? In a consideration of the rules of economic justice, one needs to take note of a heroic effort to provide an affirmative answer to this question by one of Adam Smith's well-known successors in the tradition of mainstream economics.

According to Nassau Senior's analysis of market capitalism, labor and natural resources cannot achieve their full productive efficiency without the concurrence of a third "instrument of production" (1836/1939, pp. 26, 50ff.). This third instrument is identified as the act of *abstinence*—an activity that requires the foregoing of present consumption and that is "necessary to the existence of capital." Such an activity is productive, but as a faithful follower of Bentham, Senior insists that it is also painful; it is "among the most painful exertions of the human will" (p. 60). Such painful exertion, precisely like that involved in the efforts of the laborer, must be rewarded if production is to take place. Profit is the reward savers earn by forgoing consumption and allowing the capital so accumulated to be used in production. Thus abstinence "stands in the same relationship to profit as labor to wages" (p. 59). As the reward that must be paid as the incentive to abstain, profit—or interest, in modern terminology—becomes an element in cost of production that must be paid in order to call forth productive effort.

Senior is quite insistent that a distinction be drawn between the interest income of the capitalist and the rental income of the landowner. The latter is the reward "not for having labored or abstained, but simply for not having with-held what he [the landlord] was able to withhold." Unlike wages or interest, rent is "obtained without any sacrifice" (p. 90ff.). As a natural resource, the land is available for use in production and capable of yielding a surplus (shown in marginal analysis to be the equivalent of the land's marginal product) without the intervention of human effort. Understood in terms of marginal analysis, Senior's argument suggests that it may be essential for efficient resource allocation (to fulfill the equi-VMP principle) that producers be required to pay a rent for the use of the land. But the analysis also indicates that rent does not have to be paid to call the land into existence. Land rent thus functions as an incentive payment that induces owners to transfer their property to those sectors where its use is optimal. But the payment of rent is not an incentive payment required to have the land—a productive resource given by nature—produced in the first place.

Furthermore, progress in economic analysis since Senior's day shows that what he held to be true for land rent (though he would have denied it) is also true, for the most part, for the payment of interest on capital. At the most, only that portion of interest income earned by newly produced capital goods can be considered as in any sense the reward for abstinence. In order for new capital goods to be produced, either to expand society's capital stock or (as in the reinvestment of depreciation funds) to maintain the capital stock at its existing level, saving must take place so as to divert resources from the current production of consumer goods. The return on such investment might be considered the reward for such savings, though the reasoning is not especially convincing. But for the capital stock already in existence, the income that appears in financial or legal reckoning as interest on invested capital is, so far as economic function is concerned, exactly like the rent of the land.

Capital goods are productive in the sense that they have, like any other economically significant factor of production, a marginal product greater than zero. For newly produced capital goods, the value of what such goods contribute to production, when related to their cost of production, determines the basic "real" rate of interest (or profit, in Senior's terminology) for the economic system. The competitive shifting of investment funds from one sector of the economy to another will bring interest rates on all types of investments into line with this basic real rate. For that part of the capital stock already in existence—for example, for machines and equipment produced in the past but still productive enough to have a positive marginal product—what such equipment will earn per year can be capitalized at the competitive rate of interest so as to determine the investment value in such capital goods. It follows, tautologically, that funds invested in such capital goods will earn a rate of interest equal to the going rate.

However, what such capital earns is in economic substance a reflection of what the physical capital (machines and equipment) contribute to production, though in its legal aspects it may appear as a reward for those who have saved the funds invested in them. Though a particular investor may have to make sacrifices to acquire their ownership, no incentive payment need be made to make them available to the community at large for use in production. Thus, a decrease in the rate of interest as a reward for savings will affect the exchange value of the property rights of those who own capital equipment and may also cause a change in the rate of production of new capital equipment. But a fall in the rate of interest will not affect the productivity of the existing capital stock. Once capital goods exist, their significance so far as economic function is concerned, is exactly like that of land or other natural resources. No incentive payment need be made to keep such goods available for use in production.

Our reflection on Senior's (1836/1939) attempt to treat profit as an income earned by those who abstain from consumption suggests a tentative generalization. Property incomes emerge in the distribution process of a market economy, not because capital exploits labor as Marx held, but because land and equipment are so productive (have a positive marginal product) that firms are willing to pay a price for their use. In a market economy, such factor prices serve what Rawls (1971, p. 273) refers to as an "allocative function," that is, they provide signals to the market. Response to these signals allows a market economy to achieve compliance with the equi-VMP principle. Given private ownership, factor prices also have a distributive function in that they determine the amount of income received by those who own the various means of production. It is essential to note that, unlike the wage paid to labor, such property incomes cannot be considered the reward for productive effort made by their owners and cannot be morally justified by reference to such effort. Property—natural resources and capital equipment—are productive; property owners are not. Or as an authority on neoclassical marginal productivity theory makes the point (Bronfenbrenner, 1971, p. 208), a distinction has to be made between the "productivity of my land and capital" and the "productivity of my *persona*." Whereas the second productivity might provide moral warrant for payment of a wage as reward for services rendered, the first cannot justify payment of rent or interest to those who own the land or equipment, for it is the physical productivity of these nonhuman factors and not the function performed by their owners that generates income in the market system.

Marginalism and the Liberal Conception of Justice

Such a conclusion points to a critical inadequacy in one variant of the liberal conception of justice. The fact that compliance with commutative justice in commodity markets guarantees a wage payment proportionate to worker productivity may suggest that such contractual justice is not only a necessary but also a sufficient condition for achieving economywide justice in the distribution of income. Thus, according to Nozick's interpretation of the liberal position, an individual's income should be determined not by consideration of his or her moral merit but "in accordance with the perceived value of a person's actions and services to others" (Nozick, as quoted in Sterba, 1980, p. 154). So far as wage income is concerned, marginal economic analysis indicates that such perception emerges from the play of a competitive market—the wage matches the VMP. But such analysis also demonstrates that such a principle is not sufficient to justify the receipt of property income, for such income reflects the perceived value (VMP) of physical and natural assets, not the value of those who own them. Similarly, Friedman's rule for distribution—"to each according to what he and the instruments he owns produces" (as quoted in Sterba, 1980, p. 140)—conceals an ambiguity. Instruments are productive and for the sake of allocative efficiency must earn an income proportionate to their relative VMPs. But as Bronfenbrenner's reference to the distinction between capital goods and the persona of the person who owns them indicates, there is a crucial difference between what an individual produces and what that individual's property produces. One moral principle will not justify income received from two such different sources. Posner's assertion (1981, p. 81)—"the wealthier people will be those who have the higher marginal products"—is open to the same objection. There is a crucial difference between the income derived from the marginal productivity of one's labor and that based upon the productivity of the property one happens to own.

The distinction between the productivity and ownership of capital goods, furthermore, points to an ambiguity in the wage relationship and to a necessary qualification in the principle that a payment of a wage proportionate to the worker's VMP can be justified as reward for services rendered. For the process of capital investment whereby resources are devoted to building up the capital stock can take the form of investment in "human capital." Resources can be employed in training and education that enhance skills and increase labor productivity. After such investment takes place, the reward earned by the workers may take the legal form of a wage payment, but in economic substance it will include an element of return on investment in human capital. And the worker can claim a moral right to the higher wage only if it can be shown not only that he or she earned the wage through productive effort, but also that the individual had a moral right to the educational opportunities that enhanced his or her productive efficiency.

Thus, when fully articulated, marginal productivity theory is not the simpleminded justification for the capitalist status quo that it might appear in the form given it by J. B. Clark (1902). Rather, the theory indicates that the pattern of personal or household income distribution emerging from the market process must be understood as reflecting the play of three interacting but irreducibly distinct causal factors: (a) the relative productivity of units of labor, land, and capital equipment; (b) the distribution of property rights that determines which households own the nonhuman resources; and (c) the allocation of educational opportunities.

The first determines how much a resource earns. But it is the second factor that determines which households are to receive as private income the earning generated by the nonhuman resources. And it is the third independent factor that determines which members of the community will receive the higher wages caused by investment in their training. If there is to be justice in the final end state distribution of income generated by the market, then there must be prior premarket justice in the distribution of property rights and educational opportunities. The distribution of property rights in the community's factor endowment must be established by some kind of nonmarket decision-making procedure and by appeal to nonmarket substantive criteria.

Thus, a critical question for a conception of economic justice is this: Can a market society establish procedures for distributing property incomes that would meet Aristotle's requirments for distributive justice? According to the latter, honors, offices, and the benefits of social life are to be distributed in a geometric proportion that reflects relative merit. A crucial question, of course, is the definition of merit. So far as labor incomes are concerned and if the proviso noted previously concerning education is taken into account, merit might be understood as Thurow (1973) indicates was the case for 19th-century liberal thought, by reference to a worker's contribution to production. If so, distribution of wage income in proportion to a worker's VMP might be sufficient for distributive justice. However, previous discussion was meant to show that the right to receive property income cannot be justified by reference to the productive contribution of the property owner. Thus, with respect to property income, the merit or standing in the community that determines one's position in the distribution of common goods cannot be determined by reference to the owner's economic productivity. To satisfy Aristotle's principle of distributive justice with respect to property income, a market society must come to some estimate of relative merit other than that of contribution to production.

Neoclassical marginal economics offers no guidance as to how such nonproductive merit is to be discerned and evaluated. But such economic analysis does show how a market society could provide implementation for such communal appraisal of relative merit once such a crucial decision has been made. In order to fulfill the efficiency imperative, capital equipment and natural resources must be allocated among firms and industries so as to achieve cross-sector equality in their respective VMPs. Such a rule determines the amount of rental income earned by a given unit of machinery or land. The income thus derived from the value productivity of these nonhuman resources, however, unlike the wage income that must be paid to call forth productive effort, can be distributed among society's members in whatever pattern is found to be desirable. Marginal analysis denies the Marxian claim that property income is derived from the exploitation of labor but nevertheless supports the inference that such income constitutes a disposable social surplus that the community is free to distribute to those members of society who do not make a personal contribution to production.

The conception of justice implied in marginal economic analysis can be further clarified by showing how such a conception relates to theories of justice developed by contemporary political philosophers.

Economic Marginalism: Nozick and Rawls

According to Nozick's entitlement theory, a person is entitled to ownership of an asset if it has been acquired either (a) "in accordance with the principle of justice in acquisition"; or (b) "in accordance with the principle of justice in transfer" (Nozick, as cited in Sterba, 1980, p. 149). Marginal economic analysis has no particular bearing on the second principle but does raise interesting questions about the first. Nozick's theory indicates that the worker who labors to produce additional wealth or to add value to the existing stock of raw materials has made a "legitimate first move" that gives him or her a property right in the goods produced. "Whoever makes something . . . is entitled to it" (p. 156). But marginal productivity theory indicates that the output of a productive enterprise is the joint result of the employment of complementary productive factors, capital and land as well as labor. Nozick's theory begs two questions: Who is entitled to receive the property incomes generated by these non-human factors? And on what grounds? To assert that those who have acquired them by justice in transfer are so entitled (Nozick's second principle) does not suffice for an answer but merely raises the question of justification for the income used to finance the transfer. And the assertion that "things come into the world already attached to people having entitlements over them" (p. 156) obviously does not apply to natural resources. These are immensely productive and are hence the source of income when employed in production, but no one person can claim title to them on the grounds that they are the result of his or her productive labor. And as indicated in the discussion of Senior, unless one is prepared to accept the dubious notion that interest is the legitimate reward for the sacrifice involved in capital formation, the same can be said for the capital equipment used in production.

According to Rawls (1971), the pattern of income and wages emerging from the market process would satisfy the requirements of justice if the system is "properly organized and embedded in a just basic structure" (p. 304). The proper organization required to achieve justice through the market would include such factors as enforcement of contracts, prevention of fraud, and enactment of anti-trust laws. But marginal analysis emphasizes that an additional feature of the "basic structure" is required if the market is to produce just results. That is, there must be established, by extramarket procedures and anterior to the market process, distributive justice in the ownership of productive assets. The market determines how much a productive resource should earn—for example, a rental income proportionate to the factor's VMP. But the set of factor incomes earned by nonhuman productive resources will convert into a pattern of personal income distribution that qualifies as morally just only if the premarket pattern of ownership is itself morally justified. In his model, Rawls (1971, p. 276f.) assigns responsibility for the distribution of property rights to a "distributive branch" that is charged with rectifying the pattern of property rights so as to prevent concentrations of wealth that might pose a threat to political liberty. However, careful consideration of the connection between marginal productivity theory and Aristotle's rules for distributive justice suggests that there is also a deeper conception of distributive justice implied in Rawls' model of the social system.

Rawls (1971) claims that his model for a just society is not thoroughly utilitarian. He does not believe it appropriate to make the pushpin-as-good-as-poetry assumption and then evaluate the social system solely in terms of its efficiency in satisfying given wants. On the contrary, he acknowledges that standards of excellence in culture and the arts are significant for the design and appraisal of social institutions. However, in order to avoid a possible threat to liberty, he does not allow a regard for such excellence to control the choice of first principles in the original position. Rather, concern for excellence emerges in the subsequent, postcontract functioning of the social system and is brought into operation through the activities of private associations.

From the perspective of an economist, it is important to note that the exemplification of cultural and artistic perfections cannot take place unless the actors in the scenario are provided with an appropriate supply of resources. The artist needs not only the subsistence required for survival; also, and more significantly, this individual needs the tools of his or her trade—stone for the mason, bronze for the sculptor, manuscripts for the scholar. For those whose social contribution consists of the production of useful goods sold in the market, wage income provides subsistence, and the tools of the trade are provided by their firms. The latter acquires the revenue both to pay the wage and provide the tools through the sale of marketable use values. But if the full range of human excellences is to be exemplified in the good society, there will also be a great many members of the community who need economic resources to perform their particular function but who cannot acquire them through sale of output on a market. It is this crucial relationship that finally determines what a market society must do if it is to implement the Aristotelian ideal of distributive justice.

For those members of the community who exemplify a nonproductive excellence, distribution in proportion to merit could be achieved through the allocation of property rights. Social interaction through private associations, according to Rawls (1971), allows for the exemplification and mutual appreciation of complementary perfections. The same process of social communication could lead to a specification of property rights. Community perception of the potential for a particular excellence among its members would provide the *material* context that, according to Buchanan and Mathieu (Chapter 2, this volume), must be specified in order to implement distributive justice. Such a procedure could also determine the amount of income required to permit the realization of such potential and could allocate property rights accordingly. Distributive justice in a market society would thus be achieved through a threefold process. The income earned by a nonhuman resource would be determined through the market—and for the sake of efficiency, would equate with the factor's VMP. Through interaction in private associations, the community could discern potential excellence and allocate an amount of property income required to permit its exemplification. Such a pattern of distribution in proportion to merit having been determined, the coercive authority of the state would come into play to implement and maintain the distributive decision so made.

Such a comprehensive conception of the distributive process compares favorably with that outlined by Buchanan (1975; see also Worland, 1976) wherein the initial distribution of property rights is decided by a presocial, predatory standoff. Such a combination of Rawls and Aristotle, emphasizing that distribution is a multistage process, might also resolve the apparent conflict between Rawls and the kind of "perfectionism" espoused by David Norton (Norton, 1976). Finally, a model that bases distributive judgments on communal estimates of relative excellence offers clarification for a common approach to problems of economic equity.

According to such an approach, members of the community are assumed to have preferences or desires, not only for goods consumed and work performed, but also for alternative patterns of income distribution. Desires for the latter are synthesized into a communal social welfare function, and the conditions are then specified for maximizing the latter (cf. Bator, 1957; a typical exposition is also to be found in Ng, 1980, p. 38f.). Introducing the social welfare function and isolating the necessary conditions for its maximization closes the neoclassical general equilibrium model by indicating which of the multiple Pareto optima should be selected as the target for public policy. But the procedure glosses over an underlying ambiguity. Preferences for changes in the distribution of income may be—as once suggested by Thurow (1971)—based upon a perceived connection between distribution and such factors as crime or political instability. If so, the effort to maximize social welfare implies a rather crude form of utilitarianism—society exists to maximize the satisfaction of individualistic, egoistic desires, including the desire to forestall social unrest through income redistribution. On the other hand, the analysis may invoke a critical distinction between preferences for ordinary economic commodities and those "meta-preferences" or "second-order" preferences that reflect an individual's ethical views concerning income distribution. Maximizing a social welfare function that reflects the latter does not imply egoistic utilitarianism, but it does leave open the question as to the grounds for these ethical views. Aristotle's conception of society as a communal enterprise through which complementary human excellences can be exemplified suggests what might be an appropriate grounding for such ethical judgments. They could be based, as indicated earlier, on perceptions of potential excellence.

Conclusion: Capitalist "Rationality" and the Prospects for Justice

The preceding discussion of neoclassical economics provides a comprehensive answer to the question on which the present chapter has focused: What are the rules and procedures that a market society must establish if such a community is to fulfill Aristotle's conception of justice. However, the analysis so far developed succeeds only in isolating and clarifying the rules that a market society needs in order to comply with the Aristotelian moral imperative. It does not answer the further and deeper question—an issue that pertains to moral psychology rather than to pure economics—as to whether such a society would be able to achieve the social consensus necessary for the practical implementation of such rules. Philosophers have criticized Rawls on the grounds that his model of society is in fact "want-regarding" rather than "ideal-regarding" (Barry, 1973) or because his conception of the social system does not succeed in transcending the confines of what Hegel referred to as "civic" or "private society" (Fisk, 1974; Gintis, 1983). There is a parallel line of argument that indicates that the attempts to establish Aristotelian justice in a market society will be self-defeating, because such a community, relying on supply and demand to regulate the allocation of resources, will be deprived of the crucial perspective necessary to implement such a demanding moral ideal.

Thus, according to a critique of capitalism developed by Herbert Marcuse (1964), the neoclassical justification for market institutions employs a special conception of human rationality characteristic of a "one-dimensional man." Limited to a technical or instrumental conception of causality, such a one-dimensional creature will be unable to perceive "the contrast between the given and the possible," the distinction between the world as it is and the prevalance of unrealized moral and aesthetic possibilities. Marcuse argues that inhabitants of such a "one-dimensional universe" belong to a world where conceptions of the "Good and Beautiful" are finally reduced to "matters of preference" (Marcuse, 1964, pp. 8, 12, 130, 146, 148). In a similar vein, Weisskopf (1971) points out that exclusive reliance on a technical conception of rationality (as the ability to perceive only instrumental, means–end causality) involves a "demotion of reason" that deprives society of the perspective necessary to appreciate moral and aesthetic values (pp. 37ff., 89–90). Building on Habermas's distinction between the "purposive-rational" and "practical reason," Wisman (1979) also finds that the working of capitalist institutions tends to obliterate the latter, reducing the practical vision required for the perception of the good and noble to technical means–end reasoning.

A similar analysis of the role of means–end rationality in a market society has been offered by Bruce McDaniel (1981). The historical emergence of market capitalism has produced an economic system disembedded from the rest of the social system and in the process has created a disjunction between (a) the technoeconomic, (b) the political, and (c) the cultural aspects of society. Such disembedding of the economy and concomitant reliance on means–end rationality causes grave damage to the social system because such a single-minded emphasis on efficiency tends to obliterate a crucial dimension of human activity. The structure of human needs is bifurcated—one "material part . . . satisfied by consuming a good" and another "subjective component" fulfilled by the "symbolic . . . or cultural aspects of the good." A disembedded market economy wherein performance is evaluated solely in terms of the satisfaction of consumer demand would, according to McDaniel's analysis, take account of only the first of the two components of need. Thus, he concludes that in a community relying on the neoclassical market paradigm for self-understanding, "values and meaning derived from human interaction cannot be observed . . . and are largely ignored" (p. 547ff.).

To bring matters to a conclusion—and to emphasize the moral dilemma faced by capitalist man and woman—one might note how the operation of market institutions as understood by McDaniel (1981) effectively forstalls the attainment of Aristotelian distributive justice. Such institutions are said to have "eliminated the process of creating meaning" (p. 548). Without presuming to plumb the philosophic and psychological depths such an expression suggests, it seems reasonable to conclude that inability to "create meaning" would involve a breakdown of social communication. Such a breakdown might very well preclude the discovery and articulation of possibilities for human excellence, the perception of potentialities for human perfection. But as indicated in this analysis of the relationship between neoclassical economics and the rules of justice it is precisely such perceptions of excellence that are needed to determine the allocation of property rights for a market society. Without such a first-order determination, it is indeed the case that the production, distribution, and exchange of commodities—that is, the operation of the market system—would appear to be deprived of ultimate meaning and significance.

Careful examination of a connection between neoclassical economics and the concept of justice thus terminates in a paradox: Such an examination elucidates what the rules of justice appropriate for a market society are but at the same time indicates that such a society generates psychological processes that preclude their implementation.

References

Aristotle. (1941). *Nichomachean ethics*. In R. McKeon (Ed.), *The basic works of Aristotle*. New York: Random House.

Aristotle. (1941). *Politics*. In R. McKeon (Ed.), *The basic works of Aristotle*. New York: Random House.

Barry, B. (1973). Liberalism and want satisfaction: A critique of John Rawls. *Political Theory, 1*, 134–153.

Bator, F. M. (1957). The simple analytics of welfare maximization. *American Economic Review, 67*, 22–59.

Berlin, I. (1969). *Four essays on liberty*. Oxford: Oxford University Press.

Bronfenbrenner, M. (1971). *Income distribution theory*. Chicago: Aldine-Atherton.

Buchanan, J. M. (1975). *The limits of liberty*. Chicago: University of Chicago Press.

Buchanan, J. M. (1977). *Freedom in constitutional contract*. College Station: Texas A & M University Press.

Clark, B., & Gintis, H. (1978). Rawlsian justice and economic systems. *Philosophy and Public Affairs, 7*, 302–325.

Clark, J. B. (1902). *The distribution of wealth*. New York: Macmillan.

Cohen, R. L., & Greenberg, J. (1982). The concept of justice in social psychology. In J. Greenberg & R. L. Cohen (Eds.), *Equity and justice in social behavior* (pp. 2–43). New York: Academic Press.

Danner, P. (1976). Sympathy and exchangeable value: Keys to Smith's social philosophy. *Review of Social Economy, 34*, 317–333.

Dworkin, R. M. (1980). Is wealth a virtue? *Journal of Legal Studies, 9*, 191–227.

Fisk, M. (1974). History and reason in Rawls' moral theory. In N. Daniels (Ed.), *Reading Rawls* (pp. 53–81). New York: Basic Books.

Friedman, M. (1980). The distribution of income. In J. Sterba (Ed.), *Justice: Alternative political perspectives* (pp. 140–148). Belmont, CA: Wadsworth.

Gintis, H. (1983). Social contradictions and the liberal theory of justice. In R. Skurski (Ed.), *New directions in economic justice* (pp. 90–112). Notre Dame: University of Notre Dame Press.

Harris, D. J. (1978). *Capital accumulation and income distribution*. Stanford: Stanford University Press.

Lerner, A. (1946). *The economics of control*. New York: Macmillan.

Lewis, T. J. (1977). Adam Smith: The labor market as the basis of natural right. *Journal of Economic Issues, 11*, 21–50.

Lowry, S. T. (1969). Aristotle's mathematical analysis of exchange. *History of Political Economy, 1*, 44–66.

Macpherson, C. B. (1962). *The political theory of possessive individualism*. Oxford: Oxford University Press.

Marcuse, H. (1964). *One-dimensional man*. Boston: Beacon Press.

Marshall, A. (1890). *Principles of economics*. London: Macmillan.

Marx, K. (1967). *Capital*. New York: International Publishers. (Original English edition published 1887)

McDaniel, B. A. (1981). The integration of economics and society. *Journal of Economic Issues, 15*, 543–555.

McKee, A. (1979). From a theory of economic justice to its implementation. *Review of Social Economy, 37*, 63–79.

McPherson, M. S. (1982). Mill's moral theory and the problem of preference change. *Ethics, 92*, 252–273.

Ng, Y.-K. (1980). *Welfare economics.* New York: Wiley.

Norton, D. (1976). *Personal destinies.* Princeton: Princeton University Press.

Nozick, R. (1980). Distributive justice. In J. Sterba (Ed.), *Justice: Alternative political perspectives* (pp. 148–172). Belmont, CA: Wadsworth.

Pigou, A. C. (1932). *The economics of welfare* (4th ed.). London: Macmillan.

Polanyi, K. (1957). Aristotle discovers the economy. In K. Polanyi, C. M. Arensberg, & H. Pearson (Eds.), *Trade and market in the early empires* (pp. 64–69). Glencoe, IL: Free Press.

Posner, R. (1981). *The economics of justice.* Cambridge: Harvard University Press.

Rawls, J. (1971). *A theory of justice.* Cambridge: Harvard University Press.

Robbins, L. (1932). *An essay on the nature and significance of economic science.* London: Macmillan.

Rohrlich, G. F. (1984). Community—the submerged component of economic theorizing. *Review of Social Economy, 42,* 221–230.

Schumpeter, J. A. (1954). *History of economic analysis.* New York: Oxford University Press.

Sen, A. K. (1970). *Collective choice and social welfare.* San Francisco: Holden-Day.

Senior, N. W. (1939). *An outline of the science of political economy* (2nd ed.). New York: Farrar & Rinehart. (Originally published 1836)

Smith, A. (1937). *The wealth of nations* (Modern Library Edition). New York: Random House. (Originally published 1776)

Smith, A. (1976). *The theory of moral sentiments.* Indianapolis, IN: Liberty Fund. (Originally published 1759)

Sterba, J. (Ed.). (1980). *Justice: Alternative political perspectives.* Belmont, CA: Wadsworth.

Thurow, L. (1971). The income distribution as a pure public good. *Quarterly Journal of Economics, 85,* 327–336.

Thurow, L. (1973). Toward a definition of economic justice. *The Public Interest, 31,* 56–79.

Weisskopf, W. (1971). *Alienation and economics.* New York: Dutton.

Wisman, J. (1979). Legitimation, ideology-critique, and economics. *Social Research 46,* 291–320.

Worland, S. T. (1963). Philosophy, welfare, and "the system of natural liberty." *Review of Social Economy, 21,* 117–131.

Worland, S. T. (1976). The economic social contract. *The Review of Politics, 38,* 466–470.

Worland, S. T. (1983). Economic justice and the founding father. In R. Skurski (Ed.), *New directions in economic justice* (pp. 1–32). Notre Dame: University of Notre Dame Press.

Worland, S. T. (1984). Aristotle and the neoclassical tradition: The shifting ground of complementarity. *History of Political Economy, 16,* 107–135.

CHAPTER 4

Political Studies and Justice

Arthur DiQuattro

Introduction

This chapter is about the justice of the new liberalism and disputes about its content and ethical viability. It is the prevalent theory of justice in contemporary Western political thought, not only because of its compelling defense in recent philosophy but also because it captures some of the most confidently held modern-day intuitions about justice. Indeed, the social roots of the liberal conception of justice run so deep it is said that thinkers like Rawls have simply worked up their principles from preexisting attitudes and the legal and moral codes in which they are encapsulated. Allan Bloom (1975, p. 649) writes that "Rawls begins with our moral sense, develops the principles which accord with it, and then sees if we are satisfied with the results," and Milton Fisk (1975) sees Rawls's contractualism serving the purpose of conserving the basic institutions of our society—the market economy and liberal democracy.

This may be something of an exaggeration, underestimating the critical edge of Rawls's theory and method (more about this later), but it is surely true that the liberal conception of justice owes its attractiveness and prominence in part to the fact that its theoretical expression meshes in crucial places with the consciousness (though not necessarily the practice) of many citizens in liberal democracies. It is no coincidence, then, that criticism of the liberal theory is at the

ARTHUR DIQUATTRO • Department of Political Science, Texas A&M University, College Station, Texas 77843

same time a statement of dissatisfaction with aspects of existing liberal institutions (Fisk, 1975; Sandel, 1982; Wolff, 1977), testifying to the partial truth of Fisk's point about the conservative character of the new contractualism. Unlike the radical purpose of the classical contract theorists (e.g., Hobbes and Locke), which was to undermine intellectual support for failing feudal institutions, the modern version of contract theory seeks to defend institutions already in place, although recognizing, as in the case of Rawls, the need for substantial reform to bring practice more in line with the requirements of principle. As we shall see, controversies surround the extent and nature of the reforms demanded of these institutions, and in what follows I aim to elucidate these controversies by examining some of the logical roots of liberalism; in particular, their indissoluble engagement to the values of individual autonomy and equality.

The Old and New Liberalism

In his essay, "Liberalism," Ronald Dworkin distinguishes between the "constitutive" morality of liberal theory and its "derivative" strategies. "Constitutive political positions . . . are valued for their own sake, and derivative positions . . . valued . . . as a means of achieving the constitutive positions" (Dworkin, 1978, p. 116). The principle that informs the core positions is "equality of concern and respect," which minimally requires the institutions of liberal democracy and the market. But, says Dworkin, these institutions can take on alternative shapes and their values pursued in different ways. For example, whether capitalist or socialist markets best accord with the core principle is an open question; whether the war in Vietnam was a distinctively liberal enterprise is a matter for debate (Dworkin, 1978, pp. 118–119). These are disputes about derivative positions, involving commitments to competing empirical claims about which policies and institutions can best sustain the constitutive positions and their underlying egalitarian principle. What is important is that liberals defend, as circumstances and available knowledge permit, a decentralized mode of economic allocation and the standard list of civil and political liberties.

Amy Gutmann, in her book *Liberal Equality* (1980), follows Dworkin in his distinction between a theoretical core and derivative strategies. She calls the roll of the classical liberal theorists and finds important equality assumptions. Hobbes, Bentham, James Mill, Locke, and Kant all subscribed to (though gave different weight to) "equal rationality" and/or "equal passions." Which is not to say, however, that classical liberalism was an egalitarian doctrine.

> By initially separating the basic assumptions of classical liberal theory— and central among these, postulates of human equality—from more contingent empirical claims that have transformed those postulates into inegalitarian principles of justice, we can in the end demonstrate that liberalism and egalitarian justice are not incompatible. (Gutmann, 1980, p. 119)

The postulates or metaphysical premises of classical liberalism are egalitarian and carrry egalitarian implications for distributive principles, but its theorists failed to draw them due to faulty reasoning, ignoring or being plain wrong about relevant facts, or because they recognized that historical circumstances rendered inappropriate or premature the implementation of egalitarian strategies.

Locke, for example, never made good on his assumption that equally rational individuals in the state of nature would sanction distributive inequality through tacit consent of the use of money. The distributive inequality he tried to justify stands in tension with his postulate of equal rationality that, for Locke, entailed equal rights (Gutmann, 1980, pp. 27–33). And Kant's arguments concerning property and citizenship, which falsely assumed an unalterable unequal distribution of property and aimed to justify exclusion of the propertyless and economically dependent from full citizenship, failed to square with the egalitarian potential of his theory's basic postulate of equal rationality and autonomy (Gutmann, 1980, pp. 33–41; also see Darwall, 1980, pp. 329–330). Finally, Bentham and Mill avoided the implications of their postulate of equality of passions by resting their case for inegalitarian distribution on deficient arguments about how market economies "must" work over time. By questioning Benthamite claims about motivation and incentives and how state intervention in the market might affect them, later utilitarians, pressing the egalitarian side of the theory, constructed "a framework for justifying more egalitarian principles of justice than either Bentham or James Mill explicitly sanctioned" (Gutmann, 1980, p. 27).

Put concisely, Gutmann's argument is similar to Dworkin's in holding that, despite the egalitarian directions given by the classical liberal map, its theorists trekked the wrong strategic routes and that it is only pursuant to classical liberalism—the "old liberalism," as

L. T. Hobhouse (1911/1964) put it—that "new" liberals, from J. S. Mill to thinkers like Rawls and Walzer, have put liberalism on the right, that is, egalitarian, path. Walzer (1984, p. 323), for example, speaks of and defends a "consistent liberalism—that is, one that passes over into democratic socialism," and Hobhouse (1911/1964, pp. 63, 87), in his classic exposition of liberal doctrine, stresses "the teaching of J. S. Mill as bringing us close to the heart of Liberalism" and then goes on to write of the conceptual soundness and ethical desirability of "Liberal Socialism." But is not liberal socialism a contradiction in terms? Well, not if you define the core of liberalism as Gutmann and Dworkin do and not if you interpret socialist strategy as including markets and civil liberties, as do Rawls and Walzer.

But what if you do not? Then you raise questions of the sort C. B. Macpherson explores in his penetrating analysis of liberal theory (Macpherson, 1962, 1973a, 1977). Although Macpherson is clearly supportive of the requisite civil and political liberties, he is highly dubious about markets and seeks to excise from classical liberalism elements he locates at its theoretical core. Gutmann is right that Macpherson should be taken as an immanent critic of liberalism but not altogether correct that his critique "indicates flaws in the present construction of liberal egalitarianism that are capable of being repaired without uprooting the foundations of liberal theory" (Gutmann, 1980, p. 15). If we follow Macpherson in building into the nucleus of classical liberalism the postulates of "possessive individualism," which include axiomatic assertions about human nature (infinite desire, competitive motivation, and indefatigable power seeking), then we run up against a theoretical core from which it is impossible to derive egalitarian strategies. This does not make the core contradictory for, as especially in Hobbes, equal rationality and equal passions can go together with competition and acquisitiveness, but it does rule out the derivation of egalitarian political institutions and economic arrangements. Hobbes gives us the *Leviathan*, and classical utilitarianism yields laissez-faire capitalism. It could not be otherwise, unless we purge the core of the offending postulates, which is Macpherson's project and, I take it, the enterprise of the new liberalism.

The problem with Gutmann's approach is that it either provides inadequate criteria according to which we can determine what belongs to the theoretical kernel of liberalism or, having done so, it fails to inform her analysis of liberalism about the requirements of those criteria. Why does Gutmann leave out of classical liberalism what Macpherson brings into the core of the theory? It may be because she falls short in clarifying her distinction between meta-physical postulates (the core) and empirical claims (the sphere of dispensable contingency). She says that one of her aims

> is to show how liberal theory was and might further be extended in egalitarian directions by the addition of new empirical claims about how society can be expected to work, economically and politically. Were one's reading of Hobbes correct, that the universals of human nature suffice to deduce the just state, such changes in liberal theory would be inconceivable. (Gutmann, 1980, p. 11)

But why is Hobbes's assumption about human nature empirical and his assumptions about equal rationality and passions metaphysical, with the former dispensable and the latter untouchable? One would think that Gutmann should include *all* these assumptions, call them what you will, as part of the Hobbesian core, especially in light of her (and Dworkin's) method of separating out the most general and basic (morally relevant) characteristics of human agency from the kinds of institutions that might be compatible with them.

It appears that Gutmann has simply failed, by leaving out what merits inclusion, to satisfy her own prescriptive criteria. This is not the place to settle exegetical matters, but because almost every reading of Hobbes, Mill, and Bentham recognizes in whole or in part the centrality of the Macphersonian attribution, the burden of proof lies with Gutmann. Short of some explanation to the contrary, Hobbes without egoism and Bentham and Mill minus "infinite desire" and middle-class graspiness just miss the interpretive boat. Gutmann does not succeed in demonstrating the consistency of liberal egalitarianism with classical liberalism.

The story is different with the new liberalism, and here Gutmann and Dworkin stand on firmer ground. J. S. Mill and T. H. Green set the stage for reconstitution of the core, uprooting those foundations incapable of sustaining egalitarian institutions. That is, having expunged the offending Hobbes-to-Bentham assumptions about human nature and having embellished the remaining egalitarian postulates with emphasis on an individual self-development compatible with social harmony, the theoretical center of liberalism could now be put in the service of the egalitarian program (for elaboration, see Gaus, 1983; Hobhouse, 1911/1964). But consolidation of an egalitarian core does not ensure consensus on derivative strategies.

Enter C. B. Macpherson again, this time as immanent critic of the new liberalism. According to J. S. Mill, everyone has an equal right to exert and develop his or her uniquely human capacities. As

Macpherson (1977, p. 48) says of Mill, "the good society is one which permits and encourages everyone to act as exerter, developer, and enjoyer of the exertion and development, of his or her own capacities." Yet Mill advocated economic institutions—the market—that to Macpherson give us anything but egalitarian results, not only in the sense of the maldistribution of material goods and economic opportunities but also in the less tangible sense that the market is

> a system which requires men to see themselves, and to act, as consumers and appropriators [and thus] gives little scope for most of them to see themselves and act as exerters and developers of their capacities. (Macpherson, 1977, p. 61)

In short, in Mill's model, there is a "contradiction between capitalist relations of production as such and the democratic [egalitarian] ideal of equal possibility of individual self-development. This contradiction Mill never saw" (Macpherson, 1977, p. 62). He was blind to it because he failed to "grasp the essence of the capitalist market economy" (Macpherson, 1973a, p. 175). Significantly, Macpherson says much the same thing of the most recent versions of "revisionist liberalism," in particular Rawls's theory of justice. Macpherson thinks the theory inconsistent because it requires markets that to Macpherson (1973b, p. 345) "embody a considerable element of normal capitalist motivations." Rawls, who Macpherson situates in the tradition of the new liberalism and its rejection of Benthamite assumptions, cannot have it both ways. The core postulates rule out reliance on market forces. Rawls fails to see this because, like Mill, he "does not see exploitative relations inherent in capitalism . . . or liberal market freedoms" (Macpherson, 1973b, pp. 345, 347).

These are complaints to which I will return in a later section. Whether the wedding of markets and liberalism involves some inconsistency is at the heart of contemporary controversies over the nature and worth of the liberal theory of justice. For now, however, the thing to note is the internal character of Macpherson's critique. He accepts the constitutive principles of the new liberalism; he objects to what he considers the perverse strategies endorsed by Mill to Rawls. To use the terminology of Gutmann and Dworkin, Macpherson disputes the empirical assumption of classical liberalism, that a market system can be rendered consistent with the principles of effective equality and liberty, but his critique stems from an acceptance of the constitutive principles or metaphysical postulates[1] of

---

[1] I have already questioned Guttman's characterization of core principles as "metaphysical." In the next section, I propose that they are empirical.

the new liberalism. His critique is therefore not particularly radical; it is literally inspired by the core of *true liberalism*, which is Hobhouse's (1911/1964) term for the new liberalism. As we shall see, it is different for "communitarian" critics of the left and right. Their interest lies in dismantling foundations.

The Individualist Foundation of Liberal Justice

It is an important commonplace in the history of Western political thought that liberal theory assigns a prominent place to individuals and their rights.[2] But this assignation calls into question the liberal credentials of utilitarianism, a doctrine that, despite its individualist trappings, takes seriously neither individuals nor the practice of rights. As Rawls (1971, p. 27) puts it, "utilitarianism does not take seriously the distinction between persons." It detaches from individuals their desires and aims, conflates the latter in an artificial person (the impartial spectator or ideal legislator), who then calculates the most efficient outcomes, that is, those that satisfy the greatest happiness principle. "Everyone counts as one" alright, but only in the sense that each person's interests, considered impersonally and abstractly, figure in the sympathetic imagination of a single legislator whose allocative decisions may very well discount altogether the interests of those who stand in the way of achieving maximum total (or average) utility.

> There is no reason in principle why the greater good of some should not compensate for the lesser losses of others; or more importantly, why the violation of the liberty of a few might not be made right by the greater good shared by many. (Rawls, 1971, p. 26)

Because utilitarians aim to derive principles of justice from the singular end of maximizing satisfaction among individuals, it becomes a matter of secondary importance how this sum of satisfaction gets distributed among individuals. Utilitarian doctrine is a classic case of subordinating distributive principles to aggregative ones and is

[2]"Society is made for man, not man for society; it is humanity, as Kant said, that must always be treated as an end and not a means. The individual is both logically and ethically prior. To the philosophy of the seventeenth century relations always appeared thinner than substances; man was the substance, society the relation. It was this assumed priority of the individual which became the most marked and the most persistent quality of the theory of natural law, and the clearest differential of the modern from medieval theory" (Sabine, 1961, p. 433).

bound logically to ride roughshod over distributive claims not grounded on the paramount principle of happiness maximization (Smart, 1978). Aggregative principles are in the final analysis collectivist and therefore incompatible with the individualist foundation of liberal justice.

Here we run up against one of the eclectic conundrums of J. S. Mill. On the one hand, Mill has a conception of the person akin to the best of liberal nonutilitarian theory. The emphasis is on individual self-development, and it is an individualism shorn of the egoistic postulates of Hobbes to Bentham. Yet, on the other hand, Mill's *defense* of individual interests rests on making the case for the practice of rights on utilitarian grounds. His conception of the person passes the muster of the new liberalism, but his justification of individual rights depends on appeals to "general utility," thus allowing for instances where the general welfare, as a matter of course, overrides justice. This is why, among other reasons, Sandel (1982, pp. 1–7) excludes Mill as a backup theorist of the new liberalism. For Sandel, that liberalism is instead indebted to Kant and to the deontological tradition in moral and political philosophy. Just how "deontological" modern liberalism is, or must be, is an issue I take up in what follows but bear in mind that the Kantian sort of deontology is not the only alternative to the utilitarian brand of ethical naturalism. Naturalist or descriptive ethics need not assume utilitarian form, and it may be (and I will argue) that the best of recent theories of liberal justice, though in need of some friendly amendments, escape the fatal flaws of Kantian transcendentalism while preserving the important intent of the Kantian project. What we want, to paraphrase Marx on Hegel, is the Kantian kernel (egalitarianism) without the Kantian shell (idealism, transcendentalism), and what this requires is the infusion of some empirical content into the individualist foundation of liberal theory.

"Justice," say Rawls (1971, p. 3), "is the first virtue of social institutions," and what gives it priority is its individualistic core. Individuals work up principles of justice that then apply to institutions designed to regulate the distribution of goods (rights, duties, advantages) among individuals. Liberal justice begins and ends with individuals and their interests, makes no sense without their consideration, owes its political strategies to its egalitarian conception of individuals, and radically distinguishes itself from competing (e.g., utilitarian, communitarian) theories because of that conception. Perhaps the best way of clarifying that conception is by examining how individuals are portrayed at the entry stage in social contract theory.

What qualifies someone for admission into the original position, the hypothetical state of affairs in which deliberation about and moral commitment to principles of justice takes place? According to the traditional contract theorists, what purchases the ticket for admission is the possession of a rational capacity or faculty, which includes almost everyone, although the classical contract theorists differed on how many people had *realized* that capacity to the requisite degree. Hobbes is the most radical here, including almost everyone, and Locke the most conservative, including only males and (mainly) the educated and propertied classes.[3] Not only does Hobbes's individualism side with equality and freedom irrespective of social class, but consistent with the radical implications of the liberal critique of hierarchical political and social arrangements, it argues against the discriminatory exclusion of persons on the basis of gender (Brennan & Pateman, 1979). This suggests that there is nothing in the concept of liberal individualism that is prejudicial against women, unless, of course, its emphasis on possession of rational capacity is somehow sexist, as implied in the work of Gilligan (1982) and others (for discussion, see Furby, Chapter 6, in this volume; for a recent critique of views similar to Gilligan's, see Dietz's striking analysis, 1985, of Elshtain, 1981).

So Hobbes's original position is brimming with participants whereas Locke's consists of a select number whose task is, in part, to look out for the interests of all, including the excluded mass. What really counts, then, is not so much the possession of the rational capacity but the *demonstrated* capacity to reason. But if this is so, then membership in the original position, at least for Hobbes and Locke, is determined by the display of a certain kind of performance,

[3]It is generally overlooked that Hobbes, like Locke, distinguished between explicit and tacit consent, and used the latter notion to bind the minority to the majority decision to establish the sovereign power and its rules of justice. There are some who, failing to exercise their rational faculty, perhaps because of their captivation by the "absurdities of the Schoolmen," refuse to explicitly endorse the covenant justifying the state. "Because the major part hath by consenting voices declared a Sovereign; he that dissented must now consent with the rest . . . . For if he voluntarily entered into the Congregation of them that were assembled, he sufficiently declared thereby his will (and therefore tacitly consented) to stand to what the major part should ordain . . . . And whether his consent be asked, or not, he must either submit to their decrees or be left in the condition of war he was in before; wherein he might without injustice be destroyed by any man whatsoever" (Hobbes, 1651/1968, pp. 231–232). In the conclusion of *Leviathan*, Hobbes refers to conquered peoples living under the protection of the conquering sovereign as tacitly promising obedience (pp. 720–721). On Locke's exclusion of the majority from political society, see Macpherson (1962).

empirically ascertainable and morally relevant to the task at hand, that is, deciding on the principles of justice.

I mention this because it calls attention to the empirical basis of the screening process imposed by classical contract theory. Rational capacity turns out to be a necessary though not sufficient condition for someone's passing through the screen. Only if certain facts about individual performance hold true, do individuals qualify as participating members in the original position.[4] The question arises whether possession of the rational capacity itself is an empirical issue as well, and this brings us to Kant and recent contract theory as represented in the work of Rawls.

Kant sought to provide an absolute foundation for the idea of equality among persons by making the individual's property as a moral or rational agent a transcendental characteristic. It was thought to be rockbed because it relied in no way upon empirical and, therefore, transient hypotheses. Instead, it depended upon a conceptual analysis of the necessity of the meaning of terms like *rational* and *moral*. Kant thought that rationality entailed morality and that "the ground of [moral] obligation . . . must not be sought in [human nature or contingent circumstance], but sought *a priori* in the concepts of pure reason" (Kant, 1785/1959, p. 389). But, *contra* Kant, logical necessity does not always translate into a solid justificatory basis for something, in this case human equality and equality of respect. The questions arise: Why should anyone accept or be bound by a set of definitions? What obliges someone to play according to the rules of a language game in which these concepts loom large? What, in short, obliges anyone to accept a certain conception of "rational human nature" and to live up to what it might require in practice? Not only is it difficult to appreciate how these questions can be answered without recourse to relevant matters of empirical fact (e.g., those related to human wants, need, happiness, or facts about human equality), but as Bernard Williams has argued, it is probably impossible in the first place to wield concepts like "moral or rational agent" without employing empirical criteria. It is worth quoting Williams at length. His criticism of Kant is decisive:

[4]The most important fact seems to be whether individuals explicitly agree to the respective political schemes of the contract theorists. Those who take issue with the need for an absolute sovereign, as in Hobbes, or fail to go along with the tie between natural law and private property, as in Locke, demonstrate their lack of success in realizing their rational nature. This demonstration has the ring of circularity to it, but the criteria for admission to the original position are still empirical.

> This transcendental, Kantian conception cannot provide any solid foundation for the notions of equality among men, or of equality of respect owed to them. Apart from the general difficulties of such transcendental conceptions, there is the obstinate fact that the concept of "moral agent," and the concepts allied to it such as that of responsibility, do and must have an empirical basis. It seems empty to say that all men are equal as moral agents, when the question, for instance, of men's responsibility for their actions is one to which empirical considerations are clearly relevant, and one which moreover receives answers in terms of different degrees of rational control over action. To hold a man responsible for his actions is presumably the central case of treating him as a moral agent, and if men are not treated as equally responsible, there is not much left to their equality as moral agents. (Williams, 1962, p. 116)

If Williams is right, and I think he is, then the liberal postulate of equality of rational capacity must be grounded empirically. It must be a fact that people are intrinsically equal, where this claim of equality is relevant to moral issues and where the issues are decided in favor of egalitarian strategies. This, I believe, is Rawls's view (even though, as we shall see, he muddies the water with the appearance of a relativistic turn in his most recent writing). Indeed, the room that Rawls allows for empirical theory in constructing principles of justice raises the question of just how Kantian is his theory of justice. Sandel (1982, Chapter 1) refers to the new liberalism as deontological liberalism and to Rawls's theory as "revisionist" deontology, and Rawls himself says his theory is deontological in the standard negative sense that it is not teleological. But deontological theory need not be Kantian. Rawls (1980, p. 517) says his theory resembles the Kantian view but is only analogous to it. In a characteristic passage, Rawls writes:

> To develop a viable Kantian conception of justice the force and content of Kant's doctrine must be detached from its background in transcendental idealism [and reformulated within the] canons of reasonable empiricism. (Rawls, 1977, p. 165)

In other words, Rawls is out to preserve the moral force of Kantian metaphysics (what I have called the kernel) but within the scope of an empirical theory (the new shell). Rawls's remarks on the nature of moral theory are especially telling:

> In any case, it is obviously impossible to develop a substantive theory of justice founded solely on truths of logic and definition. The analysis of moral concepts and the *a priori*, however traditionally understood, is too slender a basis. Moral philosophy must be free to use contingent assumptions and general facts as it pleases. (Rawls, 1971, p. 51)

Rawls, then, departs from Kant at crucial places, with each departure signaling an empirical turn. In the first and most important digression, Rawls takes the equality postulate to be ultimately empirical. The individuals who populate the original position are equally autonomous; that is, they are minimally capable of framing plans of life or conceptions of the good and of possessing a sense of justice, which is to say that they are moral persons who can construct principles of justice and who are entitled to the guarantees of equal justice. Rawls (1971, pp. 505–506) assumes that the "overwhelming majority of mankind" possesses these capacities and that justice protects rights based upon these "natural attributes," the "presence of which can be ascertained by natural reason pursuing commonsense methods of inquiry." Fundamental rights are based upon natural attributes that, though selected as a matter of decision,[5] are empirical in character. If human beings in fact lacked these attributes, the entire edifice of liberal justice would collapse like a house of cards.[6] If, for example, determinism were true (and compatibilism false or untenable) or if Aristotle were right about the natural propensities of most people, there would be nothing left to Rawlsian justice, and that is because at the heart of his theory is the minimally autonomous or morally free person who "constructs" justice in the original position and whose full autonomy in the well-ordered society is advanced by (and is impossible without) the application of just principles to the basic institutions that regulate individual conduct.

Now it may seem that Rawls's distinction (1980, p. 534) between a "conception of the person" and a "theory of human nature" invalidates an interpretation of his theory that stresses the empirical. Rawls says that his conception of the person as autonomous is a "moral ideal," suggesting, as it does to Galston (1980, 1982a), that its

---

[5]Of course, it is important that the choice of attributes not be arbitrary. More on this later.

[6]"'Equality' is primarily, at least, a descriptive and not an evaluative term. It [is] reasonable to suppose that equality is the cornerstone of a building whose more obvious features are made up of other political concepts: that the notion of equality, just because it is descriptive, is the essential point of departure of the road to liberalism" (Wilson, 1966, p. 18). I should add that if Rawls is one with Wilson on this point—and I have argued just that—then Dworkin's interpretation (1978) of Rawlsian justice as based on a "deep theory" of natural equality and rights is exactly on target.

In his recent essay (1985), published after I completed my chapter, Rawls dissociates himself from Dworkin's interpretation but allows that Dworkin's understanding is one permitted by, and consistent with, his theory of justice.

choice lacks a justification in which factual considerations play a part, as they necessarily would in working up a theory of human nature. Yet Rawls's recognition of how general facts of human nature and society impinge upon our judgment of the feasibility of different ideals of the person implies the subordination of the ideal to theories about matters of fact.

> The feasible ideals of the person are limited by the capacities of human nature and the requirements of social life. To this extent such an ideal presupposes a theory of human nature, and social theory generally, but the task of a moral doctrine is to specify an appropriate conception of the person that general facts about human nature and society allow. (Rawls, 1980, p. 534; also see p. 566)

This surely leaves ample space for moral construction analogous to the Kantian motif of the sort that Rawls is keen on. General facts and social theories delimit but do not specify any particular ideal from the range allowed.

But, and this is the point, the context of Rawls's discussion makes it plain that the conception of the person found in the original position and the well-ordered society is not confuted by empirical theory and that, short of evidence to the contrary, it is reasonable to accept as an ideal. And why not *the* ideal? For what conception of the person could be more relevant to the task of moral construction—in this case the generation of principles of justice? The criterion of choice of this conception is determined by the nature of the task at hand: The subject matter of justice requires agents who are capable of framing just principles and living up to them. It requires, in short, individuals who are capable of a sense of justice and conceiving aims in life. And because most people, as a matter of fact, possess these attributes, it is difficult on pain of inconsistency to justify the exclusion of anyone with the relevant attributes from participation in the construction and application of just principles. The *right* of admission to the original position stems from the *fact* of the relevant equality. From the fact that each individual has a moral will just as much as every other individual, it follows (or cannot be denied) that each individual's will should count as much as every other individual's. The problem of denying this is that there is no reason outside the wills of individuals for believing that the will of any person is superior.[7] As Rawls (1980, p. 519) put it, in speaking of

---

[7] It is important that liberals distinguish between the equal capacity to choose and the unequal possession of practical intelligence. The former is the relevant fact, providing "a natural basis for equality" (see Gewirth, 1973, pp. 361–362, Rawls, 1971, pp. 507–508). For a denial of relevance, see Singer (1979, pp. 16–23).

his Kantian constructivism, "apart from the procedure [of relevantly free and equal persons choosing just principles], there are no moral facts."

Of course, to say that there are no moral facts apart from the contractual device does not entail a lack of empirical facts that are relevant to moral choice. I have just pointed up the primacy in liberal theory of the thoroughly contingent fact of equal autonomy and, as various interpretors (Darwall, 1980; Levine, 1974) of Rawls have stressed, Rawls injects considerably more empirical content into the Kantian project than befits transcendental metaphysics. The rational beings who populate the original position are distinctly human, possessed of human interests broadly defined, and whose choice of just principles is informed by knowledge of general facts and theories about human psychology, history, and economic and political life. It is a matter for debate whether Rawls, having shed the Kantian shell, still counts as a Kantian, but my concern has been to show that there is considerably more to the principle of liberal equality than the formal (and Kantian) requirement of universalizability, which is essentially and merely a conceptual fact about the logic of moral language.[8] Liberal theory, as I have treated it, tries to offer support for this logic by appealing to relevant matters of fact. The liberal principle of equality is grounded on an empirical claim of equal autonomy, derives from this claim its practical significance for the practice of individual rights, and in combination with the procedural device of contract theory, it yields substantive principles of justice.

From the fact of equality, then, we get rights to equal consideration and duties to accord it to others. This idea is at the core of liberalism and the institutions it seeks to justify and is what new liberals like Dworkin, Rawls, and Gewirth (1973) mean by "taking rights seriously." But there is another, happily convenient though less fundamental, basis for egalitarian justice, and the liberal ideal gains strength by harking back to a recurrent theme in the history of political theory, namely that, as Rousseau put it in *Emile*, "the happy man is the just man." This suggests that there might be a supplementary rational basis for the liberal concept of the person understood as a moral ideal. This is the idea that individuals *desire* "to be the kind of person specified by the conception of the fully autonomous citizens of a well-ordered society [one regulated by the principles of liberal justice]" (Rawls, 1980, p. 533). Rawls (1971, Chapter

[8]For criticism of this view, see Richard Flathman's remarks on Gewirth's essay, cited previously. "The formal GP [generalization principle] exhausts the principle of equality" (Flathman, 1973, p. 326).

9) touches on this issue in his discussion of "the good of justice," noting the congruity of the satisfaction of natural inclinations or heteronomous desires and living within just institutions, but it is true that his emphasis is ultimately on the satisfaction of interests that individuals have as morally autonomous beings. The morally autonomous individuals who are parties to the contractual deliberations have an interest in living under social, political, and economic arrangements that foster the realization of this ideal conception. Even the concern individuals have for primary goods like income, wealth, and opportunities is, for Rawls, "born of their fundamental interest in flourishing as rational choosers of ends" (Darwall, 1980, p. 339).

However, the question arises: Why accept this ideal of the person and the interests it entails? As Galston (1982a) argues, the ideal is eminently debatable, and Rawls never adequately answers this question, although from Galston's perspective Rawls probably comes closest in his sympathetic treatment of the Aristotelian principle and its explanation of human motivation. And it is here that we return to general considerations of a factual sort. Might it not be a fact that individuals, when given the opportunity (I am aware that a lot turns on this), move to realize in themselves the ideal? Better to be Socrates dissatisfied than a pig satisfied (Mill), better to cultivate and realize complicated and intricate capacities than stick with the performance of rote and simple tasks (Rawls, inspired by Aristotle), better to relate to others as equals than as subordinates or superiors (liberalism in a nutshell). It is better to do or be all of these things because we are happier for it. A belief in intrinsic equality is rational not only because it is a fact that most individuals are relevantly equal but also because the good and satisfying life envisioned by liberals requires an egalitarian environment, one without the experience of subordination, without masters and slaves, without bowing and scraping, fawning and toadying, frightful trembling and high and mightiness (Walzer, 1983, p. xiii). "The ability to identify with other people, to communicate with them in a fraternal [and sororial] way, as equals, rather than to have a master–slave relationship with them is what lies at the root of liberalism" (Wilson, 1966, p. 23). The context of Wilson's remark implies that by "ability" he means "desire," and it is this desire that capitalizes upon the factual equality that constitutes the center of liberal theory. Do people really desire liberal equality, living in a society in which both civic and private life is characterized by relationships based on equal respect and concern (as opposed to, say, hierarchy, order, and obedience)? This is an empirical question, greatly complicated and hotly contested by advocates of competing theoretical camps (e.g., Freudians and Nietzscheans vs. the likes of J. S. Mill, Rawls, or Erich Fromm; or, politically, fascists and conservatives vs. liberals and socialists) and necessarily involving appeals to counterfactual claims.[9]

Counterfactuals are in fact extremely important to social contract methodology and, more broadly, to any ideal theory that aims to assess existing practice in light of general principles. The "state of nature" or original position is the crucial "what if" in contract theory. Its theoretical function is to press us to accept the need for political authority and obligation, for without the assurance provided by law, individuals will lack the motivation to live up to the requirements of just principles. Rawls calls this the "problem of assurance," and it receives its classic expression in the work of Hobbes. In Hobbes's state of nature, no one can be trusted to perform his or her side of covenants because there is no guarantee, backed by the state, that anyone will so perform. The unhappy consequence is that everyone seeks and acts on excuses not to perform, and that effectively eliminates the common advantage attached to the practice of contracts. The "war of all against all" is the price paid for the absence of a sovereign power (for elaboration of this interpretation, see Barry, 1972). The point for both Rawls and Hobbes (though they give somewhat different reasons for it) is that we can expect people to behave differently when the assurance problem is resolved.

The upshot, given what I have said about the desire for liberal equality, is that perhaps individuals would, even though they do not now, prefer a more egalitarian mode of life if their circumstances were changed in ways that altered their preferences. Wilson writes:

> I suspect the general relief would be enormous [if obtaining very much more money was impossible for everybody]: for there is a sense in which people do not really want to compete, but find themselves driven to do so. . . . The "rat race" is well-named. We are not happy with this style of life, and make uneasy jokes about it: but we remain compelled because we cannot picture anything else. (Wilson, 1966, p. 190)

If there were limits, imposed politically, on the extent of permissible income and wealth inequalities, the pressure to compete to maintain one's competitive position would be less than in a full-blown cap-

---

[9]What actually happens when circumstances allow individuals or groups of individuals to choose the liberal ideal as a way of life? What would happen if psychological, political, social, and economic barriers to autonomy imposed by ignorance or fostered by the powers that be were removed? On the use of a counterfactual methodology in social science, see Lukes (1974, Chapters 7 and 8).

italist market system. The state would provide the assurance that those who opt for the egalitarian way of life would not be done in by aggressive egoists. Is it unrealistic to anticipate that people's conceptions of justice might be different, and more egalitarian, in the presence of a political authority that assured an egalitarian distribution of basic goods (on why this authority must be centralized, see Rae, Yates, Hochschild, Morone, & Fessler, 1981, pp. 22–27)?

It is counterfactual questions of this kind that prompt caution in accepting as decisive the findings of polls and interviews of people's feelings about distributive justice. Hochschild (1981), for example, finds, on the basis of in-depth interviews, that Americans are more egalitarian in the "socializing" (home, family, neighborhood) and "political" (civil rights, democratic sentiment) domains than in the "economic" domain, which turns out to be the realm of the market, with all of its competitive and "autonomous" (Invisible Hand runs things) characteristics. Similarly, some very interesting research by Greenberg (1981) indicates that members of worker-owned and controlled enterprises in the United States are remarkably egalitarian in both their work organization and distributive policies, yet are notably inegalitarian in their relations with the world outside their workplace, especially competing enterprises.

> One gets the strange result . . . of a collective/cooperative/egalitarian spirit that is somewhat encouraged within the enterprise walls running up against the harsh rocks and shoals of the marketplace. (Greenberg, 1981, p. 41)

I have suggested (though I have not tried to show) that the strangeness of the result might be due to the failure to resolve an assurance problem that arises when the market is the main *distributive* institution. The market, as a distributive device, forces a self-interested rationality geared to the competitive struggle for existence. Because it provides no insurance that those who lose out in the competitive game will be compensated for their loss, it leaves its players no choice but to join in the fray in the hope of furthering advantages or maintaining positions. Indeed, given the market game, the maintenance of position translates into the seeking of advantage over others. "If you aren't competing, you're dead" (Arnold Palmer, quoted in Alchian & Allen, 1969, p. 5).

In conclusion, whatever the empirical merit of a counterfactual methodology, it is plain that liberals contest the question of people's preferences for different conceptions of justice from the side of liberal equality, from the perspective of a certain picture of the good life, and that their defense of this ideal turns in a crucial way on their making good their factual claims of intrinsic equality and the actual or hypothetical desirability[10] of what Galston (1982b, p. 621), following Barry (1973), calls the "Faustian vision."

Liberal Justice and Relativism

We find in some of the most important recent theories of the new liberalism a curious mix of rationalism and conservatism, of contractualism and the traditionalist rejection of this kind of "ideal theory." Rawls, in the Dewey Lectures (1980), has moved in a direction weakening interpretations of his theory as Archimedean, and Walzer, in his defense of the liberal values of pluralism and "complex equality" (1983), eschews altogether contractualist methodology, a universalist concept of persons, and utopian vantage points in favor of a "radically particularist" and historically specific approach to the problem of justice.

To use Oakeshott's (1956) famous phrase, Walzer (unequivocally) and Rawls (arguably) take the analysis of justice and arguments in its behalf to consist in the "pursuit of intimations." This is the idea that we cannot, or should not, proceed directly from first principles to critically assess existing institutions, for the principles are only meaningful or serviceable *a posteriori*; the principles make sense only when situated in an existing culture or tradition. On this view, it is something of a conceptual mistake to apply, say, liberal principles, to primitive societies. This is because these principles get their meaning from their historical and cultural context. They are incommensurable with and inapplicable to customs or ways of life of radically nonliberal societies. Further, on this view, it is thought to be morally askew and politically imprudent, or even tyrannical, to bring to bear abstract principles upon established practice. Recall Edmund Burke's reflections on the French Revolution, of his characterization of the unsettling and vicious effects of the ideologues, Jacobins, and assorted "political aeronauts" in their attempt to reshape institutions in light of philosophical principles and visions, drawn of whole cloth, of the good society. Then compare Walzer's refrain of the Burkean concern:

---

[10]I follow J. S. Mill here: The desirable is what is desired under circumstances conducive to autonomy (see Kretzmann, 1969).

> A given society is just if its substantive life is lived in a certain way—
> that is, in a way faithful to the shared understandings of the mem-
> bers. . . . [Justice] cannot require a radical redesign of the [society]
> against [this] shared understanding. If it had, justice itself would be
> tyrannical. (Walzer, 1983, p. 313)[11]

Walzer's argument against the radical program of ideal theory is
twofold: He casts a conceptual veto against the possibility of evaluating operative systems of distributive justice in light of the principles
of a general theory of justice, and he characterizes as tyrannical
attempts to override, intellectually or practically, the "substantive
ways of life" of people in different cultures. "Justice is relative to
social meanings," and social goods are distributed for "internal"
reasons; "every substantive account of distributive justice is a local
account"; "only [a society's] culture, its character, its common understandings can define the 'wants' that are to be provided for"
(Walzer, 1983, pp. 79, 312, 314). In some societies, piety or religious
status may be among the important wants whose satisfaction is up
for distribution. In others, for example, market societies, it may be
income, wealth, and various opportunities to realize self-determined
ambitions. It would be a mistake, according to Walzer, to follow
Rawls in drawing up a single list of "primary social goods" and
applying it, and the distributive principles of which it is a part, to all
societies. The distributive principles of the American welfare state

> do not apply to a community organized hierarchically, as in traditional
> India where the fruits of the harvest are distributed not according to need
> but according to caste. (Walzer, 1983, p. 84)

The upshot of Walzer's view is decidedly relativistic: If "justice is
rooted in distinct understandings of places, honors, jobs, things of
all sorts, that constitute a way of life" (1983, p. 314), then there are as
many just systems as there are distinct and coherent ways of life. But
if this is so, then how can Walzer also say that "to override those
understandings is [always] to act *unjustly*" (1983, p. 314, emphasis
added)? Or that

---

[11]This passage might be interpreted as consistent with Marx's views on justice but
only if one accepts a relativistic reading of Marxian justice. Allen Wood (1980), for
example, argues along these lines. I take issue with this interpretation (DiQuattro,
1984), but will not debate the disagreement here. Even if one agreed with Wood,
though, it would be difficult to attribute to Marx the sentiment that "justice itself
would be *tyrannical*" if implemented before or after its historical time. Marx would
say that different conceptions of justice might be more or less conducive to the
development of the forces of production at different historical periods but hardly
tyrannical in the way that Walzer uses the term (emphasis added).

when people [within a given society] disagree about the meaning of
social goods, when understandings are controversial, then *justice* requires that the society be faithful to the disagreements, providing institutional channels for expression, adjudicative mechanisms, and alternative distributions. (1983, p. 313, emphasis added)

Walzer cannot have it both ways. Either the meaning of justice is
exhausted by different forms of life, in which case Walzer cannot
refer to their rejection and supercession as acting unjustly, or Walzer
is assuming all along—the impressive liberal theorist he is—that
some distributive arrangements, complete with their internal justifications, are less just than others, which implies the application of
abstract principles of justice. The last passage cited is especially
telling as Walzer's conception of justice, applied in a first-order
sense, amounts to pressing the liberal case for the principles of equal
concern and respect, autonomy, tolerance, and so on. There have
been, and are, societies in which disagreements over controversial
understandings are ignored or suppressed. It is part of their way of
life. According to what criteria does justice require their resolution
according to fair procedure, where *fairness,* as Walzer uses the concept, pretty much implies the right of equal consideration for competing claims and interests?

Walzer is not alone among social scientists in trying to put to
descriptive use inherently normative concepts and, as a consequence, shifting surreptitiously and confusedly from one to the
other.[12] He prefers a descriptive account of justice—"justice" *is*
"what people in given societies consider to be just"—but he cannot
avoid using justice with the normative force that gives the concept
its raison d'être. When the people whose institutions Walzer explores apply the concept of justice to their own practices, they do not
definitionally equate "our practices are just" to "we consider our
practices just." They consider their practices just because they believe them to *be* just. To call something just is to take a position
toward it; that is, its performative function. It is no surprise, then,
that Walzer himself, in spite of his methodological pronouncements,
should use, in the most critical places in his argument, the concept
of justice in a first-order normative fashion, and when he does, he
not unexpectedly draws on the core principles of liberal theory.

If Walzer's relativism is chimerical, can the same be said of
Rawls's? Has Rawls "embraced a basic moral relativism" (see

___

[12]Walzer does to *justice* what Weber does to *legitimacy,* with the same confusing
results. Pitkin's lucid analysis (1972, pp. 280–286) of Weber's definition of *legit-*
imacy inspires my criticism of Walzer.

Buchanan & Mathieu, Chapter 2 in this volume)? In *A Theory of Justice*, Rawls allots a significant role to general principles in appraising the everyday judgments that prevail in less than well-ordered societies. Our "considered judgments" are the result of critically weighing our ordinary beliefs and institutions in light of the "regulative principles" generated in the original position (1971, p. 46ff.), principles informed by knowledge of general facts and theories about human nature, psychology, society, history, and the like. The principles of justice seem ideally suited as the vantage point from which we can project an image of a well-ordered society, which in turn serves as a model for making comparisons, enabling us to say with some confidence that some societies (say, liberal democracies) are more just than others (say, slave or feudal ones). "The principles of justice belong to the theory of an ideal state of affairs" and are "generally relevant" in ranking actual states of affairs as more or less just as well as justifying intervention, circumstances permitting, to effect their remedy (1971, p. 245ff.).

It is obvious that Rawls now discourages this reading of his theory. First, there has been a shift in intent:

> We are not trying to find a conception of justice suitable for all societies regardless of their particular social or historical circumstances. We want to settle a fundamental disagreement over the just form of basic institutions within a democratic society under modern conditions. We look to ourselves and to our future, and reflect upon our disputes since, let's say, the Declaration of Independence. How far the conclusions we reach are of interest in a wider context is a separate question. (Rawls, 1980, p. 518)

The fact that Rawls is now mainly interested in elucidating the conception of the person and the principles of justice implicit in modern democratic regimes, in organizing our considered convictions, does not altogether empty his theory of critical clout, nor does it mean that he "[has forgotten] the point of having first principles—to judge our practices, not merely to codify them" (Galston, 1982a, p. 513). The theory can still illuminate discrepancies between conception and practice (or principles and strategies, to recall an earlier formulation) and motivate both reflection and political action in shoring up or replacing less than just institutions. "Our society is not well-ordered," says Rawls, but its public culture can be made aware of the "conception of the person and of social cooperation conjectured to be implicit in that culture" (1980, p. 569). However, Rawls does seem to importantly circumscribe the critical range of his principles: In societies where conceptions of justice are not widely shared or in sharp dispute, the application of principles must await widespread agreement on the principles themselves as well as "companion agreement on ways of reasoning and rules for weighing evidence which govern the application of those principles" (1980, pp. 537–541). Now this requirement surely blunts the critical edge of the theory, disabling it precisely when it would seem most suited for service. Here the Rawlsian intent to pursue intimations contrasts starkly with the radical intent and revolutionary purpose of the classical contract theorists. One can scarcely imagine Hobbes or Locke waiting on a consensus when it was precisely its absence that prompted the application of their general principles in the first place.

In addition to a change of intent, Rawls has decided more firmly in favor of a noncommital view of the truth of metaphysical doctrines and theories of knowledge. This makes it more difficult to interpret his theory as "ideal" and opens the door to interpretations of the theory as relativist. Rawls (1980, pp. 540–542) admits into the original position and the well-ordered society only those general theories, forms of reasoning, and rules of evidence that are generally accepted as relevant to decision making about basic matters of justice. This is *not* because Rawls subscribes to philosophical skepticism (1971, p. 214) but rather because "a departure from generally recognized ways of reasoning would involve a privileged place for the view of some over others, and a principle which permitted this could not be agreed to in the original position" (1971, p. 213).

Presumably there are practical and not philosophical difficulties associated with implementing such a principle. But a question with definite philosophical and moral implications arises, and Rawls fails to deliver a response: Why identify privileged standing with *departures*? From the standpoint of minority dissidents, whose views are informed by different beliefs, theories, and modes of reasoning, it is the established beliefs, theories, and modes that are privileged. Consider what Rawls does with Aquinas's justification of the death penalty for heretics—that heretics deserve execution because they seek to corrupt or harm the safety of the souls of the faithful. Rawls (1971, pp. 215–216) asserts that Aquinas's view "is a matter of dogma," a "matter of faith" about which "no argument is possible." The problem with Aquinas's position is that it is based on theological premises that cannot be "established by modes of reasoning commonly recognized" (1971, p. 215). It therefore merits exclusion from the arena of public discourse—it gets pocket vetoed, as it were.

The difficulty with Rawls's argument should be obvious. In spite of his profession of neutrality, he accords a privileged place to certain modes of reasoning, in this case those that (a) allow for (or require) reasoned arguments as opposed to appeals to religious authority or arguments of the sort that characterize nonnatural theology, and (b) engage methods of rational scientific inquiry that predominate in modern, especially liberal–democratic, societies. This is why Aquinas or an ayotollah fares poorly in both the original position and a well-ordered society. But suppose that (nonnatural) theology is at the heart of commonly recognized modes of reasoning in a particular society and that, as is the case in the present and the past,[13] beliefs and theories about cosmology, human nature, and political institutions contrast with those justified by rational scientific modes. In this case, scientific departures would count as privileged and, in lieu of Rawls's noncommital stance, need be excluded from the realm of public justification. But can Rawls remain faithful to his conception of a "well-ordered society" while taking the position that in this case public debate about, and attempted resolution of, fundamental disagreements about justice be tabled because "a basis of public justification is still to be achieved" (Rawls, 1980, p. 596)? If a certain society, on the basis of its generally accepted beliefs and criteria of truth, denied its members "an equal right to determine, and to reassess upon due reflection, the first principles of justice by which the basic structure of their society is to be governed," and denied its members the liberty to "make claims on the design of their common institutions in the name of their own fundamental aims and highest order interests" (1980, p. 521), it would not count, on Rawls's definition (which I have just quoted), as a well-ordered society. A well-ordered society is regulated by the core liberal principles of equality of concern and respect; so societies that deny these principles are less than just. It is not true, then, that for Rawls there are as many well-ordered (just) societies as there are societies whose members widely share criteria on the basis of which they believe their institutions to be just. Despite his disclaimer that his theory presupposes no particular mode of reasoning, Rawls ap-

---

[13]In The World We Have Lost: England before the Industrial Age (1971), Peter Laslett writes of the typical 17th-century village: "All our ancestors were literal Christian believers, all the time. Not only zealous priests . . . not only serious-minded laymen, but also the publicly responsible looked on the Christian religion as the explanation of life, and religious service as its proper end" (p. 74).

pears to take sides with the prevailing forms of reasoning in liberal democracies and, in light of the beliefs and general theories sustained by those forms, denies that institutions deviating from the requirements of the liberal democratic model qualify as well-ordered. This is hardly a relativistic account of justice.[14]

Liberal Justice and Markets

Liberal theorists, both old and new, have seen in market institutions a bulwark against political interference with individual liberty. Critics of liberalism, both traditionalists and communitarian socialists, have objected that markets facilitate exploitation, thus curtailing the liberty of those who systematically lose out in market exchange and undermining the values of cooperation and community. In this section, I explore the place of markets in the justice of the new liberalism and speculate on the force of immanent criticism that reliance on the market strategy is incompatible with the demands of its core principles. Further, I comment upon the external critique that the liberal dependence on markets sacrifices the worth of "altruistic collaboration" and community.

Brian Barry (1973, p. 166) inserts markets into the very essence of liberalism.

> The essence of liberalism as I am defining it here is the vision of society as made up of independent, autonomous units who co-operate only when the terms of co-operation are such as make it further the ends of each of the parties. Market relations are the paradigm of such co-operation, and this is well captured in the notion that the change from feudalism to the liberal apogee of the mid-nineteenth century was one

---

[14]It is true that, even though Rawls's theory implies his acceptance of a rational scientific mode of inquiry, he does not defend his choice. For such a defense, as it bears on the issue discussed here, see Charles Taylor (1982, pp. 103–104), who argues the case that we can make "valid transcultural judgments of superiority" and that "[modern] culture can surely lay claim to a higher, or fuller, or more effective rationality, if it is in a position to achieve a more perspicuous order than another" (also, see Gellner, 1974). If Rawls does not subscribe to some such view as this, especially if I am right about the factual basis of the core liberal principles, his theory of justice would not carry much weight, let alone make any *sense*. Rawls (1985) elaborates on his "neutral" stance toward competing epistemologies, following what he calls "the method of avoidance." For reasons I have suggested, I find his elaboration unconvincing.

"from status to contract," and that subsequent developments reversed the process once again. . . . Rawls presses this to its logical limit by deriving the principles of justice from a notional "social contract."

Although Barry exaggerates the instrumentally motivated character of cooperation in liberal theory, especially in the case of Rawls (see Sandel, pp. 146–154), he is right in emphasizing the centrality of markets in the liberal theory of justice. But why, specifically, do liberal theorists opt for the market as an important allocative mechanism in a well-ordered society?

There is the familiar argument, common to old (Friedman, 1962) and new (Walzer, 1983) liberals, that the decentralized nature of markets works to offset the concentration of economic power and to limit the range of political power to its proper sphere. Walzer, for example, expresses concern about the "power of the planners" in centrally planned economies and allows a special sphere to money and markets, suitably constrained so that the economic sphere cannot dominate the domain of the political. Rawls, too, admires markets because he feels that, in addition to their allocative efficiency, they are less likely than planning to interfere with equal liberty and fair equality of opportunity; that is, market devices decentralize power and enhance free choice of occupation. But there is another, more important, reason for Rawls's insistence on markets. And he does insist:

> The ideal scheme sketched . . . makes considerable use of market arrangements. It is *only* in this way, I believe, that the problem of distribution can be handled as a case of procedural justice. (1971, p. 274, emphasis added)

Likewise, Dworkin (1978, 1981) designates markets as the allocative strategy most likely to satisfy the egalitarian core of liberal principles: Markets are part of the "constitutive program" of liberalism.

Dworkin and Rawls set out two related arguments in favor of markets. First, markets best accord with the principle of equal concern and respect, which secures the right of individuals to exercise their autonomy by freely choosing their particular conceptions of the good or plans of life. The state guarantees the background conditions requisite to the liberal ideal of the person as autonomous, rational, and free. Individuals, so understood, and within the bounds imposed by just principles, go about choosing, cultivating, and rationalizing their characters, preferences, and aims in life.

Dworkin's argument proceeds as follows: Suppose the state initially distributes resources and opportunities (e.g., Rawls's "primary social goods") equally, so that everyone has roughly the same share with which to satisfy self-determined aims. This is required by the core egalitarian principle because an initially unequal distribution would assume that the fate of some people is more important than that of others. Because individuals choose different conceptions of the good, however, some mechanism will be required to allocate resources in proportion to the different requirements of different choices. The mechanism that accomplishes this task automatically and without coercion is the market. An efficient market measures the costs of resources needed to realize different projects, and

> these measurements make a citizen's own distribution a function of the personal preferences of others as well as of his own, and it is the sum of these personal preferences that fixes the true cost to the community of meeting his own preferences for goods and activities. (Dworkin, 1978, p. 131)

The market thus satisfies the requirement of an egalitarian distribution, "which requires that the cost of satisfying one person's preferences should as far as possible be equal to the cost of satisfying another's" (1978, p. 131). And it does so as a consequence of each person's choices as opposed to the decisions of planning agencies, decisions based on political judgments about the desirability of certain conceptions of the good. The market, in other words, ensures the government's neutrality, within the bounds of justice, on substantive questions of the good lives.

Rawls's case for markets is similar to Dworkin's, but it proceeds from the direction of "entitlements." There is the same concern about the state imposing some "perfectionist" standard or particular view of the good on everyone, with Rawls arguing that individuals are entitled to pursue their different aims. The difference principle, combined with appropriate distributive "precepts" (e.g., payment in proportion to risk, effort, disutility, training, etc.), establishes a just system of entitlement to which individuals have legitimate expectations, and it is the market that tends to distribute income in line with these expectations. For the state to override market distribution through excessive income transfers or the excessive provision of public goods (financed through compulsory taxation) would be to interfere unjustly with the entitlement system, a system that allows individuals to expend their merited income according to their preferences. This is why

all regimes will [must] normally use markets to ration out the consumption goods actually produced [such that] the output of commodities is
guided as to kind and quantity by the preferences of households as
shown by their purchases on the market. (1971, p. 270)

It follows, I think, that Rawlsian justice requires a market in production goods as well because consumer preferences would of necessity
play a large part in determining the direction of production. Rawls
says that "there is no necessity for comprehensive direct planning"
under socialism, and the context of his remark makes it clear that
comprehensive planning that does not take its cue from market indicators violates the difference principle and its associated precepts
(1971, p. 273).[15] Again, if the market is not used to allocate resources, people would be denied the opportunity to expend their
merited incomes freely as they see fit. Justice requires the market
because of the distributional consequences of its allocative function.

   None of this is to say that either Dworkin or Rawls wants to rely
on unregulated, unfettered markets as the sole, or even main, distributive institution. The price system is used to distribute benefits
only when set against the background of just basic institutions that
set the stage for particular distributions. It is the responsibility of the
state—through taxes, income transfers, regulation of externalities,
maintenance of competitive market conditions, ensuring educational and training opportunities, provision of public goods (largely
on the grounds of Pareto optimality), and allowance for basic
needs—to maintain the appropriate setting for the operation of markets as allocative and distributive devices.[16] The particular distributions would be radically different if it were not for state activities, so
much so that it is not misleading to say that markets merely assist in
determining particular distributions. Nonetheless, once the requisite

[15]The idea that planners in a socialist economy could, and should, imitate the market
  in calculating and applying their plan was proposed some years ago by Oskar Lange
  (1938). Lange argued that a system of market socialism, in which government agencies based a planned economy on computations geared to imitate a perfectly competitive economy, would be more Pareto efficient in allocating resources than a
  capitalist market system.
[16]Although Rawls and Dworkin are in agreement on this, Dworkin has the more
  sophisticated economic argument and appears to rely to a greater degree on (hypothetical) market solutions to political questions (e.g., taxation and income distribution). Dworkin assesses actual market distributions in light of hypothetical insurance markets whose function is to mitigate the morally arbitrary aspect of actual
  market distributions. These markets, whose results would be enforced through state
  activity, yield a more egalitarian distribution of goods than actual markets (see
  Dworkin, 1981).

background institutions, or what Rawls calls the *basic structure*, are in place, "it may be perfectly fair that the rest of total income be settled by the price system" (Rawls, 1971, p. 277). Additional income transfer and provision of public goods would be unjust or, at least, place the burden of argument on those who press for their extension.

There are two senses, then, in which the market can yield an egalitarian outcome. It accords equal respect and concern to individuals by permitting them to exercise their autonomous choices, not just in their selection of consumption goods, but more importantly in their different paths of self-development. It is egalitarian also because, when suitably regulated as indicated before, it results in a distribution satisfying the difference principle that, according to my interpretation, means a distribution defined by a fairly narrow range of wealth and income differentials (DiQuattro, 1983). It is not true that markets, when situated within a system of public ownership of the means of production (market socialism) or a "property-owning democracy" (Rawls's favorite), where private property rights are widely distributed, must assume "normal capitalist motivation" (Macpherson, 1973b, p. 345) or result in the kind of maldistribution of resources characteristic of class-divided, for example, capitalist, societies.[17]

I have noted Rawls's objection to the excessive provision of public goods in a well-ordered society. He is careful to place limits on their provision and makes it difficult for the "exchange branch" of government to trade private for public goods. Indeed, he relies on Wicksell's "unanimity criterion," which calls for near-unanimous approval of legislators on the public financing of collective goods.

> There is no more justification for using the state apparatus [in an already just society] to compel some citizens to pay for the unwanted benefits that others desire than there is to force them to reimburse others for their private expenses. (Rawls, 1971, p. 283)

Or, as Dworkin would put it, liberal justice does not require, in fact it prohibits, the compulsion through political means of some by others to subsidize preferred conceptions of the good.

[17]I have argued elsewhere that the difference principle rules out the capitalist market system as just. The use of markets under socialism or a "property-owning democracy," however, fares well by the principle (DiQuattro, 1983). For more on the compatibility of markets and equal distribution, see Carens (1981) and Schweickart (1980). Both Carens and Schweickart would have *distributive* outcomes determined politically while leaving it to the market to determine *allocative* outcomes. Schweickart, though, relies less on markets as an allocative device with respect to net investment, leaving that largely to the state.

But if justice makes it tough to enlarge the public goods sector, what happens to the value of community, assuming that the latter can flourish only in the context of a sizable collective goods environment? Barry (1973, Chapter 16) suggests that the value of "altruistic collaboration" cannot long survive in a private goods (market) economy governed by the principles of liberal justice, and Wolff (1968, Chapter 5, pp. 185, 187) writes of what "conservatives and radicals alike miss in liberal society . . . [namely] the social values of community. A community is "a group of persons who together experience a reciprocity of awareness, and thus *have a community*," and an *"affective community"* is the reciprocal consciousness of a shared culture . . . that we are many together than many alone. The "rational community," which Wolff defends, incorporates the qualities of the affective community but provides, in addition, for equal participation of agents who come together to concert their wills and posit collective goods and engage in common actions. These goals and actions presuppose shared traditions and culture and work to bolster and sustain them.

> The sharing of traditions and culture takes many forms, [including] the celebration of national holidays . . . the singing of anthems or reciting of prayers [without which it would be difficult to achieve] the desired reciprocity of awareness. (1968, pp. 186–187)

If the health of the community requires public affirmation through collective activity and goods, then the market, because it makes possible and encourages diversity and independence from communal ties, emerges as an institution antagonistic to community. The result, for thinkers like Tonnies and Marx, is alienation; for the classical liberals, the consequence is liberation. And we can locate here the ethical roots of the Marxist strategy to abolish the market, through planning combined with extension of the public goods sector, and of the classical liberal opposition to the captivating effects of tradition and the translation of collective values into political fiat.

New liberals like Rawls believe they can elude theoretical conflicts or dichotomies of this kind by embodying in the liberal principles of justice the values of community and mutual benefit. In this respect, they sound remarkably like Hegel, who tries to reconcile civil with political society, except that, unlike Hegel, there is every attempt to subordinate "civil society" to the requirements of just principles. Rawls's well-ordered society is not Hegel's civil, that is, class-divided, exploitative society (see Gauthier, 1974), but Rawls does follow Hegel in trying to maintain plurality within the context of unity. For Rawls, a well-ordered society is one of differentiated unity. He sees no necessary conflict emerging between the practice of liberal justice, which includes the right of individuals to pursue their chosen life plans (as circumscribed by just principles) and the value of community. He only wants to leave it to individuals to decide whether, within the framework of just principles collectively adopted and enforced by the polity, they wish to realize whatever additional communitarian aims they may have. Though Rawls's principles are not morally neutral in a way that tolerates the cultivation and satisfaction of any and all individual ends, they do provide a defense for a pluralistic organization of society.

> Other socially collective ends may well exist besides that of being a well-ordered society; but these ends cannot be upheld by the coercive apparatus of the state. If socially collective communitarian aims could survive in no other way, why would we regret their demise, and consider the original position unfair and arbitrarily biased against them? (Rawls, 1975, p. 551)

Does this provide a solution to, or a synthesis of, one of the most important controversies that has preoccupied political theorists from Plato versus Aristotle through their adversarial counterparts in the modern period? I do not know, and I leave it to readers to hazard a response. Bear in mind though, before deciding too intuitively in favor of liberal justice, on the basis of what Rawls says in the passage cited previously, that if "socially collective communitarian aims could [not survive without a more extensive provision of public goods]," those individuals whose conception of the good or plan of life is bound up with the experience of living in an affective or rational community are out of luck if they find themselves living in a society regulated by liberal justice. The realization of their conception of the good is blocked, or severely hampered, by the "unanimity criterion." So why can we not say that the original position is unfair and aribrarily biased against them? The question is whether Rawls's implicit judgment about the superior worth of the liberal form of life is morally justified. I have tried to elucidate the justification of the slant toward market strategies and pluralist institutions by calling attention to the individualistic premises of liberal theory.

References

Alchian, A., & Allen, W. (1969). *Exchange and production: Theory in use.* Belmont, CA: Wadsworth.

Barry, B. (1972). Warrender and his critics. In M. Cranston & R. Peters (Eds.), *Hobbes and Rousseau: A collection of critical essays* (pp. 37–65). Garden City, NY: Doubleday Anchor.

Barry, B. (1973). *The liberal theory of justice.* Oxford: Oxford University Press.

Bloom, A. (1975). Justice: John Rawls vs. the tradition of political philosophy. *American Political Science Review, 64,* 648–662.

Brennan, T., & Pateman, C. (1979). Mere auxiliaries to the commonwealth: Women and the origins of liberalism. *Political Studies, 27,* 183–200.

Carens, J. (1981). *Equality, moral incentives, and the market.* Chicago: University of Chicago Press.

Darwall, S. (1980). Is there a Kantian foundation for Rawlsian justice? In H. G. Blocker & E. Smith (Eds.), *John Rawls' theory of social justice* (pp. 311–345). Athens, Ohio: Ohio University Press.

Dietz, M. (1985). Citizenship with a feminist face: The problem of maternal thinking. *Political Theory, 13,* 5–18.

DiQuattro, A. (1983). Rawls and left criticism. *Political Theory, 11,* 53–78.

DiQuattro, A. (1984). Value, class, and exploitation. *Social Theory and Practice, 10,* 55–80.

Dworkin, R. (1978). Liberalism. In S. Hampshire (Ed.), *Public and private morality* (pp. 113–143). Cambridge: Cambridge University Press.

Dworkin, R. (1978). *Taking rights seriously.* Cambridge: Harvard University Press.

Dworkin, R. (1981). What is equality? *Philosophy and Public Affairs, 10,* 283–345.

Elshtain, J. B. (1981). *Public man, private woman.* Princeton: Princeton University Press.

Fisk, M. (1975). History and reason in Rawls' moral theory. In N. Daniels (Ed.), *Reading Rawls: Critical studies in A Theory of Justice* (pp. 53–80). New York: Basic Books.

Flathman, R. (1973). Introduction. In R. Flathman (Ed.), *Concepts in social and political philosophy* (pp. 324–328). New York: Macmillan.

Friedman, M. (1962). *Capitalism and freedom.* Chicago: University of Chicago Press.

Galston, W. (1980). *Justice and the human good.* Chicago: University of Chicago Press.

Galston, W. (1982a). Moral personality and liberal theory: John Rawls' Dewey Lectures. *Political Theory, 10,* 492–519.

Galston, W. (1982b). Defending liberalism. *American Political Science Review, 76,* 621–629.

Gauthier, D. (1974). Justice and natural endowment. *Social Theory and Practice, 3,* 3–26.

Gaus, G. (1983). *The modern liberal theory of man.* New York: St. Martin's Press.

Gellner, E. (1974). *The legitimation of belief.* Cambridge: Cambridge University Press.

Gewirth, A. (1973). The justification of egalitarian justice. In R. Flathman (Ed.), *Concepts in social and political philosophy* (pp. 352–366). New York: Macmillan.

Gilligan, C. (1982). *In a different voice: Psychological theory and women's development.* Cambridge: Harvard University Press.

Greenberg, E. (1981). Industrial self-management and political attitudes. *American Political Science Review, 75,* 29–42.

Gutmann, A. (1980). *Liberal equality.* Cambridge: Cambridge University Press.

Hobbes, T. (1968). *Leviathan.* Ed. by C. B. Macpherson. New York: Penguin. (Originally published 1651)

Hobhouse, L. T. (1964). *Liberalism.* New York: Oxford University Press. (Originally published 1911)

Hochschild, J. (1981). *What's fair? American beliefs about distributive justice.* Cambridge: Harvard University Press.

Kant, I. (1959). *Foundations of the metaphysics of morals.* Indianapolis, IN: Bobbs-Merill. (Originally published 1785)

Kretzmann, N. (1969). Desire as proof of desirability. In J. Smith & E. Sosa (Eds.), *Mill's utilitarianism* (pp. 220–226). Belmont, CA: Wadsworth.

Lange, O. (1938). *On the economic theory of socialism.* Minneapolis: University of Minnesota Press.

Laslett, P. (1971). *The world we have lost.* New York: Scribner's.

Levine, A. (1974). Rawls' Kantianism. *Social Theory and Practice, 3,* 47–63.

Lukes, S. (1974). *Power: A radical view.* London: Macmillan.

Macpherson, C. B. (1962). *The political theory of possessive individualism.* Oxford: Oxford University Press.

Macpherson, C. B. (1973a). *Democratic theory: Essays in retrieval.* Oxford: Oxford University Press.

Macpherson, C. B. (1973b). Rawls' models of man and society. *Philosophy of Social Science, 3,* 341–347.

Macpherson, C. B. (1977). *The life and times of liberal democracy.* Oxford: Oxford University Press.

Oakeshott, M. (1956). Political education. In P. Laslett (Ed.), *Philosophy, politics, and society* (pp. 1–21). Oxford: Basil Blackwell.

Pitkin, H. (1972). *Wittgenstein and justice.* Berkeley: University of California Press.

Rae, D., Yates, D., Hochschild, J., Morone, J., & Fessler, C. (1981). *Equalities.* Cambridge: Harvard University Press.

Rawls, J. (1971). *A theory of justice.* Cambridge: Harvard University Press.

Rawls, J. (1975). Fairness to goodness. *Philosophical Review, 84,* 536–554.

Rawls, J. (1977). The basic structure as subject. *American Philosophical Quarterly, 14,* 159–165.

Rawls, J. (1980). Kantian constructivism in moral theory. *Journal of Philosophy, 77,* 515–572.

Rawls, J. (1985). Justice as fairness: Political not metaphysical. *Philosophy and Public Affairs, 14,* 223–251.

Sabine, G. (1961). *A history of political theory.* New York: Holt, Rinehart & Winston.

Sandel, M. (1982). *Justice and the limits of liberalism.* Cambridge: Cambridge University Press.

Schweickart, D. (1980). *Capitalism or worker control?* New York: Praeger.

Singer, P. (1979). *Practical ethics.* Cambridge: Cambridge University Press.

Smart, J. C. C. (1978). Distributive justice and utilitarianism. In J. Arthur & W. Shaw (Eds.), *Justice and economic distribution* (pp. 103–115). Englewood Cliffs, NJ: Prentice-Hall.

Taylor, C. (1982). Rationality. In M. Hollis & S. Lukes (Eds.), *Rationality and relativism* (pp. 87–105). Cambridge: MIT Press.

Walzer, M. (1983). *Spheres of justice.* New York: Basic Books.

Walzer, M. (1984). Liberalism and the art of separation. *Political Theory, 12,* 315–330.

Williams, B. (1962). The idea of equality. In P. Laslett & W. G. Runciman (Eds.), *Philosophy, politics, and society* (pp. 110–131). Oxford: Basil Blackwell.

Wilson, J. (1966). *Equality.* New York: Harcourt, Brace and World.

Wolff, R. P. (1968). *The poverty of liberalism.* Boston: Beacon Press.

Wolff, R. P. (1977). *Understanding Rawls.* Princeton: Princeton University Press.

Wood, A. (1980). The Marxian critique of justice. In M. Cohen, T. Nagel, & T. Scanlon (Eds.), *Marx, justice, and history* (pp. 3–41). Princeton: Princeton University Press.

CHAPTER 5

Sociology and Justice

Steve Rytina

Justice is more often an implicit theme than an explicit object of study in sociology. The most obvious causes of this are the strong pressures toward moral relativism and against metaphysical speculation. The effort to comprehend what is, from the point of view of those living it, lends itself to neither absolute judgments nor a unified definition.[1]

The predominant concern, which tends to fragment definitions, is with justice from the perspective of those under investigation. More narrowly, it is with their sentiments of justice about the social arrangements they enjoy (or endure). Thus the concept is often relative to the particular point of view of a participant in a particular set of social arrangements.

Social arrangement can be construed variously, but the most widely shared concern relative to the justice concept is with enduring inequalities in access to values, or stratification. The question of justification of inequality is one of distributive justice or of fair rules or procedures or processes for the allocation of advantage and disadvantage. Ideally, the issue is not whether a particular arrangement is fair, but whether or to what degree it is accepted as fair by those who live under it.

---

[1]An exception is the field of criminal justice, which is a name for studies of police, courts, and prisons. Many workers in this area would agree that what they study has little to do with justice in the normative sense, even though it goes by that name. Justice, in this instance, is mainly a label adopted from ordinary speech and not a technical term. This chapter is focused on the self-critical and not the colloquial application of the concept.

STEVE RYTINA • Department of Sociology, Harvard University, Cambridge, Massachusetts 02138.

But this ideal is disingenuous. If the truly disinterested so-
ciologist might aspire to this perfect relativism, not so many have
claimed such disinterest, and fewer yet have been so credited by
their opponents. What more often happens is that attempts to comprehend enduring inequalities embed moral elements by asserting
the inevitability or desirability of particular patterns. It may be impossible to theorize about stratification without justifying or criticiz-
ing; indeed, that is usually the motive for worrying about the problem at all.

Thus, the greater part of sociological discussion of justice is
embedded in theories of inequality. First, because these comprise
the causes and determinants of stratification, they are useful for
opponents and supporters of various arrangements. Second, most
sociologists have assumed or argued, on quite varied grounds, that
inequality must be accompanied by supporting sentiments or normative beliefs if it is to endure. The dominant problematic of justice
in sociology is an interplay of inequality and sentiment that supports
or undermines it.

Two devices will be employed in my attempt to impose coherence on this value-laden and heartily contested domain. First,
attention will be narrowed, so far as possible, to sociological views,
although the authors reviewed did not respect such limitations. Second, the review is chronologically arranged. A first section examines
the most widely followed European antecedents. A second will describe developments in Anglo-American sociology since World War
II. A third will consider recent developments with an eye on promising future paths. If I succeed in suggesting convergence, from grand
concerns to empirical studies, it is more truly a reflection of my
personal biases than the current state of the field.

The Content and Form of Classical Views

As is so often the case, the grand orienting perspectives were
laid out in the 19th and early 20th centuries by Marx, Durkheim, and
Weber. They outlined contrasting views of the sources of enduring
inequality and its ideational supports. Of course, this list is hardly
exhaustive. Each of these had predecessors. Other authors who still
are read (notably Mill, Michels, Sorel, Pareto, and Gramsci) formulated partial or comprehensive views of inequality and its supports.
Still, Marx, Durkheim, and Weber are convenient points of reference
for outlining the basic positions, and they are the dominant inspira-
tion for the positions that are vital today.

Marx

For Marx, the starting point was the human necessity of trans-
forming that given by nature through work. The necessity of work
implies that control over the conditions of work is tantamount to
control over other humans. The case that he most carefully considered, in *Capital,* was the nature of work and control in a capitalist
mode of production.

The argument in Marx's *Capital* (1867/1967) focuses on the implications of exchange of equivalent values. Productive activity, or
labor power, under capitalism is exchanged in its commodity form,
and its exchange value is its cost of reproduction. The primary
motive for such exchange is use, and in these two aspects labor
power is identical to other commodities. But a capitalist who purchases labor power and thus obtains its use value can turn a neat
trick. Because labor power can be used to produce more than its
reproduction cost, a surplus accrues to those in a position to purchase and use it. It is this surplus, realized as profit, that permits the
capitalist to set ever greater quantities of labor power and productive
capital in motion, thereby reproducing capitalism as a system on an
expanded scale.

Although there can be no doubt that Marx held caustic views
about the human costs of the extension of capitalism, his judgment
about the motives and moral character of the participants in the
system was more sanguine (see Buchanan & Mathieu, Chapter 2, this
volume). After all, in the model, all exchange was of equivalents.
Within the system as a given, neither force nor fraud was at issue.
The capitalist who deviated from the logic of the system, for example, by returning the surplus to the workers, would not long remain a
capitalist. Indeed, the capitalist who adapted to the force of competition, who by the logic of the system became an agent of expanded
reproduction, was an agent of progress. Of course, the worker who
served progress in the first instance by evading starvation had less
enviable choices but was no less compelled by the logic of the
situation.

The model in *Capital* embraces several levels. At first view, it is
a model of the microscopic process of exchange. Because this is, by
the terms of the model, exchange of equivalents by parties free to
seek the best outcome, it has the appearance of justice. At the same
time, the logic of the system's evolution appeared to imply ever
greater exploitation and immiserization even as overall social product rose but fell into the hands of a narrowing circle of beneficiaries.

Further, the system was self-justifying. Its logic appeared immanent to participants. Within a system where all useful products of labor are obtained after intermediate passage through the commodity form, nothing could appear more natural than that labor and productive means equally took this form. Because all were compelled to participate in such exchange as a condition of social life, it had the overwhelming force of necessity.

But there were two major caveats to this. First, Marx saw the system as historical creation. His inquiry into its onset, under the rubric of *primitive accumulation*, revealed quite another picture. The key to setting labor free for participation in the wage contractual exchange of equivalents was the forceful and fraudulent deprivation of preexisting rights of access to the means of production. Although the system in its present development appeared natural and fair, its origin revealed otherwise.

Second, and somewhat similarly, the exchange of equivalents presupposed an entire system of ideas, morality, law, and enforcement. It was only with these elements as givens that the entire edifice with all of its consequences was natural and inevitable. Indeed, once these givens were worked out to their conclusion, an almost completely proletarianized population would set in motion an enormous productive apparatus while being deprived of its finest fruits. This pattern would provide the basis for a higher view of the matter, which would be politically realized in the transition to socialism.

From this necessarily brief sketch, I would extract several key elements. First, once capitalism was well underway, its microscopic basis in exchange of equivalents would appear inevitable and fair, which indeed it is, from a particular point of view. Even the capitalists are not villains but agents of a process that is larger than their role. But the rapid development of this pattern would simultaneously increase its obvious human cost and lay the material and organizational foundation for an alternative. In short, an equilibrium exchange among persons produced a macroscopic dynamic that would ultimately undermine the appearance of inevitability that provided the justification for the original exchange relation.

Durkheim

Where Marx put exchange of equivalents in the center place, Durkheim's point of departure was the social, which he held took regulatory precedence over the individual and the interpersonal. Durkheim's concept of the social was both broad and prejudicial. It was broad because his project was to set apart a distinctive problem area for sociology. But it was prejudicial, albeit fraught with insight, because Durkheim nearly equates the moral and the social. This assumption in company with his functionalist outlook led to uncritical inferences of the moral necessity of existing arrangements.

One of Durkheim's major goals was to construct a science of ethics, with sociology as the foundation. In a variety of ways, he argued that collective notions (early in his career the conscience collective, later collective representations) were the source of moral constraint and the repository of moral precepts. Durkheim was most ingenious at showing how social phenomena revealed the impingement of this collective moral superstructure. Thus, for Durkheim, sociology was the determination of relations among social facts, that were always collective and normally moral.

In Durkheim, this conflation of the moral and the collective was combined with functionalism. He took as given that collective features were necessary. (He did not do this with a perfect consistency and thus evaded obvious absurdities.) Because this meant that prevalence reflected a collective fact which is both moral and necessary, the scientific necessity of morality is self-evident within his system.[2]

Durkheim's account of inequality and justice, presented in his *Division of Labor in Society* (1893/1933) follows this pattern. In this work, he undertook to investigate the sources of solidarity that were (necessarily for him) replacing the solidarity of likeness that had characterized preindustrial society. He found these in the division of labor, which was accompanied by an explosion of moral facts in the form of restitutive law. For Durkheim at this time, the preeminent moral facts were norms with diffuse sanctions (p. 491) of which the volume of law was a reflection. These facts proved for Durkheim that contract or exchange alone does not unite modern society but that exchange rests upon a broad substratum of moral guidelines. The notion that exchange presupposes moral elements lives on as a major hurdle for exchange-based theories (cf. Ekeh, 1974).

Having dismissed contractual solidarity as the moral basis of the division of labor, Durkheim addressed the obviously fractious indus-

---

[2]Circularity is an oft-noted feature of Durkheim's demonstrations. Lukes (1973) cites several critics who make this accusation. Lukes suggests that circularity is best regarded as a stylistic flaw that obscures arguments that could be stated soundly. Although Durkheim sometimes took the moral necessity of the prevalent to its logical extreme, as in his famous argument that crime is healthy because it affords the occasion for vengeful punishment that affirms shared standards, most of his arguments are more conventional in their moral implications.

trial scene of his day. Here, he achieved consistency at the price of utopianism. Under the rubric of *pathology*, he examined the "forced division of labor" wherein

> the institution of classes or castes . . . gives rise to anxiety and pain . . . because the distribution of social functions on which [the division of labor] rests . . . no longer responds to the distribution of natural talents. (p. 375)

The negation of the forced division of labor was called the spontaneous division of labor where "each social value would be judged at its own worth" (p. 377). Although conceding that "this perfect spontaneity is never met with anywhere as a realized fact" (p. 378), Durkheim foretold that

> this work of justice will become ever more complete. No matter how important the progress already realized in this direction, it gives, in all likelihood only a small idea of what will be realized in the future. (p. 381)

His confidence was based on the fact that "society . . . regards as unjust any inferiority that is not personally merited" (p. 379). In Durkheim, society gets what it wants. Durkheim was so confident of his argument that he could view contrary yet prevalent empirical conditions as a short-run aberration from a more harmonious equilibrium.[3]

For Durkheim, then, justice was a moral sentiment generated by modern conditons. This fact demonstrated that it was a necessity of those conditions. And, over the longer run, necessity would prevail, bringing reality in line with morality. But this necessity and this morality that awaited society at equilibrium was a meritocracy where all value is judged at its true worth.

This rather nebulous conception of a long-run equilibrium was only part of the story, however. For Durkheim, its precondition (the antinomy of the forced division of labor) was a system of contracts that would be spontaneously kept and was free of the moral taint of explicit force or the implicit force of necessity. Then each object would be exchanged at "its social value [which] represents the

---

[3]Durkheim's personification of society can be seen as a metaphorical trick, not as reification. The fuller passage argues that the spreading sentiment of equality, by which he meant equal opportunity, is an indication that modern conditions require it in practice. The idea that popular sentiment reflects functional necessity is not a metaphor but an implication of his scheme.

useful labor it contains" (p. 382). For Durkheim, the ideal was the fully free contract where inequalities reflected solely natural or inherent inequalities among men. In his words,

> The task of the most advanced societies is, then, a work of justice. That they, in fact, feel the necessity of orienting themselves in this direction is what we have already shown and what every-day experience proves to us. . . . Our ideal is to make social relations always more equitable, so as to assure the free development of all our socially useful forces. (p. 387)

Durkheim's view had dynamic elements, but he viewed the process as heading rapidly for an equilibrium. The two noteworthy features of this equilibrium were that it presupposed moral elements that would tame exchange and that the equilibrium would be exchange at the rates dictated by this moral background.

Weber

Weber's contribution was more textured and more ambivalent. Weber was a law professor and wrote extensively on the development of legal thought and practice. He used the term *justice* primarily to refer to the product and practices of legal specialists, as in examining the activities of jurists as the administration of justice. But Weber's subtle contributions to the questions of justice writ large went beyond the acceptance of common labels.

A source of his subtlety was the construction of comparatively modest models of societal features (known as ideal types), instead of attempting a holistic comprehension. These sketches combine analytic or conceptual distinctions with more substantive elements. The result is open-ended, leaving much to be filled in by the analyst of a concrete formation, while supplying a framework of useful distinctions and empirical expectations. The two most important for present purposes are his analysis of authority and of acting collectivities that participate in shaping it.

Weber (1979, p. 151) distinguished authority from power by noting that the former rested upon acceptance of an order or framework of rules and assumptions that specified the personnel and the domain of unquestioned control. The scale and depth of acceptance by a subject population was the extent of legitimacy of that order. The subjectivity involved is comparable to Durkheim's because legitimacy corresponds to a mental state of the individual but is insofar as it is widespread.[4] Authority, then, was power among persons that was a result of the enmeshing of dominated and dominator in a single set of rules. Although this relationship is not voluntarily entered, once it is entered it can proceed without much force or fraud.

For Weber, the rules were not static or causally grounded in either economic or functional necessity. Though they might appear static and be proclaimed static by those who benefited from the appearance of inevitability, the rules changed variously according to inner logics or as the result of contest among competing groups.

Weber's conception of group competition was derivative but more encompassing than Marx's. He recognized the reality of class (or shared life chances) as a determinant of action but stressed that class was not the sole or even prevalent basis of acting together. An alternative basis for cooperative action was status, or position in a hierarchical order of honor, where membership and internal standing were presumed to be based on conformity to a moral code. Because such codes prescribe conduct within and among groups, their prevalence makes group membership salient and binding.

In addition to this stress on isomorphic groupings with differences in world view, Weber's addition to class opens a new realm of conceptual possibilities. Within such a scheme, persons no longer have unique memberships but multiple memberships defined by different dimensions. Any particular set of co-members can then be subdivided by differing positions on other dimensions. Thus there are various levels of inclusion and patterns of overlap at each level. This leaves open the issue of the potency of the various social distinctions or, obversely, the internal coherence and cohesion of the collectivities so defined.

Weber does not argue for a single, final equilibrium or a self-sustaining equilibrium that precedes a massive transformation but for perpetual damping following bursts of instability. Legitimacy in his scheme was partly traditional, and one can infer that it was enhanced by duration. But there was always the possibility that it would be unmade and remade in the jockeying among groups that were themselves becoming more or less potent in shaping members' views and action.

---

[4]Weber is clear that obedience does not solely rest upon rules. People may obey out of habit, from custom, for lack of a better idea, and because it is in their self-interest. Despite these qualifications, the emphasis on rules has been transmitted as the central Weberian idea.

The Classics Summarized

The classical views do not converge, but together they narrow the range of possibilities. All emphasize that to understand society, one must analyze the way that tasks are allocated and coordinated. Partly this rests upon the distribution of control over material means, but it is ultimately control over people. All agreed that such control was rooted in or worked through meaningful symbol systems. For Marx, this was the exchange of equivalents, which was both necessary and preparing the ground of its own demise. For Durkheim, interdependence was generating equitarian sentiments, and these would summon up a society evolved in its own self-image. For Weber, there were the politically derived rules and understandings that made an "ought" of obedience but that embedded the dominant as well as the dominated.

Thus, all agreed that people achieve ends through social relationships, but that these relationships, and the motives that activate them, are socially defined and socially derived. Within these constraints, construed differently of course by each author, people do what they want.

Each in his own way grappled with an apparent circularity, one that may be captured in the paradox of social action. Insofar as it is social, it is constrained, but insofar as it is action, it reflects choice. What this means is that every individual comes into a world already existing. That priority is, to the person, constraint, in such forms as shared language, moral codes, and technical arrangements. At the same time, everyone has choice, although only relative to these givens. The paradox is that in an analytically closed world, the aggregate of all the choices is the constraint.

This totality of constraint, which can be understood in various ways, corresponds to social structure.[5] In each of these classics, structure was understood in terms of a small number of fundamental building blocks. For Marx, the triad of productive means, its owner,

---

[5]*Social structure* is hardly a consensual term. I take it as having two central properties. First, it refers to that which is empirically independent of the will of the actor, although in a sufficient time scale, it is not necessarily independent of the will of all together. Second, structure refers to analytic constructions that provide insight into the orderliness that is observed empirically. Thus language is a structure in both of these senses. First, in any linguistic community, communication requires conformity to a set of rules, the greater part of them tacit. Second, structural linguistics has brought to light patterns that account for some of the order to be observed in language production. These two senses are related but hardly identical. The structures yet

and its activator was the core from which all else followed. For Durkheim, the moral codes that made interdependence feasible and regular were the core elements. For Weber, the central concern was domination, with its basis in orders or rules and the consequent control over things and command over people.

For each of them, there exists a fundamental residuum of choice, nicely summarized by Marx's aphorism "men make their own history but they do not make it under circumstances chosen by themselves" (Marx, 1959, p. 320). This implies that the social relationships that are elements of social structure are contingent on commitment. That is, without motive to comply with requirements, the entire edifice is rent by friction, and in extremum, subject to dissolution and reformation.

The ideological expression of commitment is sentiments of justice, that is, belief that the pattern of rights and obligations, of debts and payments, of give and take, are as they should be in the joint interest of the partners and not the expression of the capacity of the one to coerce the compliance of the other.

Although all agree that commitment, which is manifested in sentiments of justice, is a necessary lubricant in the world as we find it, they differ about the source and moral standing of that commitment. For Marx, the free wage contract is not morally culpable interpersonal coercion but a collective coercion that is an artifact or result of the structure that shapes the world we inhabit. For Weber, somewhat similarly, legitimate command is not coercion, although the extant pattern is established by coercion and shaped by the distribution of control over coercive resources. Durkheim, however, believed that the absence of coercion, which he equated with justice, was both immanent and imminent.

To summarize, each of the three held that free or uncoerced commitment rested upon sentiments of justice, that is, was just from the point of view of all parties to the relationship. Each agreed that major features of the world rested upon widespread sharing of such sentiments. Where they part company is whether this empirical necessity was evidence of transcendental justice. Durkheim, true to his positivist principles, was willing to equate the empirical with the transcendental, even where the "fact" was only a prediction. The others were not so ready to follow.

---

proposed by linguists cannot account for all the effect of structure observable under the first sense. Thus to assert that some particular set of intellectual constructs accounts for features of the world is structuralism but one that falls far short of embracing the totality of structural properties.

But together they defined the fundamental questions of justice in sociology. As a variable but important empirical regularity, the inequalities inherent in the division of labor are likely to be accompanied by supporting sentiments. But the transcendental question of justice rests upon whether the relationships that bridge the division of labor may be regarded as uncoerced. This is not the empirical question of whether arrangements rest upon commitment but the theoretical questions of how those arrangements, with their empirically consequent commitment of whatever degree, are, in the first instance, constituted.

What they share, then, is an image of unequal social positions that are united in reciprocal relations that are, must be, or tend to be defined as inevitable and morally binding or just so long as the arrangement endures. They differed on how they defined the key positions, Marx emphasizing classes, Durkheim a multiplicity of functions, and Weber the variety of differentiating dimensions that ultimately referred back to power. They disagreed on whether this perception of reciprocity was an illusion, a reality, or a prevalent and stabilizing adaptation. They disagreed widely about the course and desirability of future developments.

Finally, they share a common deficiency. Sentiments of justice are, in the final instance, an individual matter. Yet they help unite people into collectivities and collectivities into societies. This gives rise to a certain ellipsis in theoretical presentation. The ideas that are attributable to individuals are sometimes rather cavalierly attributed to collectivities. What is true of an analytically typical individual often is rather freely taken as a collective property. Thus classes, societies, and groups sometimes act, or pursue goals, because their coherence is taken as given or proved. Although the classical authors, especially Weber, recognize the problem, the combination of persons into ascending levels of collective coherence has received ever more careful treatment, as I hope to show later.

Refinements of the Classical Views

Structural-Functional Theory

Following World War II, a self-proclaimed synthesis of these classical views held sway in sociology under the leadership of Talcott Parsons. Parsons's views are important both because he held that reciprocity in social relations was analytically necessary and because his views formed the backdrop for a thesis that was both controversial and enduring—that inequality is a self-justifying necessity of society. Somewhat after the fashion of Durkheim, Parsons and his followers uncovered the scientific necessity of reciprocity uniting inequality, and in those starry-eyed days of progress, this necessity spilled over into morality.

The analytic necessity of reciprocity is summarized in the argument leading to the "fundamental dynamic theorem of sociology" (Parsons, 1951, p. 42). People meet each other in roles where ego's responses are alter's environment and vice versa. The stabilization of this rests on value standards that assume a moral significance. Those who share values "constitute" a collectivity so that the theorem states that the integration of shared value standards with personal need dispositions is the source of social stability. In slightly more ordinary language, because each person depends on others, social stability depends on the degree that each may take the other's motives as like their own and thus as predictable. Although the problematic is the scientific question of predictability, the result is none other than the golden rule, that all must do unto others as they expect them to do unto one's self.

The original passage is horribly obscure. (This argument is the one that Mills, 1959, "translated" into English in his devastating critique of Parsons's awkward profundity.) But it seems clear that for Parsons the collectivities in question were large. If so, the argument is fallacious in a fashion that illustrates what might be called the fundamental fallacy of integration.

Although it is enormously handy to be able to predict others' behavior, for each of us the set of others whose acts we must predict is far short of the totality of our fellow citizens. Those with whom one actually comes in contact are a small and highly nonrandom sample of that population. Certainly the stability of such relationships rests, in part, on mutually satisfied expectations. But, as bad but durable marriages or prisoner–guard relations illustrate, choices can be relative. And even if there were sufficient fluidity to guarantee mutual satisfaction in pairings, it is a great logical leap that the relations of each to all is inherently so guaranteed. Yet it is only by this leap that any overarching commonality in motive is necessary.

A highly influential and controversial theory that grew out of Parsons's work seemingly argued for such a guarantee. In their functional theory of stratification, Davis and Moore (1945) argued that inequality of rewards was an "unconsciously evolved device" whereby society insured that the most talented were supplied with means and motivation to undertake the training that would insure that the most important functions were properly carried out.

Davis and Moore, following Parsons, believed that every social order rested upon consensual values. These, they felt, defined collective goals that, by definition, were in everybody's interest. Those best able to contribute to those goals had to be induced to contribute, and thus inequality of rewards was in everybody's interest. Of course, it was "obvious" to them that prostitutes and mafioso were not contributing in quite the manner of brain surgeons. Thus they emphasized the prestige or moral reward that inhered in various occupations or functions and not just the economic returns.

The emphasis on prestige is one of the major sociological themes transmitted through the functional theory. Prestige, if it is to be coherent, is a function of widespread convergence in moral evaluation. This has crucial implications for justice. If differential rewards in prestige exist, these rest on convergent evaluations of the moral standing of different positions in the division of labor. Thus differential rewards in prestige mean that this inequality that arises from the division of labor is viewed by all as just.

This theory sparked an extended controversy. Many critics thought that the theory was an apology or justification of inequality. Although the original authors did not say so, it is hard to avoid the implication that attempts to protest or do away with the inequality that supplies motive and allocates talent in the division of labor are as futile (and irrational) as calls to repeal Darwinian evolution or the law of gravity.

Through the many exchanges (Bendix & Lipset, 1953), one can detect a gradual agreement that practically all complex systems had some trade-off of equality and efficiency so that inequality was a nearly unavoidable response to scarcity. In that very weak sense, the theory was true, although it seems to have largely escaped commentators that the necessity of some trade-off has no bearing on the magnitude of extant trade-offs. One reason that magnitude was not addressed was the equally widespread impression that functional importance was a nearly circular concept that could not bear such precision. At first, it seems obvious that the functions regarded as more important are more rewarded, especially if rewards are to be measured in prestige because perceived contribution to the common good is a source of prestige. But it was noted that many lowly occupations are indispensable when regarded as functions. This is shown by the thought experiment of comparing society's survival chances faced with a loss of neurosurgeons versus a loss of garbage collectors. What was needed but not found was a criterion of importance that was conceptually independent of the rewards obtained. (Stinchcombe, 1963, does derive predictions from the theory but his criteria do not readily suggest comparisons among all occupations.)

In fact, a plausible criterion is rather obvious if one replaces the emphasis (unchallenged by Davis, Moore, and their defenders) on a collective construal of functions. In the spirit of the original argument, the issue for society is not collective performances but motivated and skilled individual performances. The rewards used to induce talent and training should minimize the costs from failed performances by persons in jobs. An error by a judge or neurosurgeon may well be, on average, considerably more costly than a dented garbage can or even a smashed truck.[6]

This solution, if it is adequate, highlights a central but implicit tenet of the theory: that justice obtains when individuals are competitively allocated among positions whose rewards rest upon consensus. This is a two-unit proposition. One unit is society, conceived as a system of positions and a congruent consensus on rewards. The other is the individual for whom the system is a given. As a member of society, the individual partakes of the consensus. Then, as a person, he or she is allocated an outcome that reflects merit from the collective point of view, which is equally the point of view of all persons, including the person, himself or herself.

The two poles of this package have undergone separate development. A vast body of status attainment research (Blau & Duncan, 1967; Hauser & Featherman, 1977; Jencks et al., 1972, 1979) has examined how test-taking ability, educational attainment, aspirations, and, debatably, luck determine how individuals are sorted into jobs along the dimension of status, which is theoretically and

---

[6]Although this might appear to rescue the functional theory, I think that implication is too extreme. First, it almost equally evades the question of quantitative trade-offs. Second, it does not escape embedding in the world as we find it, that is, that people are rewarded for the potential costs of accidents that actually never occur. (Although I prefer to fly on airplanes with highly experienced pilots, I suspect that in the present state of automation this is a waste of money.) Third, an obvious corollary is that people are rewarded, in part, to fend off demonstrated capacity for errors, so that disruption potential in forms like work stoppages (or even sabotage) surely makes a difference (Perrone, 1984). Fourth, the argument has overtones of consumer sovereignty. Providing services (in the broad sense) to those who control many resources is worth more because they control such resources, so that oil billionaires can establish a class of evasive drivers, the worth of whose skills depends on beliefs about ideal life expectancies for oil billionaires. Fifth, explaining the hierarchy of occupations has only indirect bearing on the implications of inequality transmitted through families over generations.

empirically close to prestige (Hope, 1982). It has been suggested (Horan, 1978) and denied (Bielby, 1981) that this paradigm rests upon the functional theory. Certainly it shares with the functional theory a concern with the allocation of persons along a dimension of social honor that rests upon consensus (Hodge, Siegel, & Rossi, 1966). Thus, attaining socially dominant positions becomes success in the pursuit of honorable vocations. However, with the notable exception of Jencks *et al.* (1972, 1979), most of this analysis parallels the functional theory with a scientific emphasis, in this case heavily empirical, that is far more concerned with what is than with the implications for justice. But Goldthorpe (1980) has pointed out that concerns for justice and social stability are rarely very far beneath the surface of the scientific investigation of social mobility.

Another line of development, sometimes explicitly in response to the functional theory, emphasized the importance of power and social struggle in setting the rules within which individuals competed for life chances. Here the primary movers were classes variously defined (Dahrendorf, 1959; Lenski, 1966), status groups (Collins, 1975; Parkin, 1979), ethnic groups, or even classes within a system of states that often take on the attributes of status or ethnic groups (Hechter, 1974; Wallerstein, 1974, 1979). These described the basic hierarchical givens as derivative of a sequence of coerced "bargains." The acceptance of these bargains, and thus of the broad outlines of stratification, is adaptation to necessity, and not the voluntary acceptance of the advantages inherent in reciprocal cooperation. Against this backdrop, there have been almost innumerable studies of how people are seduced or coerced into accepting such bargains, under the rubrics of ideology or false consciousness. Such notions lend themselves to tautology, which recent authors have taken much care to avoid. The result is a convincing body of evidence that subordination is partly maintained by imposition of delusory or immobilizing views (e.g., Gaventa, 1980; Hochschild, 1981; Lukes, 1974; Willis, 1977).

Exchange Theory

Although the functional theorists, and Parsonians more generally, took the transaction of the individual and society as a point of departure and the antifunctionalists emphasized the coercive bargains among groups, an intermediate alternative was to examine exchange among individuals. This was carried out, in contrasting fashion, by Homans (1974) and by Blau (1964). By breaking down the problems into more levels, they were able to see how social arrangements could be both fair and unfair, or voluntarily accepted and imposed from without, at the same time.

Both Homans and Blau examine microsociological processes, although both, especially the latter, also pursued macrosociological questions. For each, the starting point is that each of us may do things that are pleasing (or hurtful) for others, and they may do likewise for us. Some pleasing behaviors correspond to scarcity. In Homans (1974), a person who may provide a greater value than received can wield power or command compliance by the principle of least interest. In effect, the voluntary ability to withdraw produces voluntary compliance, although this includes the case of money at gunpoint. For Blau (1964), any item obliges the other to a fair return, and value in excess of what can be returned must be compensated by compliance. In both instances, control over scarcity translates to power.

For both, though by different arguments, exchange in groups is regulated by shared standards or norms. The most critical of these is distributive justice (Homans, 1974, Chapter 11) or fair exchange, which Blau (1964, p. 156) directly likens to Homans's distributive justice. This is formulated as a proportionality rule, following Aristotle, so that returns are proportional to costs and investments. In both cases, the rule itself is something that is a given (that is, it is not explained), and the evaluations of different items (e.g., the "worth" of investment in education or in a "white" skin) ultimately rest on expectations. These derive from individual and collective history because "what is, is always on the way to becoming right" (Homans, 1974, pp. 98, 253). Thus expectations and the norm of distributive justice are prior to the face-to-face group, and neither author claims that the history incorporated in expectations is inherently fair.

With this major caveat, justice prevails in the short run in the small group because even unilateral monopolies are balanced by the collectively provided good of social approval (which sanctions fair or just exchange). Although Blau emphasizes more than Homans that this happy equilibration is retarded by commitments to occupations and organizations that impede the search for the best rates of exchange, both emphasize that over the longer run, in larger collectivities, going rates become fair rates even if their moral basis is deficient. Thus historical accident and naked exploitation enter into exchange as verities made moral by the weight of persistence. As Homans baldly states, "There is no just society" (1974, p. 251). In other words, where choice is free and the weaker control the coin of social approval, the world tends to justice, but the scale and durability of inequality in a complex society has only the justice of inevitability and not that of universal voluntary exchange. It appears as just, most of the time, but this is adaptation to necessity.

Yet each of them exempt legitimate authority from this difficulty. For Blau (1964), power becomes legitimate authority when subordinates positively sanction its use. One is then both obliged to obey and be subject to sanctions by co-members for disobedience; that is, obedience is a norm of the group of subordinates. Homans suggests that obedience is fundamentally the same (1974, pp. 278–279) as compliance with a norm. When obedience to either serves to further collective goals, sanctions by co-members reflect their interest in the fruits of the norm or of the principle of command. Of course, both of these tame power because legitimacy rests upon conformity by superiors with rules upheld by subordinates. Neither of these authors is naive about the ultimate sources or potential for abuse of power, yet each agrees that it is substantially regulated by the necessity of assent governed by rules.

Thus, for the exchange theorists, proportional distributive justice is a normative standard that is popularly accepted. However, its application rests upon evaluations of groups and activities that are derivative of the surrounding social environment. Within this not necessarily just constraint, distributive justice is popularly enforced (given fluidity in seeking partners) within face-to-face groups. In particular, authority is grounded in rules that have popular assent. But neither is very successful at unpacking the "rest of the world" because each sees a somewhat indeterminate mix of adaptation to inevitability, consensus about the evaluations that justify distributed inequality, and dissent from these evaluations and resistance to extant arrangements. In sum, under fluid exchange, individuals will obtain and believe in justness, and power will tend to become legitimated authority, but at a macroscopic scale this is a mixture of delusion and inevitability.

Contracts and Bargains

A macrosociological variant was presented by Moore (1978). He argues that there is a more or less universal social contract between rulers and ruled, whereby the latter must provide some measure of security against foreign and domestic depredation, supernatural, natural, and human threats to the food supply and other material supports of customary daily life. In return, the obligations of the subject are obedience to orders that serve these ends, contributions toward the common defense (lacking in those few societies where war is unknown), material contributions toward the support of the rulers who do not as a rule engage in straightforward economic production. Finally, subjects are generally expected to make some contribution through their own social arrangements toward keeping the peace. (1978, p. 22)

Moore leaves no doubt that such contracts are political settlements that vary in time and space. The core of his argument is that failure to live up to this contract is the source of moral outrage, which in turn is the wellspring of revolt.

Moore's macrosociological argument is complementary to that of the exchange theorists, focusing on the bargain that shapes the world outside the work group. But the bargain itself is different. In particular, it has neither the quantitative or rationalist flavor of compleat distributive justice. Compliance is "exchanged" for security, but the equivalency is very rough.

This suggests another way of conceptualizing authority and its complement of long-term commitment to organizations. Although Homans and Blau describe the social contract mandating distributive justice as quantitative, the quantities are very fuzzy. Both agree that social exchange does not have a currency and that prices or exchange ratios are not the exact quantities of economic exchange. Blau, (1964) in particular, emphasizes that social exchange runs by obligation spread over time, not just because there is a norm of reciprocity but because of a pervasive interest in presently indefinite future exchanges (1964, p. 92). Thus one must reciprocate to preserve reputation, which is like a credit rating. Homans, in his discussion of Mauss's essay on gifts among primitives (1974, pp. 217–219) argues that reciprocation preserves status, which is a summary public expectation of one's capacity to reward and is for Homans also much like a credit rating.

What neither does is recognize the combined implications of fuzzy rates and an indefinite future for norms and for authority. Norms, for each, have the character of public rules. For Homans (1974, p. 99), they are statements, that is, linguistically encoded generalizations. For Blau (1964), they also appear to have the character of law, that is, that the nature and degree of violation may be linguistically expressed by any social competent. In the spirit, and perhaps imitation, of Weber, this means that the charter of authority is codified.

But this is exactly what authority is not, and in two different senses. First, the Milgram (1974) experiments revealed an enormous discrepancy between what linguistic competents would expect based upon a verbal report of the situation and what actually occurred. And this fact is central to Milgram's explanation. Most of his subjects fell into an "agentic state" where they disattended or did not perceive the implications of their actions while their attention was directed to how well they were complying.

Second, it is obvious that the Milgram subjects did not do this on the basis of a formal contract that men in white coats may, for a fee, command you to do damage to others. Seemingly, the subjects complied because they were disattending the specificities of their action. Economists (Simon, 1957) have recognized that this is inherent in the purchase of labor power. Willing subordination, as in a labor contract, is an agreement to respond to unspecified commands within unspecified limits, albeit sometimes only for a specified period of time. As Williamson (1975) has pointed out, it is the practical impossibility of prespecification of all contingencies that makes fuzzy contracts necessary and efficient.

There is evidence that ordinary folk will assert limits to compliance (Gamson, Fireman, & Rytina, 1982) but that these do not rest on inspecting the fine print of the social contract. This research showed that groups presented with an "obviously" illegitimate demand often will converge on disobedience but that the process is hardly inevitable and rests as much on a shift in gestalt, or point of view, as in a careful weighing of evidence. Another finding, which suggests a limiting condition of Milgram's result, was strong group effects. The reaction of similarly situated others was critical for individuals so that groping resistance often snowballed into unanimous dissent. Thus, both psychologically and factually, authority is less an agreement for specific services than a diffuse obligation to obey where limits are not, indeed cannot, be laid out in advance. In this research, different limits emerged from highly variable group processes.

Two aspects of the authority relation are present indefiniteness that is embedded in a future of uncertainty. What takes place is less like market exchange than the barter of present compliance against future consideration. The negative aspect, that compliance forestalls punishment, is widely recognized, although it is quite clear in Milgram (1974) that this threat is not clearly thought, although maybe it is felt. The other side, as Moore (1978) points out, is that authorities insure against uncertainty. Partly, this has a negative character when the uncertainty inheres in the potential of authorities to inflict indefinite damage. But it often has a positive character. Compliance can be an investment in future benefits of promotion and reward or an investment in protection against evil fate or evil people. The good will of those controlling the levers of power can be very useful, but their centrality allows them to bargain for compliance today as insurance against events that may never come to pass.

Rules matter because they are communication devices that finely texture expectations, with potential gain in efficiency. Rules work best when those scrutinizing their application find evidence that sustains faith in the future. Just as insurance companies must appear to pay claims to keep the premiums flowing, power holders who honor obligations are lending motive to compliance.

But the formal contract sustained by rational self-interest is the limiting case. Much more typical is an inability to calculate the future (technically uncertainty, and not risk) and the consequent necessity to cope in the face of ignorance. Unquestioning obedience is a strategy that supplants the inability to calculate with faith that someone else will somehow insure an acceptable outcome. Thus professional expertise, which converts uncertainty to risk within the supposed domain of competence, is a potent source of unquestioning obedience. Magicians, warlords, and corporate chiefs are often looked to with faith that they can transmute uncertainty into favorable outcomes. In a more negative vein, even those herded by force into the clutches of an utterly brutal and arbitrary figure have most to gain by attending to clues for evading the direst consequences. This surely can produce unquestioning obedience and even some measure of "oughtness" in the minds of the victims. This can be "reciprocated" insofar as even concentration-camp guards have some interest in motivated compliance (Kogon, 1950/1980). But this has not the same rosy fragrance as the happy equilibrium of the American office.

Indeed, the uncertainty that compliance evades can be imposed by dominants. Hay (1975) describes 18th-century English criminal justice where harsh sentences were brokered by intervening notables in a rough bargain of deference against the possibility of dire legal straits. The vulnerability of Southern blacks to private- and state-sponsored coercion similarly produced dependence, sometimes to the point of internalized servility, on white patrons (Dollard, 1957). Experts in totalitarian practice like Paraguay's Stroessner (Vinocur, 1984) have not missed this trick. One should not overemphasize such extreme cases, but they cannot be overlooked.

Implications of Indefinite Contracts

All of this suggests important modifications to the exchange theorist's views. First, uncertainty heavily shapes local social contracts. People develop rich rhetorics about the payoffs, like promotion, for certain ways of behaving. Pleasing bosses and/or furthering the collectivity's interest figure among these. But some environments are too disorderly and irregular to sustain an accurate rhetoric of the local contract. Second, the local contracts are decoupled, not universal. Different uncertainties mean the local details are different. Local equilibrium does not extrapolate to global. Because organizations must sometimes share similar or identical training environments, certain abstract universals (like the framing device that supposes that work comes in jobs of contracted remuneration and duration) must be accommodated. But much of the person's worth to an organization rests on acquired knowledge of the local situation.

From this viewpoint, the exchange theorists analyzed a special, and not universal, case. Their arguments rest on something like the knowledge requirements of the Weberian model of bureaucracy, where calculability prevails. In such an environment, justice calculations can also rest upon rules and consensual (i.e., socially objective) evaluations. As uncertainty increases, the balance of faith and calculation shifts in favor of the former. The result, by this argument, is the displacement of reason by ritual. The pressure to believe in fairness and rightness may well increase, even as the scientific capacity to pierce uncertainty and judge the claims declines.

It is probably fruitful to regard the pressure toward voluntaristic fairness as variable. The exchange theorists have called attention to comparison levels (resting on reference persons or groups) and available alternatives. These emphasize the importance of realizable, and known, choices. I would add several additional considerations. First, the pressure toward fairness rests upon the desire for motivated compliance. When mistakes are more costly, and/or evadable by application of human, not mechanical, capacities, that is, when the task requires knowledge, then the dignity and self-concept of the subordinates must be protected. Second, when the extremity of uncertain outcomes is greater, in a disorderly environment, where great riches or great defeats are plausible, dependence and thus the capacity of authority are enhanced. Third, because the leverage turns about the indefinite future, as the horizon of termination of the relationship nears, authority will diminish.

Even though this suggests that obedience to authority can be nonrational, that is, that the trade-offs may lie beyond present limits of knowledge, there are two possible implications that must be explicitly disavowed. Compliance may often be the best available, though imperfect, strategy. It is not necessarily irrational, nor does it entirely revolve around inscrutable elements. By the same token, one hardly need sacrifice all possibility of moral judgment. In particular, the uncertainties to which persons are subject range from the intentional and therefore avoidable to those truly beyond human control. Although there is a grey area of socially imposed uncertainties, like the chances of unemployment in a capitalist economy, where necessity is debatable, other uncertainties are far less problematic. In short, those who agree that knowledgeable free choice is the wellspring of justice, probably should also agree that unnecessary uncertainty is the antagonist of justice.[7]

Leaving aside such speculations about the future state of opinion, I would like to summarize the extant sociological comprehension of justice. A repeated theme is that voluntary exchange of equivalents attracts to itself the sentiment of justness. Put another way, such exchanges are regulated by motives of justice, but they also fulfill them. However, the very notion of equivalents presupposes some degree of consensus on what counts for how much. Although some have attempted to derive this from social necessity, the more common view is that it is somewhat historically arbitrary. Proponents of either position would agree that popular sentiments matter because they delimit the tolerable from the infuriating. However, there is increasing recognition that the problems of justice embrace different levels of analyses. The exchange theoretic analysis of the exercise of options gives way to the recognition that these options are embedded in larger structures and longer durations, which shape exchange in two ways. First, consensual evaluations of various items sets limits on what certain people, through their acts, can command. Second, and far more complex, is the fact that exchange commits people to collectivities, and it is the collectivities that compete for

---

[7]The possibility and application of this scientific capacity is part of the massive project of Habermas. In *Knowledge and Human Interests* (1968), he exposed the political bias of purely technical criteria. As a new ideal, he offers the uncoerced communication situation, which I take to be a condition like exchange uncontaminated by the inheritance of past hierarchies or the exploitation of differential control over uncertainty. The grandeur of this vision is attractive, but the reconstruction of sociology from this basis is an immense task barely begun.

scarce goods and services (Coleman, 1982). As Blau recognized, this extra layer forbids simple extrapolation from the happy office to the just world.

This second position is one that sharply distinguishes the outlook of sociologists and of economists. Economic arguments tend to take as given the existence of individuals with stable preferences over outcomes. The chapter by Worland in this volume (Chapter 3) displays how this can be used to generate models of superior equilibria that follow in the absence of limits on pursuit of self-interest (including that constraint on Peter that is freedom for Paul summarized by the concept of liberty). Sociologists give far more weight to collectivities.

One variant emphasizes some obvious empirical facts concerning firms and occupations. It is fairly clear that many people experience careers, that is, an orderly sequence of roles where access to later ones is only open to those occupying adjacent positions. But the absolute promotion rates are determined by openings produced by growth and the rate of exit and are therefore independent of individual qualities, even though relative promotion rates may reflect such qualities (Baron, 1984). Thus armies during wartime and universities during the 1960s exemplify successful collective enterprises, whereas an air of defeat can sometimes be discerned among junior faculty today. Some occupations, which can limit entry and/or bargain collectively, similarly alter life chances independently of individual qualities. This imagery suggests that collectivities bargain for resources and then redistribute them to members. Although some of this corresponds with the model of many competing firms compensating mobile labor at the margin, many of the collectivities are monopolies, like the American Medical Association, or oligopolies like General Motors. Many, like universities and government bureaus, are not firms facing markets, and many demand lifetime commitments, or careers, and deny or restrict labor mobility.

Another more speculative line of reasoning emphasizes that participation in social circles is not merely a source of satisfaction but is constitutive of ends. To put it starkly, values that are not sustained by participation and mutual recognition tend to fade. It is probable that most of us overestimate the stability of our preferences because we do not have to experience radical changes in our social environment. The literature on total institutions (Goffman, 1961) suggests that most people's identities are quite malleable. Less dramatically, a history of participation in a distinctive religious, ethnic, or class position imposes costs upon exit. But these are not costs commensurate with rational choice models. Among the incalculable sacrifices are the loss of interpersonal validation for past choices, that is, the loss of autobiographical meaning. Ethnographic studies suggests that anticipated loss restrains economic mobility (Gans, 1962) or that mobility produces self-estrangement (Sennet & Cobb, 1972), whereas less selective sample survey data do not detect such effects (Goldthorpe, 1980).

The deeper point is that taking ends as given (for example, middle-class propensities to save) assumes away the different conditions that are historical givens for different groups. The assumption of preferences as given is agnostic on whether people pick preferences, and hence "deserve" the benefits, or whether preferences are imposed by environments. For example, a well-documented source of greater educational attainments by middle-class youth is a greater desire for education (Jencks *et al.*, 1979).

This poses a great puzzle for issues of justice. From a collective perspective, it may appear advantageous to reward the accumulation of individual skills that results from such motivation to reinforce the motive in succeeding cohorts. But this view overlooks the fact that extant patterns of rewarding education are differentially inspiring to youth of different social backgrounds. It is unconvincing to attribute this to individual preferences as if these are independent of environments. But then the attribution of merit to the educated entails rewards to the effortless fact of family background. Thus, extant patterns of rewarding individuals in fact reward inheritance, and one cannot easily dismiss the suspicion that this happy coincidence may account for some of the preferences of those who exercise power to sustain such a system. Education can convincingly be interpreted as a game that legitimates inheritance by imparting individual capacities to the wellborn that are denied to others (Bourdieu & Passeron, 1977). This gives rise to two different versions of justice, or of the fair return. Once the system is operating, differences in capacity among adults are real, and one can and should expect voluntary contracts to reflect those differences. But this does not mean, imply, or require that such differences are free of original sin, that is, of differences in life conditions that allowed the differences to develop.

This suggests two contrasting agendas for investigating justice, regarded as popularly sanctioned fair returns to personal assets. First, one can examine current, popular notions of fairness. Second, one can look at those rarer occasions where popular perceptions of injustice are conspicuous. Implicitly, it is the latter that, through collective contest, determined the former but, in current practice, the two domains of study are discrete. It is to a review of these that I now turn.[8]

Living Issues in Justice Research

Current Popular Sentiments

One lively line of research focuses on the forms, contents, and implications of present popular sentiments of justice. The originator and most active executor of such studies is Peter Rossi. (Some of the most recent developments are reported in the collection edited by Rossi & Nock, 1982.) This research rests on surveys using vignettes, or descriptions of social acts and actors with outcomes that random samples of adults can assess for fairness. Much effort has been devoted to research design. The most sophisticated designs present each sample member with a portion of a model universe in which each relevant attribute is combined with each other. Rossi and Anderson (1982) describe how such fully crossed designs can be extended over larger model universes using a random procedure to generate combinations that are orthogonal (uncorrelated) in the probability limit. This allows for the investigation of a very large number of factors with a single sample.

---

[8]Although the primary topic of this essay is approximately *social justice*, which is near the heart of sociology, a brief review of the application of these concepts to problems of crime can be added.

Although most portions of the division of labor are supplied with positive motive, certain strategies for gaining access to goods, services, or satisfaction are subject to negative or criminal sanctions.

The definition of crime has been laid to two sources, the common outrage felt by all against certain acts, which was explicitly proposed by Drukheim, or as a result of the interests of dominant groups in control. In fact, both have elements of truth and fiction. Threats to control, or controlling myths, whether symbolic *lèse majesté* or the organization or furthering of resistance, have often been subject to the same sanctions (and sanctioning apparatus) as acts that are offensive to most citizens, such as theft. Indeed, arguments over the political character of various acts indicate that the boundary of laudable resistance and unwarranted intrusion on ordinary lives is, itself, a political tool.

The point is that elites may well try to define acts threatening to their position as threatening to a general interest. At the same time, as Moore (1978) points out,

Two results from this approach are quite relevant. First, Americans assess fair income mostly on criteria of merit; that is, those with more education and with jobs higher on the empirically consensual scale of social standing are popularly awarded more pay. (Hochschild, 1981, and Coleman & Rainwater, 1978, report similar results.) However, the top of the fair scale falls quite short of the highest incomes actually received. At the bottom, there is acceptance of a floor below which even the undeserving should not fall, and there is some support for such need-based criteria as number of dependents.

The second result is an absence of dissensus. For Rossi, *dissensus* is defined as disagreements that are systematically related to

---

protecting citizens from acts that non-elites deem offensive is a chore that is neglected at peril. The problem of the definition and treatment of crime is similar to the problem of authority. There are definite forces that favor definitions grounded in popular sentiment, but the special problems of power holders also receive special attention.

There is considerable evidence that popular sentiment on the seriousness of crime is largely consensual (Rossi et al., 1974) and that this is linked in orderly fashion with desired punishment (Hamilton & Rytina, 1980). The deeper source of the hierarchy of seriousness is not known. One possibility is that people evaluate crime on a "victims-like-me" principle. The more severely dislodging (and undeserved) acts from one's own point of view are viewed as more serious. Thus threats to persons are more serious than threats to property; women tend to view rape as more serious; and white collar crimes that damage many victims slightly or involve activities beyond the comprehension or involvement of most citizens are seen as less serious. Victimless crimes may be seen as jeopardizing relations that are altruistic or involuntary, such as with kin and neighbors, but there presumably is less popular agreement about such two-step arguments.

Criminal activity can be seen as a form of noncompliance. Force and fraud bring short-run benefits but entail the certain sacrifice of cooperative future relations with the victim, and the uncertain possibility of criminal sanction, with the possibility of coercion into a highly unpleasant environment followed by nearly indelible marking as an unreliable exchange partner. (There is, for some, a "society" of criminals to fall back upon, which is reflected in widespread recidivism.) Attention to and faith in the long run increases with present and expected rewards (social standing), intelligence, obligations to others or family status, timidity, criminal incompetence, or ignorance of criminal routines, age, superior ethnic status, and to a declining degree, femaleness. Because most of these are correlated with residence and associates, crime is rooted in neighborhoods, ethnic groups, and cliques. Crime rates in American cities increase with inequality (Blau & Blau, 1982), which may reflect the fact that inequality implies greater relative profit for predation in the average stranger contact. Finally, crimes within enduring relationships, including victimless and organized crimes as well as abuses of power (sexual, parental, political, and economic), fall under exchange theory and have much in common with more savory activities.

components of social standing or cleavage such as race, income, and religious affiliation. (For a modest and apparently exceptional finding of group differences, see Hamilton & Rytina, 1980.) This absence of structured dissent is not to be confused with detailed agreement among individuals. Although differences among persons are not correlated with membership in demographic categories, large but uncorrelated differences are implicit in most reports that have been published. (Such results are often implicit in published work because of Rossi's influential, and debatable, argument that uncorrelated differences should be regarded as statistical error or noise.) This suggests that someday a profit will be turned by successfully linking this variation in ideals with more refined measures of social membership.

Methodological differences notwithstanding, the evidence to date strongly supports Homans's (1974) assumption that agreement on principle is widespread although there is disagreement on the application of the principle to cases. For example, most people agree that the better educated deserve more pay, but they do not agree on how much more. We yet await the study that examines the application of such abstract quantitative justice rules to oneself.

There has been some dispute about the exact mathematical form of the justice equation (probably somewhat reflective of the parallel theoretical dispute among social psychologists, on which see Furby, Chapter 6, this volume). Jasso (1978), reanalyzing earlier work with Rossi (1977), discovered that the logarithm of fairness produced a better statistical fit than the raw measure. From this foundation, she proceeded to a theory of justice sentiments (Jasso, 1980) that rested upon shape properties of various statistical distributions, which in turn were attributed to popular sentiments. Whether there exists a social consensus with such exact properties might be doubted, but this work may foreshadow efforts to pin down the quantitative properties of justice judgments more exactly.

The Rossi method allows the researcher to force responses to various combinations of attributes so that different standards, such as need versus desert, are reflected only as popular weights for attributes like family size and education. Hochschild (1981) used less structured interviews to gather evidence that different principles are applied to different domains. She reports that egalitarian principles are supported within families and for politics, whereas distributional principles are more popular for economic outcomes. The ethical desirability of noncomparable domains for different principles was argued by Walzer (1983).

Collective Responses

Although much of this work follows the exact tradition hoped for by Homans and Blau, another developing area has been more after the fashion of Moore's concern for historical studies of folk beliefs about justice and reciprocity. Among these are Aminzade (1981), Hanagan (1980), Rudé (1980), Sewell (1980), and Bonnell (1983). For all their differences, these share a concern for the little tradition, located in particular geographical and social regions.

These support a common theme, which derives from the influence of Tilly (1978) and is summarized by Calhoun (1983). The activists of 19th-century radical collective action were not dislocated, recently urbanized proletarians, but artisans and skilled workers. The reason, to put it simply, is that such people are embedded in long-established networks that sustain a collective definition of fair play and provide an easily activated pattern of selective incentives to overcome Olson's (1965) dilemma of "free riding."

A model or ideal image of this pattern may be formulated in terms of White's (n.d.) concept of a cat net (which is discussed by Tilly, 1978, and Calhoun, 1983). A cat net exists when a set of people are both rhetorically distinguished by a common label and are interconnected by social ties. A necessary and sufficient condition for this is that the label delimits a small group, where small is relative to the number of social relations, and that in-group preference or like choosing like is substantially true. Thus, if a label delimits a distinct set of people whose social relations reflect self-selection, the result is a category with the constraining property of a group (Rytina & Morgan, 1982). Such a configuration facilitates the enforcement of group standards of conduct, including contribution to collective action.

A second condition is that the occupants of the labeled and knitted position must share a common antagonist, again to be understood as a category, with which each member has an antagonistic relation. This often is a market relation, in Weber's sense, where a relatively unitary factor price makes the zero-sum quality of the relation transparent. But it could also be an authority relation, where the shared label implies that the treatment of another is a harbinger for oneself.

A third condition is negative. The configuration must not be crosscut by other categories or other relations that would allow the antagonist(s) to play off different factions within the category. The absence of crosscutting patterns is a necessary, but not sufficient condition, for Stinchcombe's (1977) solidarity. In his view, commitment to a group is greater when the group is institutionally complete, that is, when the arrangements that provide for sociability, reproduction, spiritual solace, and so forth are internal. This means that problems can be solved without alliance with outsiders and conversely that other cat-net members control many benefits. Perhaps one sufficient condition is that the category has had a sufficiently lengthy history to develop such institutions. But it may be that any master status that is not overlaid with competing role systems will collectively control the bulk of the individual's social rewards. This suggests that populations with restricted access to different role systems, such as prisoners, students, and youths are more at risk to such configurations.

Under such conditions, a threat (or opportunity) for the master status is not just to an aggregate of individuals but to a network or a potential collective actor. In contrast, a change in the returns to some categorical distinction that is crosscut has contrasting effects within a social network and cannot provide the occasion for a unified response. A slightly sharper consideration is that when those with the most resources are those whose social relations provide the glue uniting the category, then the category is likely to produce a collective response. Thus, a farming community, where the more successful tend to be older, with more children and hands, but still local, stands in contrast to a suburb where the women and children have the bulk of the local relations.

With these considerations, I can suggest two contrasting situations that are particularly prone to perceptions of injustice that coincide with network cleavages. First, if membership in a category is partially passed on by inheritance, categories that are declining in size, which often means they are being economically undermined, will have very high rates of inheritance.[9] The effect is that the bonds of kinship will strongly coincide with the boundaries of the category. Second, if a category expands dramatically in a restricted geographic location that it does not have to share, then social relations will tend to coincide with the boundary and, in the short run, crosscutting bases of affiliation will be absent. In the first case, a rhetoric of tradition, as analyzed by Calhoun (1983), is to be ex-

---

[9]An example of this is independent farming in the United States. Against the backdrop of a declining number of farmsteads, a small number of future farmers per present farmstead suffices to saturate the available spaces. The paradoxical implication, which has held for several generations, is that most family farmers at the second millennium will be the descendants of farmers, even though most farm offspring are being forced into other occupations.

pected. Because the decline in size is likely to be accompanied by, or caused by, shrinking returns, enthusiasm for return to a better past is predictable. The second case, which describes such "new" populations as northern urban blacks, students, and homosexuals, is conducive to the advance of novel claims to new advantages or, to put the same thing differently, relief from traditional disabilities that were insured by the lack of sufficient autonomy, interdependence, and mass to allow, enforce, and struggle for a better deal.

In sum, I think what these studies are uncovering is both that rebellion is rooted in attempts to redress the treatment of an attribute and that only attributes that correspond to networks can react or act collectively. The reasons are related. Spontaneous resistance, which is a frequent starting point for longer movements, requires an unambiguous violation or injustice (Heirich, 1971). The cat net without crosscutting is a conducive configuration for a shared point of view that can be inadvertently (accidentally) transgressed by social control agents even as it facilitates the collective participation that makes an issue of injustice. Over the longer run, it is such incidents and the movements that they spark and highlight that underlie the process of collective readjustment of the rights and prerogatives of various groups.

These collectivities are exceptional insofar as their interknittedness may negate Olson's dilemma—that the negligible impact of any person's contribution to achieving a collective good implies that rational self-interest restrains contributions. There are at least three versions of this negation. One may claim, following Calhoun (1983), that the structures of a community provide ample selective incentives. Less in the spirit of Olson's rigor is the reinterpretation of rebellion as a self-affirming act of moral witness that can be an end in itself. Interknittedness tends to insure that significant others are also present as witnesses. But several recent works, such as Hardin (1982) and Margolis (1982), have suggested that collective action can be self-interested. And Axelrod (1984) has shown that altruistic behavior can evolve even among agents playing the notorious Prisoner's Dilemma, if they are embedded in an indefinite sequence of repetitions. To reduce this to a phrase, the either-or solution to the problem of voluntary cooperation that goes back to Hobbes is slowly yielding to issues of degrees, emphasizing overcoming the uncertainty of the long run.

The import of this innovative work may be less scientific than ethical (although the authors take great pains to point out empirical applications). I would express this as an unsolved paradox that is at the center of the problem of justice. If, following Olson, the contribution to collective bargaining power will be suboptimal in collectivities that do not coerce (or manipulate) their members, then the social bargain among collective units will favor those units whose internal practices bear the least resemblance to the ethical optimum of the absence of coercion. It is only by dissolving this dilemma that we can find cause for hope that the actual bargains people make could ever resemble the ideal bargain that individuals would reach in the absence of arbitrary constraint.

Conclusions

It should be clear that justice is no simple matter on which sociologists agree. For all of that, I believe a simple summary of the problem may be offered.

Justice obtains when individuals reach (and uphold) a bargain governing cooperation that is fully voluntary. (Rawls, 1971, and Habermas, 1968, who have both been quite widely read by sociologists, base their ethics on, respectively, a bargain reached prior to undertaking social positions or a consensus achieved in a conversation sheltered from the distortions of domination. These embody different analyses of the preconditions of a fully voluntary agreement.) Because cooperation is advantageous and problematic when people are different, the bargain balances diverse contributions and outcomes so that the several parties are better off by their own lights. This is the central sociological concern because such a bargain would motivate voluntary cooperation in the division of labor that is more or less equivalent to making society possible.

It is currently taken as common sense (cf. Geertz, 1983) that all social units enjoy some degree of voluntary cooperation that implies an empirical problem of justice, namely the degree of consensus on forms and contents of trade-offs motivating continued cooperation.

But just as there is no excuse for confusing the *is* with the *ought*, that which is believed just may reflect adaptation to necessity, and to domination, and not any process that is more ethically inspiring. The empirical agents that can undertake bargains, with their assets, their attributes, their cognitions, and their evaluations, are the results of the world as we find it—with all of its flaws.

Thus one can pursue the implications of bargains among individuals, as the exchange theorists have, only by taking the world outside the dyad as substantially given. Or one can examine the historical settlements among collectivities that determined those givens. These remain distinct problems. One of the greatest current challenges is integrating these different analytic levels (Blalock & Wilken, 1979; Collins, 1981).

The sad irony remains that if free bargains are the wellspring of justice, it is all too evident that it is mainly individuals who concretely bargain. This is against a backdrop of implicit bargains among collectivities that set the terms of trade. These greater bargains are not often renegotiated and to do so is a rare and costly process. Collectivities cannot easily act or bargain so that the absence of activity is no assurance of individual satisfaction. Unless one believes, as few do today, that the present is an equilibrium condition that would return even after profound disturbance, one is left with the conclusion that current bargains are, at best, somewhat arbitrary. The fluid bargain among groups, categories, and classes that is the ideal of the philosophers is most noteworthy for its contrast with the world we inhabit.

References

Aminzade, R. (1981). *Class, politics and early industrial capitalism.* Albany: State University of New York Press.

Axelrod, R. (1984). *The evolution of cooperation.* New York: Basic Books.

Baron, J. (1984). Organizational perspectives on stratification. *Annual Review of Sociology, 10,* 37–69.

Bendix, R., & Lipset, S. (1953). *Class, status, and power.* New York: Free Press.

Bielby, W. (1981). Models of status attainment. In R. Robinson & D. Treiman (Eds.), *Research in social stratification and mobility* (Vol. 1, pp. 3–26). Greenwich, CT: JAI Press.

Blalock, H. M. Jr., & Wilken, P. (1979). *Intergroup processes.* New York: Free Press.

Blau, P. M. (1964). *Exchange and power in social life.* New York: Wiley.

Blau, P. M., & Blau, J. (1982). Metropolitan structure and violent crime. *American Sociological Review, 47,* 114–28.

Blau, P. M., & Duncan, O. D. (1967). *The American occupational structure.* New York: Free Press.

Bonnell, V. (1983). *Roots of rebellion.* Berkeley: University of California Press.

Bourdieu, P., & Passeron, J. (1977). *Reproduction in education, society and culture.* Beverly Hills, CA: Sage Publications.

Calhoun, C. (1983). The radicalism of tradition. *American Journal of Sociology, 88,* 886–914.

Coleman, J. S. (1982). *The asymmetrical society.* Syracuse: Syracuse University Press.

Coleman, R. P., & Rainwater, L., with McClelland, K. (1978). *Social standing in America.* New York: Basic Books.

Collins, R. (1975). *Conflict sociology.* New York: Academic Press.

Collins, R. (1981). The microfoundations of macrosociology. *American Journal of Sociology, 86,* 984–1014.

Dahrendorf, R. (1959). *Class and class conflict in industrial society.* Palo Alto: Stanford University Press.

Davis, K., & Moore, W. (1945). Some principles of stratification. *American Sociological Review, 10,* 242–249.

Dollard, J. (1957). *Caste and class in a southern town* (3rd ed.). New York: Doubleday.

Durkheim, E. (1933). *The division of labor in society.* New York: Free Press. (Originally published 1893)

Ekeh, P. (1974). *Social exchange theory: The two traditions.* Cambridge: Harvard University Press.

Gamson, W., Fireman, B., & Rytina, S. (1982). *Encounters with unjust authority.* Homewood, IL: Dorsey Press.

Gans, H. (1962). *The urban villagers.* New York: Free Press.

Gaventa, J. (1980). *Power and powerlessness.* Urbana: University of Illinois Press.

Geertz, C. (1983). *Local knowledge.* New York: Basic Books.

Goffman, E. (1961). *Asylums.* New York: Anchor Books.

Goldthorpe, J. (1980). *Class structure and social mobility in modern Great Britain.* New York: Oxford Clarendon.

Habermas, J. (1968). *Knowledge and human interests.* Boston: Beacon Press.

Hamilton, V. L., & Rytina, S. (1980). Social consensus on norms of justice. *American Journal of Sociology, 85,* 1117–1144.

Hanagan, M. (1980). *The logic of solidarity.* Urbana: University of Illinois Press.

Hardin, R. (1982). *Collective action.* Baltimore: Johns Hopkins University Press.

Hauser, R., & Featherman, D. (1977). *The process of stratification.* New York: Academic Press.

Hay, D. (1975). Property, authority and the criminal law. In D. Hay, P. Linebaugh, J. Rule, E. P. Thompson, & C. Winslow (Eds.), *Albion's fatal tree* (pp. 17–63). New York: Pantheon.

Hechter, M. (1974). *Internal colonialism.* Berkeley: University of California Press.

Heirich, M. (1971). *The spiral of conflict.* New York: Columbia University Press.

Hochschild, J. L. (1981). *What's fair?: American beliefs about distributive justice.* Cambridge: Harvard University Press.

Hodge, R. W., Siegel, P. M., & Rossi, P. (1966). *Occupational prestige in the United States: 1925–1963.* In R. Bendix & S. M. Lipset (Eds.), *Class, status, and power* (2nd ed., pp. 309–321). New York: Free Press.

Homans, G. (1974). *Social behavior: Its elementary forms* (rev. ed.). New York: Harcourt Brace Jovanovich.

Hope, K. (1982). A liberal theory of prestige. *American Journal of Sociology, 87,* 1011–1031.

Horan, P. (1978). Is status attainment research atheoretical? *American Sociological Review, 43,* 534–543.

Jasso, G. (1978). On the justice of earnings: A new specification of the justice evaluation function. *American Journal of Sociology, 83,* 1398–1419.

Jasso, G. (1980). A new theory of distributive justice. *American Sociological Review, 45,* 3–32.

Jasso, G., & Rossi, P. (1977). Distributive justice and earned income. *American Sociological Review, 42,* 639–651.

Jencks, C., Smith, M., Acland, H., Bane, M. J., Cohen, D., Gintis, H., Heyns, B., & Michelson, S. (1972). *Inequality.* New York: Harper & Row.

Jencks, C., Bartlett, S., Corcoran, M., Crouse, J., Eaglesfield, D., Jackson, G., McClelland, K., Mueser, P., Olneck, M., Schwartz, J., Ward, S., & Williams, J. (1979). *Who gets ahead?* New York: Basic Books.

Kogon, E. (1980). *The theory and practice of hell.* New York: Berkely Books. (Originally published 1950)

Lenski, G. (1966). *Power and privilege.* Chapel Hill: University of North Carolina Press.

Lukes, S. (1973). *Emile Durkheim.* New York: Harper & Row.

Lukes, S. (1974). *Power: A radical view*. London: Macmillan.

Margolis, H. (1982). *Selfishness, altruism, and rationality*. Chicago: University of Chicago Press.

Marx, K. (1967). *Capital* (Vol. 1). New York: International Publishers. (Originally published 1867)

Marx, K. (1959). *Basic writings on political and philosophy* (L. Feuer Ed.). New York: Anchor.

Milgram, S. (1974). *Obedience to authority*. New York: Harper & Row.

Mills, C. W. (1959). *The sociological imagination*. New York: Oxford University Press.

Moore, B., Jr. (1978). *Injustice: The social basis of obedience and revolt*. White Plains, NY: M. E. Sharpe.

Olson, M. (1965). *The logic of collective action*. Cambridge: Harvard University Press.

Parkin, F. (1979). *Marxism and class theory: A bouregeois critique*. New York: Columbia University Press.

Parsons, T. (1951). *The social system*. New York: Free Press.

Perrone, L. (1984). Positional power, strikes, and wages. *American Sociological Review, 49,* 412–426.

Rawls, J. (1971). *A theory of justice*. Cambridge: Harvard University Press.

Rossi, P., & Anderson, A. (1982). The factorial survey approach. In R. Rossi & S. Nock (Eds.), *Measuring social judgments: The factorial survey approach* (pp. 15–67). Beverly Hills, CA: Sage Publications.

Rossi, P., & Nock, S. (1982). *Measuring social judgments: The factorial survey approach*. Beverly Hills, CA: Sage Publications.

Rossi, P., Waite, E., Bose, C., & Berk, R. (1974). The seriousness of crimes. *American Sociological Review, 39,* 224–237.

Rudé, G. (1980). *Ideology and popular protest*. New York: Random House.

Rytina, S., & Morgan, D. L. (1982). The arithmetic of social relations. *American Journal of Sociology, 88,* 88–113.

Sennett, R., & Cobb, J. (1972). *The hidden injuries of class*. New York: Vintage Books.

Sewell, W., Jr. (1980). *Work and revolution in France: The language of labor from the Old Regime to 1848*. New York: Cambridge University Press.

Simon, H. A. (1957). *Models of man*. New York: Wiley.

Stinchcombe, A. (1963). Some empirical consequences of the Davis–Moore theory of stratification. *American Sociological Review, 28,* 805–808.

Stinchcombe, A. (1977). Social structure and politics. In F. Greenstein & N. Polsby (Eds.), *Handbook of political science* (Vol. 3, pp. 557–622). Reading, MA: Addison-Wesley.

Tilly, C. (1978). *From mobilization to revolution*. Reading, MA: Addison-Wesley.

Vinocur, J. (1984, September 23). A republic of fear: Thirty years of General Stroessner's Paraguay. *The New York Times Sunday Magazine* pp. 20–32, 36–40, 93–94, 101.

Wallerstein, I. (1974). *The modern world system I*. New York: Academic Press.

Wallerstein, I. (1979). *The capitalist world economy*. New York: Cambridge University Press.

Walzer, M. (1983). *Spheres of justice*. New York: Basic Books.

Weber, M. (1979). *Economy and society* (G. Roth & C. Wittich Eds.). Berkeley: University of California Press.

White, H. (n.d.). *Notes on the constituents of social structure*. Unpublished paper, Harvard University.

Williamson, O. (1975). *Markets and hierarchies.* New York: Free Press.
Willis, P. (1977). *Learning to labor.* New York: Columbia University Press.

CHAPTER 6

Psychology and Justice

Lita Furby

The Study of Justice in Psychology: Historical Perspective

Introduction

Most work on the psychology of justice has failed to state explicitly, let alone justify, its underlying definitional assumptions. This failure has inevitably led to conceptual confusion and to inconsistent use of terminology. The definition adopted in this chapter is that justice involves an evaluative judgment about the moral rightness of a person's fate: that is, a person's treatment by others (including nonhuman forces) is judged to be just if it corresponds to some standard or criterion of what is morally right.[1] Some psychologists have implicitly assumed more restricted definitions of justice, such as the objective and impartial treatment of persons (i.e., fairness). This definition limits the concept of justice to an evaluative judgment of how people should be treated only when there are competing claims and conflicts of interest. In my view, such a restriction places undue emphasis on scarcity and competition in human in-

---

[1] The first definition of justice in a standard dictionary (*American Heritage Dictionary*, 1981) is "moral rightness," and Aristotle defined justice as "the whole of virtue" insofar as it concerns relations with others (Loomis, 1943). As defined in this essay, however, justice and morality are not always synonymous because justice is a concept limited to phenomena involving the treatment of a person or persons, whereas morality is not (e.g., promiscuity might be considered immoral but not unjust).

LITA FURBY • Eugene Research Institute, 474 Willamette Street, Eugene, Oregon 97401. This work was partially supported by a grant from the Center for the Study of Women in Society, University of Oregon.

teraction, an emphasis that is pervasive but also distorting (see Gross & Averill, 1983). I am assuming that justice refers not only to fair treatment but also to respect for the needs and rights inherent in human nature—an assumption that is shared by some (e.g., Adler, 1981) but not by all (see Buchanan & Mathieu, Chapter 2, this volume). Justice is usually said to exist when people receive what they are due, and they are due not only fairness but treatment consistent with their natural rights as human beings. When discussing other authors who have defined justice more narrowly, I have placed single quotation marks around the word *justice* in order to distinguish their usage from my own.

Although philosophical analyses have focused on how we *should* determine what is just, modern psychology has focused its attention on the standards that people actually *do* use. Several recent volumes provide good summaries of empirical studies and current theories (Folger, 1984b; Greenberg & Cohen, 1982a; Lerner & Lerner, 1981; Mikula, 1980b). Rather than attempting yet another summary of psychological research, this chapter offers a framework for examining the relation of research on justice in psychology to that in other disciplines. The first section briefly reviews how justice has been studied by psychologists. It is intentionally sketchy, and the four volumes mentioned previously should be consulted for elaboration. The second section discusses several major controversies that have emerged, including (a) the validity of "equity theory"; (b) the relative importance of procedural justice; (c) the development of justice concepts in childhood and adolescence, as reflected principally in Kohlberg's theory; and (d) the nature and implications of gender differences in reasoning about justice. The last section highlights issues that psychologists might profitably address in the immediate future, including (a) the common meaning of justice, (b) the nature of rights and their role in conceptions of justice, and (c) experiential and interpretive aspects of perceived injustice.

Distributive Justice

By far, the largest amount of empirical work has been devoted to *distributive* justice—the comparative allocation of goods and bads to people. This research developed out of social exchange theory, at the interface of sociology and psychology. Exchange theory emphasizes the role of distributional or exchange considerations in shaping the dynamics of interpersonal interactions (see Rytina, Chapter 5, this volume). It views essentially all social interaction as transactions in which rewards and punishments (or goods and bads) are exchanged among individuals (or groups of individuals).

Equity Theory

Several seminal works in this tradition (Adams, 1963, 1965; Blau, 1964; Homans, 1961) prompted a flurry of empirical research in the 1960s and 1970s within a framework that has come to be known as "equity theory" (cf. Adams & Freedman, 1976). At the heart of equity theory lies the *contributions rule* that states that justice judgments reflect the relative ratio of one's contributions (or inputs) to one's receipts (or outcomes). Justice is achieved when this ratio appears equal for all the individuals involved in a given distribution or exchange.

A further proposition of equity theory is that people try to maximize their outcomes, that is, they always try to get as much as possible. Another is that the perception of inequity causes psychological distress and efforts to restore equity. The leading proponents of this view (Walster, Walster, & Berscheid, 1978) claim that these propositions are applicable to so many areas of human interaction that they provide a general theory of social behavior (for reviews, see Cook & Hegtvedt, 1983; Greenberg & Cohen, 1982a).

Alternative Views

A common criticism of equity theory is that people often use standards of justice other than the contributions rule, especially *equality* (Deutsch, 1975; Mikula, 1980a; Sampson, 1975) and *need* (Deutsch, 1975; Leventhal, 1976b, 1980; Schwinger, 1980). These three justice standards—equity, equality, and need—are found in much of the empirical research on justice, although as many as 9 (Lerner, 1980) or even 17 different criteria for justice have been delineated (Reis, 1984).

A focus of this research has been to specify when these different standards are employed. For example, it appears that an equal division of resources is more likely to be considered just under conditions emphasizing interpersonal harmony and cooperation, whereas a standard of equity is more likely to be adopted when productivity or competition is salient (Deutsch, 1985; Greenberg, 1982; Leventhal, 1976a). More generally, the choice of a justice standard seems to depend on (a) the level of intimacy among the individuals involved; (b) the degree of interdependence and cooperation required in obtaining the goods in question; and (c) individual and group difference factors such as social class and gender (Austin & Tobiasen, 1984; Deutsch, 1985; Greenberg & Cohen, 1982b; Lerner, 1980; Major & Deaux, 1982; McClintock & Keil, 1982).

The Development of Justice Concepts

Although studies of distributive justice have dominated psychological inquiry on justice, there is increasing acknowledgment that a broader approach is necessary (Hogan & Emler, 1981), one that goes beyond distributional characteristics per se and probes the ontogeny of the justice concept: How do people develop a concept of justice?

Belief in a Just World

One answer to this question evolved from Lerner's (1980) empirical observations that (North American) adults display a need to believe that people get what they deserve in the world. He proposes that this "belief in a just world" is rooted in the universal childhood experience that it is often advantageous to give up immediate (but lesser) gratification for delayed (but greater) gratification. In so doing, children acquire the ability to anticipate various alternatives for actions and their consequences, and they also learn to expect certain outcomes if they meet the preconditions for obtaining them. Such expectations form the basis of the concept of deserving and entitlement: If an individual fulfills certain preconditions, then certain outcomes should be obtained (i.e., are deserved). These expectations also require belief in a stable and consistent environment in which everyone receives what they deserve. According to Lerner, the need to believe in a just world is so powerful that it can overshadow other strong motives such as maximizing one's own benefits.

Cognitive-Developmental Approach

Another approach to the development of justice concepts has been part and parcel of Piaget's (1932/1965) study of moral development that describes two basic levels of moral reasoning. One, the "morality of constraint," equates what is right with what conforms to the commands the child receives from the adult. Piaget believed that children initially have a unilateral "respect" for adults' rules defining what is right and wrong. Then, principally as a result of experience with peer interactions, the child moves on to a "morality of cooperation" based on considerations of reciprocity. Justice is achieved when everyone's interests can be balanced.

Lawrence Kohlberg and his colleagues have spent the past 25 years extending Piaget's initial efforts by refining a method for eliciting moral judgments and for categorizing them into a series of developmental stages. Kohlberg's method involves presenting hypothetical stories describing moral dilemmas. For example, in the well-known Heinz dilemma, a pharmacist has a special drug that could save a woman's life. However, the drug is too expensive for the woman's husband to buy. The dilemma to be addressed is whether the husband should break into the pharmacy and steal the drug to save his wife's life.

Kohlberg maintains that it is not the specific course of action advocated by interviewees that indicates their "level" of moral development but rather their reasoning about why that course is the right thing to do. This approach is based on an assumption that the determination of what is just is realized by applying logical rules that develop "naturally" as the child's thinking matures. Very briefly, Kohlberg's developmental stages may be characterized as follows:

1. The first stage is one of *obedience*, with right defined by obedience to authority, avoiding physical damage, and avoiding punishment.

2. The second stage emphasizes *instrumental purpose and exchange*, with right defined as satisfying one's own desires while letting others do the same (through equal exchange, mutual agreement, etc.).

3. The third stage is one of *mutual interpersonal expectations, relationships, and conformity*, with right defined by being "good" (meeting others' expectations).

4. The fourth stage is one of *social system maintenance*, with right defined by laws and duties.

5. The fifth stage emphasizes considerations of *social contract and individual rights*, with right being defined more by self-chosen principles than by the rules and expectations of others.

6. Finally, the sixth stage is one of *universal ethical principles* where right is wholly defined by logically consistent principles satisfying criteria of comprehensiveness and universality.[2]

---

[2]Kohlberg has repeatedly refined his scoring procedures and resulting developmental stage characterizations; the most recent description of his framework can be found in Colby, *et al.* (in press) and in Kohlberg, Levine, and Hewer (1983).

Kohlberg's approach (like Piaget's) fits squarely in the structuralist tradition and claims that the justice structures represented by the six stages are universal and underlie much of the cognitive organizing we do of our social worlds. Justice concepts are understood as progressing from an initial hedonistic orientation emphasizing external consequences, to a conventional orientation dominated by conformity to social rules, and then finally to universal principles constructed either autonomously or in a type of social contract.

Distributive Justice

A number of studies within the tradition of equity theory have also addressed the developmental question, focusing on children's behavior with respect to the fair allocation of resources. The results have generally been interpreted as demonstrating that (a) very young children make allocations on the basis of self-interest; (b) between the ages of 5 and 10 they become progressively more equalitarian; (c) children can understand the contributions rule by age 5 or 6 but wait until midadolescence to apply it as their standard of distributive justice (Hook & Cook, 1979; Keil & McClintock, 1983).[3]

It is usually argued that this developmental progression reflects the development of cognitive abilities that enable the child to compare proportional inputs and outcomes (and thus to make equity calculations). However, there is some evidence that children as young as 4 years of age can make equity-based judgments (Anderson & Butzin, 1978). Furthermore, it has been demonstrated that children's distributive justice behavior is determined also, at least in part, by culturally transmitted beliefs. Nisan (1984), for example, found that Israeli kibbutz children, for whom equality is a central norm in socialization and practice, favor equal distributions more than do nonkibbutz Israeli children. Furthermore, at least one investigator (Montada, 1980) has questioned whether a developmental trend from equality toward equity actually exists. He emphasizes the important effects of situational characteristics in determining alloca-

---

[3]Children's concepts and judgments about distributive justice have also been studied using a clinical interview method similar to that of Piaget and Kohlberg but employing more child-oriented stories. Damon (1977) is responsible for most of this work, and he has delineated a series of developmental levels dealing with concepts about what he calls "positive justice" (i.e., who should get what portion of the available resources and other rewards in a society). The developmental progression he outlines is quite similar to the one described here for children's distributive behavior.

tion preferences, and he argues that drawing conclusions about concepts of *justice judgments* solely from observation of *allocation decisions per se* is overly simplistic because the integration of several (sometimes mutually incompatible) justice principles into a single decision is probably quite commonplace even among 4- to 5-year-olds.

Current Issues and Controversies

Equity Theory

Although equity theory has dominated psychological studies of distributive justice, it has increasingly come under attack, and it is instructive to review, if only briefly, the principal lines of criticism.

Multiplicity of Standards

In order for equity theory to accomodate a variety of justice criteria that people actually use, the concept of inputs (or contributions) must be so chameleonlike as to be of questionable theoretical or practical utility (Sampson, 1969). For example, if "equal portions to all" is to be interpreted within the equity framework, then the relevant input becomes something like "being a member of the human species" (and because all people are equal on that input, the equity formula results in equal amounts for all).

The problems with the equity formula become even more complicated in a situation where multiple inputs are involved (e.g., when both age and years employed are used to determine retirement benefits). In such cases, people may use multiple standards for a single situation (Cook & Yamagishi, 1983; Jasso & Rossi, 1977). Although some work has been done attempting to model how people apply a single justice standard to multidimensional inputs (Farkas & Anderson, 1979), how they integrate multiple justice standards has yet to be addressed.

Ideological Assumptions

Sociohistorical Bias. Equity theory has also been criticized on the grounds that (a) it reflects an ideology surrounding particular economic practices (Sampson, 1975; Wexler, 1983); and (b) it embodies a basically conservative viewpoint, reflecting the views of those who are relatively advantaged in the existing economic distribution (Martin & Murray, 1984). These arguments are based on the position that justice standards reflect social consensus arising from particular societal and historical circumstances (Murphy-Berman, Berman, Singh, Pachauri, & Kumar, 1984; Sampson, 1980, 1981b; Schwinger, 1980) and function to minimize social conflict in allocating resources.

Individualistic Bias. Basic to the contributions rule is the assumption that the contributions of each individual can be assessed in a quantitative and unbiased manner (thereby permitting comparisons among individuals). The appropriateness of this assumption has been challenged on the grounds that the very meaning of individual contribution to any endeavor involving some degree of cooperation is problematic (Miller, 1976). Furthermore, Cohen (1983) has shown how the experimental paradigms typically used by psychologists to study distributive justice impose the assumption of task independence on the situation. In so doing, they virtually assure that people in an experimental setting will view allocations "in terms of retaining what they have been led to believe is the rightful and direct consequence of their own, individual action" rather than in terms of "meting out just shares resulting from a common enterprise" (p. 16). This individualistic bias has been evident in other areas of psychology as well (e.g., Furby, 1979) and is consistent with the individualistic ideology in Western, industrialized society (Weber, 1930).

Methodological Shortcomings

The vast majority of distributive justice studies bring together a small group of strangers (usually college students), have them work on a task and receive information about each other's productivity or other characteristics under study (e.g., ability, need), and then ask each individual (privately) how the specified payoffs should be distributed among the individuals in the group. Frequently, the individuals do not actually work together or even see each other—they are simply given (usually fictitious) information about the other individuals (who, in some cases, are also fictitious). Such situations tell participants little about their relationships with the others involved (Utne & Kidd, 1980) or about why there is variability in outcomes and/or in inputs. In the artificially simple world of the laboratory, people are denied access to a myriad of "irrelevant" pieces of information and provided with only that information considered relevant to equity theory.

Another difficulty with psychological experiments on justice is the fact that they are interpreted solely in terms of justice concerns, whereas one or more other motives are often involved such as politeness, fear of retaliation, status assertion, and impression management. Part of the reason for confusing these other concerns is that many empirical studies deal with allocation behavior per se and not with the justice of such allocation. An empirical demonstration of the importance of this distinction is presented in Nelson and Dweck's (1977) study with 4- to 5-year-olds. When told to share "as you want," results were much different than when told to share "so it's right." Follow-up interviews indicated that children knew perfectly well that their self-interested allocations in response to the former instructions were not necessarily "fair." Given that a large number of studies on distributive justice instruct participants to allocate the goods in question "as you see fit," it is clear that the findings from empirical studies of distributive justice need to be interpreted with caution.

Another potential difficulty in experimental work concerns the respondent's understanding of what is being asked. It has been shown in empirical studies of related areas, such as economic choice behavior, that framing a question in a somewhat different (but formally equivalent) way can have dramatic effects on people's expressed preferences (Kahneman & Tversky, 1984). A study by Harris and Joyce (1980) suggests that empirical studies of justice may be subject to comparable framing effects. They obtained results that were quite different, depending upon whether respondents were asked to allocate outcomes or to allocate expenses for a group task.

Quantifying Equity

There has been considerable controversy over exactly how to define equity, that is, over precisely which mathematical function describes people's beliefs about the just relationship between inputs and outcomes. Although most theorists have accepted an ordinal relationship (i.e., if I contribute more than you, then I should receive more than you, although it doesn't matter exactly how much more), such a simple definition leads to a number of conceptual as well as practical measurement problems (see Harris, 1983). For instance, one of the most interesting difficulties for Adams's (1965) original ratio definition of equity (i.e., [outcome level]/[input level] must be equal for all participants) is its inability to handle either negative inputs or negative outcomes. The following example, adapted from Harris (1983), demonstrates the problem.

Suppose Person A contributes 20 *positive* units of input, whereas Person B contributes 30 *negative* units (e.g., Person A works hard and sells enough inventory to make $20 for the company, whereas Person B is not only lazy but also careless and manages to lose $30 worth of inventory). If Person B receives 60 units of outcome (e.g., $60) and Person A receives 40 negative units of outcome (i.e., is actually fined $40), equity has been achieved according to Adams's formula (because $[20]/[-40] = [-30/[60]]$), even though the person who contributed the least received the most.

Limits of the Exchange Viewpoint

Equity theory insists on viewing all social interactions as transactions in which rewards and punishments are exchanged among individuals. Even within the area of distributive justice, this view seems untenable (Heath, 1976). Rather than equity theory's "exchange orientation" that assumes a two-way transfer of goods, many transactions consist of a one-way transfer evoking a "distributive-pattern orientation" (Folger, 1984a) that ignores inputs and only examines outcomes. Unlike equity, criteria such as equality and need reflect a distributive-pattern orientation. In such cases, the shape of the resulting distribution of resources may be at least as important as the ratio of inputs to outcomes in determining judgments about justice (Brickman, Folger, Goode, & Schul, 1981; Furby, 1981).

Gender Comparisons

There is no basis in equity theory for expecting males and females to use different standards in judging distributive justice. However, gender differences have appeared in numerous empirical studies, and the explanation of these differences merits a separate section.

Summary

A common theme in these criticisms of equity theory is that the flexibility regarding which inputs are to be considered "relevant" evades defining justice. By describing inputs only as "the participant's contributions to the exchange, which are seen as entitling him to reward or cost" (Austin & Hatfield, 1980, p. 27), equity theory sidesteps the question of perceived entitlement, which is at the heart of the concept of justice. It is necessary to know which contributions to an exchange are perceived as entitling one to reward. One response to these limitations of equity theory has been to develop more elaborate schemes for describing the circumstances under which different distributive justice standards are evoked (e.g., Lerner, 1980; Leventhal, 1976b). There has, however, been little agreement about how to construct such an alternative framework.

Procedural Justice

Another growing controversy in psychological studies of justice concerns the relative importance that decision-making procedures play in determining people's judgments about justice. It took a surprisingly long time for psychologists to look beyond the resource *outcomes* involved in distributive justice and to examine the decision-making *procedures* used to determine those quantities (Deutsch, 1974, 1975; Folger, 1977; Thibaut & Walker, 1975).

Thibaut and Walker (1975) found that perceived fairness of procedures affects satisfaction with those procedures, independent of outcomes. Furthermore, in adjudicatory proceedings they showed that procedures are judged as more fair to the degree that they incorporate "process control"—the ability of disputing parties to determine the information and evidence upon which a verdict will be based (see also LaTour, 1978; Lind, Lissack, & Conlon, 1983; Thibaut & Walker, 1978). Process control was distinguished in this work from "decision control," the ability to determine the verdict itself. In the context of typical legal disputes it was judged more just to leave decision control in the hands of an impartial decision maker than to leave it in the hands of the disputing parties themselves. Where the disputants necessarily have decision control themselves (as in mediation), process control is still an important determinant of justice evaluations (Lind *et al.*, 1983).[4]

In a series of studies, Tyler (1984) has found that evaluations of

---

[4]Thibaut and Walker's work has not gone without criticism. A methodological problem in the studies on procedural justice is that people are presented with alternative procedures that vary along only a single dimension (e.g., process control), and thus we do not know what dimensions people spontaneously use to evaluate procedures. It has also been charged that the empirical methods used in this research incorporate certain cultural assumptions about what kinds of disputes are suitable for litigation and that a number of non-American societies hold quite different views on that issue.

political leaders and legal authorities depend more on the distributive procedures used by those leaders than on the specific outcome that the evaluator obtains from them (Tyler & Caine, 1981).
Tyler argues that these results call into question the wisdom of relying on economic models emphasizing incentives and punishments
to implement public policy (Brigham & Brown, 1980; Shapiro, 1969)
while neglecting the importance of perceived procedural justice.

In an insightful analysis, Cohen (1985) has emphasized the importance of examining the organizational and institutional context
within which procedural and distributive justice are examined. In
particular, he contrasts the effect that *participation* (a form of procedural justice) has in legal disputes with its effect in hierarchical,
profit-oriented enterprises. In the former, increased participation legitimates the distributional outcomes, thereby increasing disputants'
commitment to those outcomes. In the context of hierarchical and
profit-oriented enterprises, however, increased participatory practices can sometimes actually decrease the acceptance of outcomes,
referred to as the "frustration effect" (Folger, Rosenfield, Grove, &
Corkran, 1979).

A somewhat broader conception of procedural justice is represented by Haan (1983) who argues that dialogues that "promote
accurate and full exchange of views" are the only way of achieving
justice. Her interpretation is very similar to that of Young (1981) who
suggests that Habermas's "ideal speech situation" represents well
the idea of justice because it consists of institutional relations that
are devoid of domination and thus permit free and complete expression of everyone's interests. A somewhat different analysis that
also uses procedural legitimacy as the ultimate standard of justice is
John Rawls's (1971) notion of the "original position." According to
his account, justice is defined by those standards that would be
adopted by people if they were behind a "veil of ignorance" as to
their particular situation in society. What little empirical evidence
there is tends to support these claims for the importance of procedures to justice evaluations (Brickman, 1977; Haan, 1983), but
psychologists have only begun to explore this issue in any systematic fashion.

The Development of the Concept of Justice

Discontent with equity theory is now fairly widespread, and
attention is shifting to developmental theories. Kohlberg's study of
the development of reasoning about justice has become the focal

point for a major controversy with important implications for understanding people's concepts of justice. After summarizing the major criticisms of Kohlberg's general formulation, I will discuss the more far-reaching controversy arising from it, that of the nature and significance of gender differences in moral reasoning.

Methodological Weaknesses

For a number of years it seemed that only Kohlberg and his associates had the necessary knowledge to score interview protocols accurately. Once a complete scoring manual appeared, it was long and complex. There have been repeated, seemingly endless modifications in the scoring system. Even the most recent version (Colby et al., in press) has been criticized for methodological weaknesses—including ill-defined criteria for scoring the six stages, internal inconsistency, and questionable construct validity (Cortese, 1984b). Moreover, Phillips and Nicolayev (1978) suggest that "a fundamental methodological failing of the Kohlbergians is their insistence upon seeking evidence that confirms rather than refutes their hard core" (p. 299). That is, they assumed the universal inner logical order of moral concepts, rather than discovering (let alone proving) it empirically. Somewhat different methodological approaches that do not make such an assumption have obtained different results. Damon (1975), for example, concluded from his empirical work with 4- to 8-year-olds that "the priority of logical to moral reasoning does not appear necessary in development: Even among normal subjects, the pattern may be quite the reverse" (p. 312). Furthermore, several studies (Emler, Renwick, & Malone, 1983; Yussen, 1976) have indicated that individuals can give justice arguments at more than one of Kohlberg's stage levels. Most importantly, they can reason at a level above their own position (when asked, for example, to consider a philosopher's perspective or that of a political radical), thereby suggesting that cognitive competence might not be the only or even the major determinant of one's reasoning about justice.

Cross-Cultural Variation

Kohlberg's assumption of a universal ordering of justice stages has naturally led to cross-cultural studies using his methods. As summarized by Turiel, Edwards, and Kohlberg (1978), the evidence is very encouraging for the theory. The vast majority of cross-cultural studies (including those done in Kenya, Mexico, Honduras, the Bahamas, India, England, Israel, Canada, Turkey, New Zealand, and

Nigeria) report finding essentially the same stage sequence as that found in the United States, although the mean stage for any given age group is frequently higher in the United States than for samples from other cultures.

Yet some critics argue that things are less tidy upon closer scrutiny. Gorsuch and Barnes (1973) reported that the actual responses they categorized in a given stage for Honduran subjects were qualitatively different from those typical of subjects in the United States at the same stage. They concluded that Kohlberg's moral dilemmas did not adequately capture the nuances of moral reasoning in that collectivistically oriented culture. Harkness, Edwards, and Super (1981) found that among a group of rural Africans, community leaders who were considered morally outstanding were in the range of Stages 2 to 4, well below what would be expected of moral leaders in Western, industrialized countries. Harkness et al. argue that the conventional moral reasoning demonstrated by these community leaders "fit well with the assumptions of a small, face-to-face society based on close and continued contact among people, stable authority of older over younger, and networks of cooperation and reciprocal obligation" (p. 602). In contrast, Stages 5 and 6 in Kohlberg's scheme "are an abstraction of the ways in which Western concepts of law and government have evolved in response to the requirements of social heterogeneity and a more distant government" (p. 602). Thus, Stages 5 and 6 may not be "higher" or developmentally more advanced than the "lower" stages but rather reflect differing social arrangements and institutions.

Consistent with the culture-centric charge, Dien (1982) has argued that Kohlberg's system is hardly appropriate for understanding the Confucian view of morality (embraced by a large portion of humanity) that justice is achieved only by a delicate balancing of feelings, reason, and law. Confucians argue against universally applied standards (which Kohlberg sees as the most advanced stage) because such standards undermine natural distinctions and therefore cannot possibly cover all possible circumstances. In contrast, Kohlberg's emphasis on rational thought and individual responsibility seems to reflect its roots in Western Judeo-Christian tradition emphasizing human freedom and self-determination, coupled with the Greek emphasis on using reason to judge moral good and evil.

In sum, cultural and ethnic differences in moral judgment suggest that Kohlberg's stages may simply reflect the Anglo life-world in which they were developed (Cortese, 1984a; Edwards, 1981a, 1981b).

Historical-Ideological Bias

The comparisons across cultures have helped force psychologists to examine some of the hidden assumptions in Kohlberg's stage model. Newman, Riel, and Martin (1983) argue that the formal operations required by Kohlberg's highest stage do not develop as a general cognitive mode. Rather, individuals learn the rules for specific content domains through concrete experiences. For example, Saxe (1982) demonstrated that the introduction of trade stores in a society prompted greater abstraction in the numeration system for related behaviors. Some have even argued that Kohlberg's higher stages simply reflect the abstract language of higher education in Western societies (e.g., terms such as justice, equality, reciprocity) and that use of the higher stage reasoning is a direct result of exposure to that abstract language (Simpson, 1974).

More generally, it is argued that Kohlberg's entire system of stages is a reflection of the social and economic arrangements of our particular society (Buck-Morss, 1975; Edwards, 1975, 1981b; Hogan, 1975; Nicholson, 1983; Reid, 1984; Sampson, 1983; Sullivan, 1977). The separation of form from content inherent in Kohlberg's analysis is consistent with the technical interests of Western, industrialized society (Sampson, 1981a). Knowledge is oriented toward the generalizability and repeatability of experience in order to obtain technical control over nature. The technical precision of means becomes the primary focus, rather than normative concern with ends. Accordingly, rather than asking what the goals of moral actions are, Kohlberg's scheme focuses on the cognitive operations used to achieve whatever goals have been adopted. This focus is almost inevitable, given Kohlberg's emphasis on reasoning. As Simon (1983) notes,

> Reason goes to work only after it has been supplied with a suitable set of inputs, or premises. If reason is to be applied to discovering and choosing courses of action, then those inputs include, at the least, a set of should's, or values to be achieved, and a set of facts about the world in which the action is to be taken. (p. 7)

Given the convergence between Kohlberg's system and that of philosopher John Rawls (1971; see Buchanan & Mathieu, Chapter 2, this volume), it is not surprising that similar criticisms have been leveled against both (Barry, 1973; Shweder, 1982). Both theories attempt to establish a rational foundation for an objective definition of justice. In contrast, some philosophers (e.g., MacIntyre, 1982) argue that when we give a reason why something is right or wrong, we imply that there are objective standards for that evaluation, but actually there is no rational foundation for it. Consistent with this view, Emler (1983) claims that the themes of rationalism, individualism, and liberalism are overemphasized in Kohlberg's scheme. His moral dilemmas concentrate on issues of property, liberty, life, and individual rights, all of which are traditonal liberal values.

Gender Comparisons

Several female investigators who had conducted research in the Kohlbergian tradition and become aware of significant gender differences in their own and others' empirical studies suggested that such gender differences raised questions about the validity of Kohlberg's system. This issue has developed into a major area of controversy, one which I shall now examine as it relates to our more general understanding of how people think and reason about justice.

Gender Comparisons

Historical Overview

Distributive Justice. The generally accepted finding in the experimental literature on distributive justice is that men are more likely to distribute resources according to a principle of equity (i.e., proportional to inputs), whereas women are more likely to distribute them equally among recipients (for reviews, see Kahn & Gaeddert, 1985; Major & Deaux, 1982). The most prevalent explanation of these gender differences is that males and females have different social interaction goals (cf. Deaux, 1976; Sampson, 1975). The fact that women more often allocate equally is interpreted as reflecting their concern with harmonious interpersonal interactions, whereas men's more frequent use of equity is seen as reflecting their concern with efficient task performance and competition. This interpretation is consistent with the empirical finding that equality is more often used to promote interpersonal harmony within the group and equity to elicit and maintain high performance (Leventhal, 1976a; Stake, 1983).

A slightly different explanation of the gender differences is implied by Lerner's (1975) view that people distribute according to an equality principle when the recipients are perceived as persons but use equity when the recipients are viewed simply as occupants of positions. From this perspective, men focus more on (impersonal) positions, whereas women focus on the person (Kidder, Fagan, & Cohn, 1981).

A weakness of early studies reporting gender differences was that most studies looked only at women allocating to other women and men allocating to other men. The differences might, therefore, reflect gender stereotypes regarding the status, power, and so forth of the recipient, or people might simply be doing what they think is expected of their own gender (Kidder, Bellettirie, & Cohn, 1977; Reis, 1981; Reis & Jackson, 1981).

All gender differences in allocation behavior, however, cannot be explained by gender stereotypes and expectations. For example, Austin and McGinn (1977) found that when subjects were led to anticipate continued future interaction with the other person (and thus had an interest in keeping the other happy), both females and males allocated in a way that maximized the other's outcomes (equity when the other's inputs were large and equality when they were small). When no further interaction was anticipated, however, males tended to prefer equity, whereas females were more likely to prefer equality. In other words, even when there was no need to worry about keeping the other person happy so that future interaction would be pleasant, females still acted in a way that maximized the other's well-being. This suggests that perhaps it is not only (or even principally) harmonious interactions that concern women but rather the other's well-being or happiness. Because insuring the other's well-being is one way to promote harmonious relations, these two concerns often coincide; however, the Austin and McGinn results imply that it may be the other's well-being per se that is the principal motivator for females. In contrast, there is evidence from a study by Greenberg (1983) that when males expect future interaction with the other person, they are more generous simply because they fear retaliation.

Moral Development. One of the earliest reports of gender differences in moral development was Haan, Block, and Smith's (1968) finding that about twice as large a percentage of college females as college males were at Stage 3 whereas more males were at "higher" stages. Kohlberg and Kramer (1969) interpreted these results as showing that "Stage 3 appears to be a stable adult stage for women" and that "while girls are moving from high school or college to motherhood, sizeable proportions of them are remaining at Stage 3, while their male age mates are dropping Stage 3 in favor of the stages above it" (p. 108). Other studies also seemed to support the contention that female moral development is more likely to be "arrested" at Stage 3 (or 4), whereas males are more likely to move on to Stages 4 and 5 (Fishkin, Keniston, & MacKinnon, 1973; Gilligan, Kohlberg, Lerner, & Belenky, 1971; Holstein, 1976; Kuhn, Langer, Kohlberg, & Haan, 1977). However, in 1977, both Norma Haan and Carol Gilligan began to question this generally accepted finding.

Gilligan's Contention

The core of Gilligan's (1977, 1982) claim is that there are two different approaches to reasoning about morality, one focusing on interpersonal caring and responsibility, and the other focusing on individual rights and equality. The former, an "ethic of care and responsibility," emphasizes the avoidance of hurt. The latter, an "ethic of 'justice'," focuses on individual freedom and rights to impartial treatment.[5] This distinction was highlighted for Gilligan when she realized that the primary moral imperative for many of the women she interviewed was to *care about others' well-being*, whereas the more typical imperative for adult men seemed to be to *respect the rights of others*. Gilligan maintains that men give priority to autonomy and objectivity, that is, equal and fair treatment regardless of what the specific consequences might be for particular individuals, whereas women have a "relational bias" that focuses on the consequences of decisions and actions for individual suffering and hurt.

Gilligan reasons that a woman's sense of identity is involved in a network of relationships, whereas a man's is more related to a process of individuation, that is, of defining one's own position vis-à-vis others. The transition from Kohlberg's Stage 3 to Stage 4 is particularly difficult for women because it requires subordination of the interpersonal definition of the good (i.e., interpersonal harmony) to an impersonal one (law and order). Gilligan's claim is not that Kohlberg's formulation of 'justice' is wrong but only that it is incomplete. She maintains that there is a fundamental dialectic within every individual, a natural tension, between Kohlberg's notion of

---

[5]Gilligan consistently uses the word *justice* in a narrow sense, that is, universal principles of objective and impartial treatment. She uses *morality* in a broader sense, so that it encompasses both her "ethic of 'justice'" and also her "ethic of care." The reader is reminded that throughout this essay, justice is defined in its broad sense, which is equivalent to Gilligan's use of the term morality. When referring to Gilligan's more restricted use of 'justice', I will indicate that narrower use with single quotation marks.

'justice' as fairness and the concept of justice as care and responsibility.

Support for Gilligan

Sociohistorical Analyses. Gilligan's characterization of the ethic of 'justice' corresponds well to Kohlberg's own description of his higher stages (1981; Kohlberg, Levine, & Hewer, 1983) and is thus relatively noncontroversial. However, her contention that the ethic of 'justice' fails to represent adequately the full scope of morality (justice in its broader definition) is very controversial.

Gilligan's position is supported by the fact that the primary developmental sample upon which Kohlberg's work is based consisted of males only. Furthermore, her characterization of the bias in Kohlberg's framework is consistent with Sampson's critique (1978, 1981a, 1983) of cognitive-developmental theory. This theory, he contends, sees knowledge as abstract, general, and universal, that which he calls "Paradigm I" knowledge. In contrast, Paradigm II holds that knowledge is necessarily historical, that is, embedded in a particular culture and set of circumstances (see also Gergen, 1973; Habermas, 1971; Kurtines & Gewirtz, 1984; Wexler, 1983). Cognitive-developmental theory defines development as involving increasingly abstract and universal principles. Concrete and particularistic reasoning (i.e., Paradigm II), which Gilligan argues is more typical of females, is viewed as less developmentally advanced. Thus, for example, reasoning about the logical priority of one principle over another (such as life over property rights in the Heinz dilemma) is considered to be more developmentally advanced than reasoning about the specific consequences that an action would have on particular people in a particular situation (such as the consequences that Heinz's stealing the drug would have on his wife and the druggist).

It is further argued that the growth of the nuclear family and of the nation-state has led to a presumed domestic versus public division and to the importance of large bureaucracies and nonpersonal law. Because males have dominated the public world of work and government in Western civilization, it is not surprising that they might emphasize abstract knowledge and universal principles. Females, on the other hand, have been excluded from the public sphere and have been relatively more focused on caring for personal needs and others' well-being in one-to-one relationships, principally within the context of the family (Blum, 1982). As a result, we should not be surprised to find that females' reasoning about justice often focuses on the relative well-being (pain and/or happiness) of the particular individuals involved.

Robyn Dawes (personal communication, 1985) has suggested that the public–private distinction is important for a slightly different reason: Men are required to make decisions in the context of large-scale social dilemmas much more often than are women. These dilemmas include situations where attention to the actual consequences of an act for the well-being of particular individuals could undermine the well-being of society as a whole. For example, a soldier might be tempted to stop and care for his injured friend on the battlefield, and his absence from the ranks would hardly be missed. But if all soldiers reasoned this way, their collective absence *would* be missed, and the perceived larger "good" of saving the world from fascism (or communism, or capitalism, as the case may be) would be undermined. Another example is the voter's dilemma: A single voter knows that his or her vote will not make any difference in the well-being of his or her co-citizens, and yet if voters refrain from voting for this reason, their well-being will indeed be affected. Because men participate more than women in such large-scale social dilemmas (presumably because they have more political and social power), they are encouraged and learn to ignore the particular and immediate consequences of an act and instead act according to an abstract rule or principle. A critical feature of social dilemmas is that they involve large groups (i.e., the public sphere) with small numbers of people (i.e., the private sphere); there is usually no dilemma because attention to a particular set of consequences rarely undermines some other concern. It is important to emphasize that this analysis does not imply that the reasoning fostered by experience with social dilemmas is in any way superior. Indeed, such "lifeboat ethics" (Hardin, 1972) have recently been challenged as leaving much to be desired, and interestingly, the alternative solutions consist of breaking large groups into smaller segments (Fox, 1985).

Gender Development. It is important to distinguish two aspects of Gilligan's argument. One is that there are two fundamentally different ways of reasoning about justice. The other is that males and females tend to differ in the degree to which they engage in each of these approaches.

In evaluating the latter and more controversial claim, one clue from the general psychological literature on gender development[6] is

----

[6]See Furby (1985a) for a more detailed review of the gender development literature that is relevant to Gilligan's thesis.

that females are more empathic than males from a very early age (Hoffman, 1977a, 1977b). This gender difference does not seem to be a cognitive one, insofar as there is no difference in ability to assess another person's state. Rather, it appears to reflect a more prosocial affective orientation including a greater concern over hurting others.[7] The gender differences in empathy have generally been attributed to different socialization experiences, with girls being socialized into an "expressive" role that has traditionally been required for family harmony and boys being socialized into an "instrumental" role that is appropriate to the function of linking the family to other social institutions (Hoffman, 1977b; Johnson, Stockard, Acker, & Naffziger, 1975; Parsons, Bales, & Shils, 1954). These differences are certainly consistent with the gender differences in justice reasoning described by Gilligan.[8]

Universal Principles versus Particularity and Relativism. Gilligan's description of the "ethic of care and responsibility" includes an emphasis on the particular; moral judgments are characterized as being context-specific. In contrast, the "ethic of 'justice'" emphasizes abstract, universal principles. Kohlberg's system assumes that universality is a characteristic of more advanced justice systems. A rule or principle that can be applied to all cases is assumed to be superior to judging each case according to its specific features, but this assumption is highly questionable.

Flanagan and Adler (1983) have eloquently discussed the need to consider the particular in any conception of justice, demonstrating how even the understanding of formal universal laws depends upon specific content. Substantive background knowledge and values are invariably required in a moral reasoning situation (Baumrind, 1978). Thus, for example, it may sometimes be judged just to treat people unequally—as with minority quotas, school busing, or fair housing, when there has been prior group discrimination—whereas at other times, the same treatment may be judged unjust (e.g., when no prior group discrimination had occurred). Of course, one can always argue that there is really some all-encompassing principle of justice underlying both cases. However, such arguments run into the same problems (discussed before) that equity theory

[7]For example, Hoffman (1975) found that consideration for others is a more salient value for females than for males (among both children and adults), and some evidence from the Milgram obedience paradigm suggests that women will resist pressure to harm others more than will men (Kilham & Mann, 1974).

[8]Gilligan also refers to Chodorow's (1978) theoretical account of gender identity to help explain the gender differences in moral reasoning, but this account has thus far been untested empirically.

faces in attempting to reinterpret every justice principle as an instance of the contributions rule. For such reinterpretations to succeed, the conceptualization must be so vague that it neither explains nor informs the phenomenon we seek to understand.

The application of universal principles precludes consideration of their effects in specific instances. An exception cannot be made just because one may not like some of the consequences in a particular case. Gilligan's ethic of care, in contrast, is characterized by a consideration of the specific outcomes in determining what is just.[9] So, for example, if distributing according to effort leaves someone without enough to eat, an ethic of care would say that this is unjust—we cannot let the individual die.

Other Empirical Studies. In an analysis surprisingly parallel to, but independent of Gilligan's, researchers studying justice in helping behavior have also proposed that two types of issues are involved in justice judgments, one being the fairness of the help and the other being its effectiveness (Rabinowitz, Karuza, & Zevon, 1984). The former concerns the morality of the helping act itself and is judged by deontological principles.[10] The latter concerns the effect the helping act actually has on people (reflecting teleological concerns). No reference is made to Gilligan's work, but these two aspects of justice in helping closely parallel the two delineated by Gilligan.

Additional empirical support for Gilligan's distinction between two types of justice comes from Bloom's (1977) study demonstrating the operation of a "social principledness" dimension corresponding to Kohlberg's moral autonomy but also a "social humanism" dimension reflecting the importance of the individual consequences of justice decisions. Bloom found evidence for both of these dimensions among Chinese, American, and French groups.

Haan (1978) has also presented empirical support for the simultaneous operation of both formal (Kohlbergian) moral judgment and "interpersonal morality," moral solutions achieved through dialogue among participants. Indeed, Haan argues that interpersonal morality represents the more fundamental way in which people morally relate to each other, whereas formal morality in the Kohlbergian sense "is one particular, late-developing branch of in-

---

[9]In some sense, "caring for others" could be considered a universal principle, that is, applied to all instances. But it does not really represent an *abstract standard* allowing one to specify in any substantive way what constitutes justice across a number of different cases.

[10]Principles based upon reason as exemplified in the theory of Kant.

terpersonal morality, preferred by specialized problem solvers and used in special kinds of rule-governed impersonal situations" (1978, p. 304).

The Nature of Justice. In an insightful discussion of the nature of justice, Edney (1984) points out that in a relationship involving sympathetic mutual awareness of each others' conditions, needs, and feelings, justice would "almost be redundant." After all, if you care for and are aware of other people's well-being, it follows almost by definition that you will treat them in a way that conforms to your standards of what is morally right (that is, justly). Although Edney makes no reference to Gilligan's work, he argues that exchange formulations such as equity theory suffer from inadequacies analogous to those Gilligan has identified in Kohlberg's formulation. Significantly, their point of departure is not empathy, trust, and caring but rather an assumption that individuals are psychologically separate from each other and are basically selfish.

This perspective suggests to me that specific standards of justice such as an equity rule, or 'justice' in the Kohlbergian sense, may be attempts to obtain the same (just) result that would be obtained if people did in fact care for each other as Edney describes. 'Justice' standards may be rules of thumb or heuristics to help people who do not care for each other (either because they are selfish or because they find themselves in a large-scale, impersonal social setting such as a bureaucracy and simply cannot take all the particulars of each case into account) behave as if they did.

In an ingenious study of preschoolers' reasoning about justice, Smetana (1985) found that preschoolers use information about the consequences an action has on others when judging whether the action was just. Indeed, it was the presence or absence of such information that determined whether or not a given action's rightness or wrongness was considered to be a question of justice. In other words, the very definition of justice involved the effects that an action has on another's well-being.

Critiques of Gilligan

Interpretation of Data. A number of authors argue that Gilligan's claim of gender differences in moral development is flawed because it is not substantiated by the data. Indeed, several comprehensive reviews of studies conducted in the Kohlberg tradition now claim that there is no evidence for significant differences (Brabeck, 1983; Walker, 1984). Combining the results of multiple studies is, however, a delicate affair because of differences in data collection procedures, numbers of participants, and types of statistical tests reported. Haan's (1985) more careful examination of the studies reviewed by Walker (1984) revealed that although only a minority of studies found significant gender differences, those that did involved a total of 1483 people, whereas those finding no significant differences involved only 522. Baumrind (1986) likewise demonstrated errors in Walker's methods and in his conclusions.

It has sometimes been argued that the gender differences obtained in Kohlbergian studies reflect differences in the educational opportunities of the two genders, rather than any basic difference in their moral reasoning or orientations (Rest, 1983). However, recent studies obtained gender differences despite matching males and females for educational level and occupation (Baumrind, 1986; Lyons, 1983). Furthermore, we might be wary of any theoretical framework that finds the more educated to be more "advanced" in reasoning about justice (Haan, 1985).

Yet another line of criticism concedes the existence of gender differences but argues that they are too small to represent "a global dichotomy between the life orientations of men and women" (Colby & Damon, 1983, p. 476). Deaux's (1984) review of the relevant literature led her to conclude that 5% may be the upper boundary for the size of gender differences in social and cognitive behavior. However, Gilligan does not claim there is a global dichotomy between the genders, rather that the use of the two major modes of moral reasoning is only gender-related (Gilligan, in press). Referring to her ethic of care, she states:

> I do not mean to argue that this ethic lies solely in the feminine domain.
> In the past as well as in the present, a morality of responsibility and care
> had been articulated by members of both sexes and speaks to a series of
> concerns shared by both. (Gilligan, 1983, p. 35)

Why These Critiques. In historical perspective, it is instructive that no one minimized the gender differences as long as the differences seemed to suggest that women's moral development was "arrested" relative to men's. It was only when Gilligan suggested a reason for the gender differences that implied (in at least some people's minds) that women might be superior to men[11] that the validity

---

[11]Caring for others is a positive value in our culture, and Gilligan's formulation not only states explicitly that women incorporate standards of caring into their moral judgments more than do men, but her formulation also suggests implicitly that maybe women care more than do men. Women care, whereas men are merely just. The latter is an implication that, I suspect, is particularly hard to swallow for "liberated" men who see themselves as unusually sensitive. But the evidence indeed suggests that even in intimate relationships, women provide more care and concern than do men (Kidder, Fagan, & Cohn, 1981).

and significance of gender differences in justice reasoning was seriously questioned.[12]

In addition, if Gilligan's analysis is correct, then the existing studies fail to provide a clear test of her theory, for their methods do not capture women's experience. Kohlberg's analytic scheme does not adequately represent the ethic of care, and even Gilligan's critics recognize that it is unreasonable to expect "a flawed science to provide an accurate view of reality" (Colby & Damon, 1983, p. 476; Smetana, 1984b). Furthermore, Kohlberg's moral dilemmas are all hypothetical ones, in contrast to Gilligan's emphasis on real-life moral judgments.

Although Kohlberg has recognized that "the 'principle' of altruism, care, or responsible love has not been adequately represented in our work" (Kohlberg et al., 1983, p. 20), he seems to distort unwittingly the meaning of Gilligan's ethic of care by interpreting it as applicable only to "special relationships and obligations." He sees it as involving care responses that are attributable to the fact that one is dealing with family, friends, or co-members of a group. Kohlberg rejects, however, the proposition that there are two generalized justice orientations, as suggested by Gilligan, and instead argues that justice as rights and duties is primary (Kohlberg et al., 1983). He recognizes that the ethic of care should be included as an aspect of moral development, but he suggests that it is only relevant to "personal decisions" and "special obligations" such as those involving friends and family. Yet the very essence of Gilligan's formulation is care for the other that is based not only on a special affective relationship with that individual but also on a basic empathy and concern for the other's well-being.[13] Thus, Kohlberg sees the contractual "responsibilities of caring" undertaken at the time of the marriage as an example of the caring orientation. Kohlberg's interpretation shifts the emphasis from concern for the other's well-being per se to more impersonal obligations with respect to honoring formal commitments.

---

[12]Broughton (1983) has suggested that gender differences are less controversial when they deal with objectively measured, value-free assessments such as cognitive abilities and more controversial when they deal with subjective, value-laden areas such as morality. However, there seems to be more to the controversy than just its value-laden characteristic, because as long as the suggested differences had men looking superior, there was little controversy.

[13]It is important to note, in this context, that Gilligan's analysis suggests that women's focus on the interpersonal does not mean that they are "arrested" at Kohlberg's Stage 3. In her scheme, their concern develops from one of interpersonal approval (which is a defining characteristic of Stage 3) to a concern with interpersonal care, responsibility, and the quality of group life.

Summary

The most lasting contribution of the focus on gender comparisons will undoubtedly be the identification of the ethic of care and responsibility as an approach to reasoning about justice issues that deserves equal consideration along with the previously dominant formulation of justice as fairness. The caring dimension was not a new discovery but rather one that was ignored until several female investigators insisted on examining it because Kohlberg's formulation simply did not jibe with their personal experience. Even Piaget suggested that "the primary condition of moral life" is a need for reciprocal affection. Apparently, he ignored affective considerations in his work because he could not handle them as neatly as the rational considerations of justice as fairness.

The degree to which two different views of justice should be differentially identified with males and females is an important but perhaps secondary issue. The point is that there do seem to be some significant gender differences in reasoning about justice. Two very different theoretical and empirical approaches reviewed here—equity theory and Kohlberg's theory—have produced remarkably similar results with respect to gender differences in the meaning of justice. It would be foolish to ignore them—obviously they have something to teach us about the nature of concepts of justice.

Identifying the sources of gender differences is also an important but secondary issue. Candidates include hereditary, biological differences, socially learned gender roles (or stereotypes), historic differences in life circumstances of the two genders, and various combinations thereof. At any given point in time, our understanding of these gender differences will depend upon the variables examined and how they are studied: Any understanding will always be not only a scientific question but also a political one (Kahn & Gaeddert, 1985; Parlee, 1981).

The merits and shortcomings of moral relativism have long been the subject of philosophical debate, but modern Western moral theory has generally looked down on particularity and relativism and has sided with abstraction and universal principles. Gilligan's suggestion that we give equal weight and attention to the ethic of care and her contention that it constitutes a view of justice on equal footing with a view based on universal, abstract principles, challenges not only Kohlberg but the mainstream of philosophy as well.[14]

[14]Gilligan's challenge to Kohlberg's work on the basis of its male bias bears some
   resemblance to similar charges against long-standing philosophical theories (Blum,
   1982; Garside-Allen, 1971; Lange, 1983).

Gilligan's choice of words to describe the two orientations may have been unfortunate. Giving impartial consideration to the rights of individuals (Gilligan's ethic of 'justice') is certainly one way of manifesting a sense of responsibility and caring for how people are treated (Prakash, 1984), and thus it is perhaps unwise to *contrast* it with an "ethic of care and responsibility."

Future Directions for the Study of Justice in Psychology

The Meaning of Justice

Implicit Understandings

So much of the early research on the psychology of justice was focused on identifying which distribution rules are considered just that the field has generally neglected to examine people's understanding of the concept of justice itself. Those interested in the development of concepts about justice among children address this issue to some extent (Kohlberg, Lerner), but there has been almost no effort to examine implicit definitions of justice among adults.

Reis (1984) recently provided one example of how the definitional issue might be studied empirically, within the context of distributive justice. He had people judge the degree of similarity of every possible pair of 17 distinct distributive justice rules drawn from the literature on justice. Using a multidimensional scaling procedure, he identified several underlying dimensions that people were implicitly using as a basis for making their comparisons. With sufficient comprehensiveness in the initial set of rules to be judged and with enough people doing the judging, this approach may hold some promise.

With respect to the more general concept of justice, however, there is a notable absence of studies examining exactly what falls within people's understanding of the domain of justice and what falls outside it. In the course of writing this chapter, I found great disagreement among my colleagues regarding the difference between justice and morality. Is slavery unjust? Were concentration camp victims treated unjustly? Some answer in the affirmative to both of these questions, but others claim they are not cases of injustice but rather of immorality.

Although the psychological meaning of justice has been neglected empirically, I believe that much of the evidence reviewed here suggests that the concept of justice involves at least two components: (a) fulfillment of previously learned or explicitly stated expectations, and (b) humanitarian treatment of persons.

Fulfillment of Expectations

One difficulty that plagues any general theory of justice is identifying objective standards of justice, a difficulty that is exacerbated by the large cultural and historical differences in what people consider just. If the concept of justice exists in all cultures (Nader & Sursock, Chapter 7, this volume), what could be the defining features of that basic concept?

A possible answer lies in the conditions that lead to learned expectations, somewhat along the lines suggested by Lerner (1980) in his analysis of "belief in a just world," where justice is conceived as fulfilling promises, meeting expectations, honoring contracts. According to Lerner's formulation, agreeing to give up an immediate reward now, in order to obtain a larger one later, establishes the notion of a "personal contract" with the world and motivates the belief in a just world. The prominent role given to delay of gratification, however, may reflect Lerner's sociohistorical setting rather than something fundamental about the nature of justice. In particular, Weber's (1930) well-known analysis of the symbiosis between the growth of capitalism and the emergence of the Protestant ethic (with its asceticism, strict control of impulses, and emphasis on hard work to obtain the better life) suggests that the practice and importance of delay of gratification may have reached an extreme in industrialized Western countries during the past century. If so, it may be unwise to propose delay of gratification as the basic building block for a universal concept of justice.

By contrast, a fundamental fact about our world is the correlation between the actions we take and the events we experience. One of the major tasks for all infants and children is learning a multitude of such correlations in both the physical world and the social world. At the simplest, physical level, these learned expectations involve the unconscious messages we send to muscles and the resulting movement of some part of our own bodies. The learned nature of these expectations has been demonstrated dramatically by experiments that suddenly alter those correlations by reversing one's perceptual input (e.g., wearing glasses that turn the entire visual world upside down). In such instances, physical movement is at first awkward and ineffective, but with experience the individual adapts remarkably well to the new set of correlations (Kohler, 1962). Exactly which actions one believes are correlated with which consequences depends on one's own experience, what one observes others experiencing,[15] and what one is told explicitly in the form of promises, contracts, and the like.

Of course, a large number of learned expectations are not based on perfectly predictable relations between an action and a consequence. But there are innumerable such relations that have a high degree of predictability. Indeed, the fact that we are motivated to be active at all is probably the best evidence for such correlations. If we did not have reasonably invariant action–outcome relations, goal-oriented behavior would be unknown. Studies of "learned helplessness" have demonstrated how humans (and other animals) become inactive when their actions do not lead to somewhat predictable consequences (Seligman, 1975). The essence of the injunction against arbitrary treatment in most justice formulations (see Buchanan & Mathieu's discussion of the "consistency" requirement, Chapter 2, this volume) is the provision of predictable contingencies.

The principal difference between learned expectations and a promise or a contract is that the former are implicit (at least at first) and learned from experience, whereas the latter are explicitly stated correlations. We are indignant when the expectations of a promise are not fulfilled. Perhaps we are also indignant when previously learned relations between actions and outcomes are suddenly altered.[16]

The differences between the implications of social and nonsocial expectations (humanly mediated contingencies) for perceptions of justice are still an open question. Although some would argue that justice is necessarily a social concept, I would allow that it can be a wholly personal experience (for empirical support, see Folger, Rosenfield, Rheaume, & Martin, 1983; O'Malley, 1983). Thus, for example, if a farmer did a superb job of planting and cultivating one year and still got no harvest (due, for example, to a draught), and if his crop was ruined by a tornado the next year, and if a midsummer freeze devas-

---

[15]There is good evidence that people learn vicariously from others' experience of behavior–outcome correlations (Bandura, 1977). Thus, observing what happens to other people is an important source of the expectations we learn, and has been shown to be a component of the justice concept from both the "relative deprivation" perspective (Crosby, 1976; Davies, 1969; Martin, 1981) and the "status-value" one (Berger, Zelditch, Anderson, & Cohen, 1972), even when conflicting expectations (e.g., from explicit contracts) are present (O'Malley, 1983).

[16]A possibly significant difference between implicitly learned expectations and promises is that the latter always involve another human, whereas the former do not necessarily (see following paragraph in text).

tated his crop the third year, it would seem unjust, even if there was not another individual involved.

The specifics of these learned relations vary from culture to culture. Doing X may lead to Y in one society but to Z in another, making justice seem relative. What is considered unjust in either culture, however, is the nondelivery of the expected Y or Z because that would constitute a broken (implicit) contract—an unfulfilled expectation.

This formulation differs from Lerner's view that learning to delay gratification prompts the concept of deserving and the need to believe in a just world. His notion of deserving, and thus of justice, would only be applicable to situations where Action X is something one does not want to do, whereas Y is something one desires. This may be too restricted a view of justice. Perhaps any action–outcome relation that has become a strong expectation for the individual can be the source of perceived injustice if it is nullified.

Both Reis (1981, 1984) and Mikula (1984) have also identified the action–outcome relation as important to justice, but they emphasize the role of a desire for control over outcomes (in order to obtain positive ones) as central to just behavior. From this point of view, however, the indignation over an injustice (i.e., breach of expectations) should be nothing more than dissappointment over not getting the positive outcomes. It is important to distinguish between the dissatisfaction resulting from not having something one wants and the injustice experienced as a result of an unfulfilled expectation. Many times the two coexist, but they should not be confused (see Furby, 1985b, for a more complete discussion of this issue).

Another problem with viewing control as a necessary component of justice conceptions is that some people seem to believe that justice is determined by fate, by a just deity, or by some other external forces. Indeed, people with strong belief in a just world have been found to be more religious, more authoritarian, and less politically active than those with less belief in a just world (Rubin & Peplau, 1975). They are not people who tend to think that they can control their own fate (Zuckerman & Gerbasi, 1977). Further work is needed to identify more precisely the relation between control and justice, but we must be attentive to the possibility that the notion of control may be most relevant to, but also overemphasized by, researchers in our own society (Furby, 1979).

Several philosophers, who otherwise hold quite differing views of justice, have all argued that justice requires sufficient stability in expectations about which actions lead to which outcomes, so that the execution of rational plans is possible (Buchanan, 1975; Nozick, 1974; Rawls, 1971). Although their emphasis has been on long-term planning, their core concept is also the fulfillment of expectations.[17]

The strength and breadth of people's adherence to the contributions rule in distributive justice judgments also attests, I believe, to the universal experience of action–outcome correspondences. The peasant who works hard cultivating a crop is likely to have a bigger harvest than one who loafs. That is a fact of nature we all experience. In a sense, the contributions rule merely reflects this universally experienced fact of nature. I have heard even the most ardent supporters of egalitarianism in Mao's China express resentment at the fact that those who loafed got just as much as those who worked hard. As Moore (1978) suggests, sanctions against the idler are probably universal.

Support for the notion that meeting expectations is central in the definition of justice also comes from the practice of attempting to convince people that they should continue to believe in the justness of their world even when expectations are not met. The biblical story of Job is a case in point. Although the lesson Job must learn is to have faith that his God is a just one even though Job's expectations are not fulfilled, the fact that this lesson must be taught (and that such a big deal is made of teaching it) suggests that unfulfilled expectations are central to our concept of injustice.

Unfulfilled expectations do not always result in judgments of injustice because the reason for the unfulfilled expectation is critical to people's justice judgments (Folger, Rosenfield, & Robinson, 1983). For example, if I am not paid by my employer on the first of the month as I expected to be, my judgment of whether an injustice has occurred will depend upon the reason my employer fails to pay me. If a fire destroyed all the company's records that morning, I would not consider failure to meet the payroll on time to be an injustice because I do not consider the company responsible for the failure (i.e., my expectation was not that I would be paid on the first of the month even if there was a fire). Reasons are something that have all too often been ignored by contemporary psychologists (Buss, 1979), but clearly they must be examined as part of any comprehensive understanding of justice judgments.

---

[17]A breach of expectations, be they explicit contracts or expectations learned from one's own or others' experiences involves deceit: One is provided with (and acts upon) information that turns out to be false. I suspect that deceit may be universally considered unjust.

Humanitarian Treatment

The expectation component of justice helps to explain how justice might be a universal concept, and why, although specific standards can vary from group to group, indignation will still accompany injustice (because in all cases it consists of a breach of contract). Does this then imply that any established action–outcome relations are considered just? That is, as long as the expectation is met, will Y be considered a just consequence for X, no matter what X and Y are?

If we take the view that standards for justice consist simply of whatever expectations one learns from the environment, then the answer must be in the affirmative. But perhaps we also judge justice on the basis of the nature of the expected consequence. There is a sense in which beating a child is considered unjust no matter what expectations have been established between actions and beatings. Are there not some "humanitarian" standards of justice, the essence of which is an injunction not to cause others hurt and suffering? If so, it might explain why beating a child is considered unjust, no matter how consistent the expectation of the beatings might be (i.e., even though no implicit contract is broken). It might also be the reason why incinerating people is considered an injustice, even though an expectation (e.g., that those practicing Judaism will be incinerated) may have been very explicitly established.[18]

Some may protest that people have been known to inflict the most atrocious pain and suffering on others, thus demonstrating that humanitarian standards of justice are not universal. However, we must be careful to distinguish between what people judge to be just and what they do. People often behave in ways that they do not consider to be just.[19] Also, people's judgments about what is just can

---

[18]The nature of the X–Y relation itself may also sometimes be subject to justice evaluations (e.g., it is unjust when a woman must tolerate sexual harrassment in order to obtain a promotion).

[19]Rest (1983) distinguishes judging what ought to be done in a situation from deciding what one actually intends to do. He claims that these are two separate components of morality and that formulations such as Gilligan's ethic of care are relevant to the latter component, whereas Kohlberg's theory speaks to the former. Rest's conceptualization distorts, I believe, the essence of Gilligan's contribution. Like Kohlberg, she studied what people think they ought to do. The fact that she has examined real-life dilemmas, and Kohlberg hypothetical ones, does not make Gilligan's results less applicable to the realm of the *ought*. It may, however, explain why Kohlberg's subjects can more easily ignore the actual consequences to particular people—it is less likely that their affective sensibility will be aroused in a hypothetical story.

change over time (in some cases the earlier judgments might be viewed as reflecting "false consciousness"). Such changes can be due either to temporal changes in what are considered to be legitimate expectations or to modifications in one's conception of what a human being is and should be.

What might be the underlying determinant of a humanitarian standard that would account for its being universally associated with justice judgments? A likely candidate is empathy. The developmental origins of empathic feelings for others are only beginning to be understood (Hoffman, 1977a, 1982), and their role in determining concepts of justice is as yet largely unexplored. But evidence from a number of sources suggests that standards of humane treatment may play a role in our judgments of just and unjust events. It seems reasonable to assume that certain physical and psychic experiences (e.g., lack of food, physical battering, absence of favorable responses from others, lack of sensory stimulation) are innately noxious. To the degree that judgments of justice are based on empathic feeling for the well-being of others, at least some minimal humanitarian standard might be universally associated with such judgments.

The sum total of humanitarian standards corresponds to what Moore (1978) refers to as "the prevailing conception of what a human being is or ought to be." The psychological research reviewed previously has shown that the effect an action has on an individual is an important consideration when judging the justice of the action. I propose that the standard one uses in such judgment is a humanitarian one based upon one's conception of what it means to be human.

That conception may have implications not only for what a person should not have to suffer but also for what is necessary to achieving positive personhood. There is very little empirical work by psychologists on a possible positive aspect of the humanitarian component of justice, though it does play an essential role in some theoretical formulations, most notably that of Rawls (1971). A basic premise in his concept of justice is the notion that a person has a right to be treated in a way that contributes to certain essential components of positive personal development (e.g., a right to self-respect). Several studies reported by Smetana, Bridgeman, and Turiel (1983) suggest that children and adolescents do, in fact, view certain positive or "prosocial" acts as issues of justice, based on the effect they have on another's welfare.

Surely the historical and cross-cultural variation in what has been considered just treatment suggests that at least some of our humanitarian standards are learned and specific to our own culture (and thus gives some validity to the notion that justice involves preferences). However, perhaps there is a set of universally noxious experiences that are found everywhere. Gilligan's ethic of care, emphasizing an imperative to avoid hurting people, may capture the essence of this aspect of a humanitarian standard of justice. Turiel and his colleagues (Smetana, 1983; Turiel, 1983) have found that American children distinguish between morality (or justice) and social conventions[20] based on whether rightness or wrongness of an action is evaluated solely by arbitrary social rules (e.g., it is wrong to go through a red light, but only because it is an agreed upon social rule), or whether it depends upon factors "intrinsic to the action" (principally the degree to which it inflicts harm or otherwise negatively affects the welfare of others). There is evidence that children as young as 2 years of age make this distinction (Smetana, 1984a), lending support to the universality of the humanitarian component of justice.

Differences in people's beliefs about what a person is and ought to be undoubtedly result in different humanitarian standards of justice (e.g., some would not agree with Rawls that diminishing another's self-respect has anything to do with justice). Indeed, Rawls himself concedes that his principles of justice may be valid only for those who hold his specified ideal of the person (see Buchanan & Mathieu, Chapter 2, this volume). Furthermore, an individual can simultaneously hold more than one conception of what a person is, depending on the social group to which the latter belongs (Lerner, 1975; Tajfel, 1984). For example, a slave owner undoubtedly had a different conception of "person" with respect to a slave than he did with respect to his fellow slave owners. Similarly, many men's conception of what personhood means for a woman is different from their conception of what it means for a man.[21] These conceptions of two (or more) kinds of people—different basic characteristics, different feelings, different self-actualizing goals, and thus different rights—can lead to the application of differing humanitarian standards to different groups of people (just as one might apply a differ-

---

[20]The equation of morality with justice is fairly explicit in their work: The moral domain is defined as "a prescriptive system, based upon an underlying conceptualization of justice, that is concerned with how individuals ought to behave toward one another" (Smetana, 1983, p. 131).

[21]One consequence is that women, who constitute half of the world's population, perform almost two-thirds of the world's work, yet receive only one-tenth of the world's income (United Nations, 1980).

ent standard of what kind and degree of hurt should be avoided for the just treatment of an animal as compared to that of a human being). This explains one way that oppressors can construct belief systems that permit them to judge their behavior as being just even though they would consider it unjust if anyone behaved in that same way toward them.[22] It also speaks to the essence of affirmative action programs, which is to require a distribution of rewards that is consistent with a single conception of what a person is, regardless of group membership.

Overview

There is a certain similarity between the fulfillment of expectations formulation and other analyses in which objective and equal treatment for all plays a central role, most notably the work of Rawls and Kohlberg. At the heart of the latter's concept of justice is the notion of establishing consistent action–outcome expectations, so consistent in fact that they should be applied impartially and universally.

There is also a certain similarity between Gilligan's "ethic of care" and the humanitarian standard of justice outlined here; both are concerned with individual well-being *per se*, and in particular with avoiding hurt and suffering. A humanitarian standard may also include those positive aspects of personhood that are essential to one's conception of what it means to be human (e.g., self-respect in Rawls's theory of justice; see also Worland, 1977, Chapter 3, this volume).

How these two dimensions interact in determining people's concepts of, and judgments about, justice is an issue that needs greater attention in future studies. Neither dimension is sufficient by itself to represent what people mean by justice; simultaneous consideration of both takes place in any given judgment. Obviously, there can be a tension between the two: The standard of realizing expectations can contradict the standard defined by the physical and psychological well-being of the particular people involved. Milgram's (1974) well-known studies highlighted exactly this tension (fulfilling the implied contract with the experimenter meant causing a particular person to suffer painful electric shocks; preventing the

[22]Of course, the oppressed can also hold more than one conception of what it means to be a person, believing that the oppressors actually are superior beings. One of the common goals of "consciousness raising" efforts is to eliminate this double standard about what it means to be a person.

suffering meant breaking the contract). Further empirical work is necessary to understand how such contradictions are resolved. In a given instance, if both standards are met, justice is obtained; if neither standard is met, injustice is perceived. What we still do not fully understand is how judgments are made when one standard is met and one is not. The seemingly irresolvable philosophical debates over whether the essence of justice concerns fairness (in the rationalist tradition of Kant, 1785/1959) or whether it concerns effectiveness of consequences (in the spirit of the utilitarians like Mill, 1861/1957) reflects this same tension between two constitutive components of justice.

Entitlements

Justice and rights are almost inseparable; yet there has been remarkably little work in psychology on the notion of right or entitlement (Friedman, 1971). Equity theory assumes a role for entitlement in justice judgments, by defining inputs as those contributions that are seen as "entitling" one to the outcomes in question, but it never discusses the concept in any detail. Likewise, theories relating relative deprivation[23] to perceptions of injustice have proven inadequate, due in large part to their failure to specify the meaning and determinants of entitlement (Crosby, Muehrer, & Loewenstein, 1984).

The concepts of *deserving* and *entitlement*, though frequently used interchangeably need to be distinguished. Entitlement is a broader concept, with deserving typically being limited to situations involving some notion of merit. In terms of the framework presented here, deserving refers mainly to the expectations aspect of justice and in particular to situations where a person takes some *action* based on the expectation that she or he will obtain a particular consequence as a result. Entitlement, on the other hand, can also refer to the humanitarian aspect of justice (e.g., a person is *entitled* to not be beaten) and is essentially synonymous with a right.

Consider the prevalent notion that abused children do not feel a sense of injustice about the way they are treated. This might suggest that they have a different set of entitlement standards than do those of us looking on from the outside who do feel that an injustice is

---

[23]Relative deprivation formulations, and derivatives thereof such as Folger's (in press) referent cognitions theory, have much in common with the expectancy component of justice (if one receives less, relative to what one expected to receive, then injustice is experienced).

taking place. It also might question the universality of any human-itarian standard of justice. However, Smetana, Kelly, and Twen-tyman (1984) found that abused children judge actions that cause harm to others to be morally wrong, just as do nonmaltreated chil-dren. In other words, the humanitarian standard seems to be oper-ative for them. Furthermore, abused children were more likely than neglected children to judge psychological distress as universally wrong for others, suggesting that their own experiences of hurt and pain have made them even more sensitive to the humanitarian stan-dard of justice. An interesting parallel between the justice concepts of women and of abused children can be seen here. The abuse and physical destruction of women is horrifyingly widespread through-out many cultures (Daly, 1978), and the evidence reviewed pre-viously suggests that women emphasize the humanitarian standard of justice more than do men, much as do abused children. These examples emphasize the importance of examining concepts of jus-tice among the oppressed, something that has generally been ne-glected by psychologists studying justice.

An interesting question concerns the developmental origin of the general concept of a right and also of beliefs in specific rights. Some relevant studies in psychology have examined the origin of possession rights (Bakeman & Brownlee, 1982), but it has been very difficult to separate empirically a sense of property rights *per se* from a simple desire for an object. It has also been difficult for researchers to shed their own particular beliefs about rights, thereby leading to some confusion in the literature. For example, in studying the devel-opment of a distinction between moral standards and social conven-tion, it has been assumed by some researchers that the loss of an object is a moral injustice equivalent to personal injury (e.g., Smet-ana, 1983; Turiel, 1983). Yet property rights are not as inalienable everywhere as they are in our own society.[24] Indeed, even within our own culture there is considerable variation in the degree to which property rights are thought to supercede other rights (Barton, 1985).

Political and economic theorists have wrestled with the justice of private ownership of property (Held, 1979; Worland, Chapter 3,

---

[24]The fact that children react to the loss of objects in the same way they react to personal injury (with physical retaliation, emotional upset or statements of the object loss) and that they insist stealing would be wrong even if there were no rule against it is taken by some researchers as proof that both injury and loss concern moral rights. However, it seems perfectly plausible that a young child will react this way to the loss of an object merely because the child really wants the object and not necessarily because she or he perceives an entitlement to it.

this volume). It is not the right of ownership *per se* that is controversial, but the inclusion of ownership of property (e.g., of a business) as relevant in determining entitlement to the values produced by that property. For the capitalist, the distribution principle is "to each according to what he and the instruments he *owns* [italics added] produces" (Friedman, 1962, pp. 161–162). For the socialist, of course, private ownership of the means of production is not a valid "contribution," and therein lies the heart of their disagreement (see Worland, Chapter 3, this volume). Despite the enormous political and economic implications of this issue, psychologists seem to have totally ignored it in their numerous studies of the contributions rule.

The Sense of Injustice

The Role of Attributions in Perceiving Injustice

One of the principal disagreements between Rawls's (1971) and Nozick's (1974) views on justice concerns the degree to which individuals are responsible for their current ability and skill levels. Responsibility attributions often involve a judgment of causality, requiring an assessment of the individual's effective causal contribution to a given state of affairs. If the individual is judged to be responsible for that state of affairs, he or she is perceived as more deserving than if he or she were not responsible for it (Lamm, Kayser, & Shanz, 1983). Responsibility attributions also involve judgments about social roles and expectations. Different roles can entail different rules for attributing responsibility, with high-status roles generally involving more stringent rules (Hamilton, 1978). There are a number of findings from the empirical work on attribution that are directly applicable to the study of justice (see Cohen, 1982) and that suggest that diverse attributional perspectives may account for some of the individual and group differences in justice perceptions.

One of the most theoretically influential findings from the study of attribution is the tendency for individuals to see their own behavior as caused by situational (environmental) factors, whereas when observing someone else's behavior, they see it as caused by stable, internal dispositions of the actor (Jones & Nisbett, 1972). This effect engenders a difference in the attribution of personal responsibility, with observers being more likely to view the actor as responsible for her or his behavior than is the actor herself or himself. This discrepancy in the attribution of responsibility can obviously result in a disagreement about what constitutes just treatment of an individual.

Certain historical shifts in the attribution of responsibility, such as the fact that Americans today are less likely to blame themselves for poor housing or unemployment than they were earlier in the century (Lambert & Curtis, 1979), also have obvious implications for justice judgments.

From Perceiving to Redressing Injustice

An issue of enormous importance to any society is the behavioral consequences of perceived injustice: When do people take action (e.g., revolt) in response to injustice, and when do they remain passive? Although this question has received some attention from other disciplines (Gurr, 1970; Hirschman, 1970; Moore, 1978), psychologists have been slow to tackle it (but see theoretical discussions in Cohen, 1986; Deutsch, 1974; Fine, 1979).

In psychology, a critical tenet of much of the work on justice is that the perception of injustice leads to internal discomfort, which then motivates efforts to redress the injustice (Adams, 1965; Lerner, 1980). The assumption of inequity-induced distress has generally been tested empirically only indirectly, by looking for either cognitive distortion (e.g., blaming the victim) or compensatory actions aimed at minimizing the (perceived) injustice. Recent empirical studies by Fine (1983), however, suggest that cognitive or behavioral attempts to minimize the perception of injustice may be more typical of nonvictimized observers than of the victims themselves. The latter are more likely to see the injustice, but they are also more likely to consider the costs of trying to do something about it as too high (see also, Mikula & Schlamberger, 1985).

Interpreting Injustice

In order to understand better when action will be taken to redress a perceived injustice, we must realize that injustice often exists in the context of relations between groups, and it is essential to examine the nature of the power relations between those groups (Cohen, 1986). Physical force is only one of several types of power that can affect reactions to injustice. One of the most insidious types is the ability to determine how people interpret injustice.

Two crucial factors affecting justice interpretations are the prevailing societal beliefs as to what constitutes legitimate expectations and the prevailing conception of what it means to be a person (and thus the nature of humanitarian standards). It is reasonable to expect social and political power to play a central role in determining the nature of these prevailing beliefs and conceptions. The powerful have an interest in promoting a social philosophy that perpetuates their control in the community. If a given justice criterion is perceived as legitimate, it will be accepted and supported. The establishment of legitimacy is, at least in large part, a social affair: People must be convinced that specific justice criteria are proper.

An important implication of this view is that the source of cross-cultural differences in justice beliefs lies in cultural variations with respect to power and authority. Different groups hold power in different societies, and because each manages to erect an ideology that serves its own particular case, different justice ideologies evolve in different societies.

The degree to which the powerful can successfully establish an ideology of justice that is in their own interests remains an open question. There is some empirical evidence that those in disadvantaged positions are less likely than those in advantaged positions to judge the prevailing distribution of outcomes as fair (Cook & Hegtvedt, 1986; Hamilton & Rytina, 1980). Rawls's "veil of ignorance" is, of course, designed specifically to eliminate the role of self-interest in establishing justice principles. However, in the real world, where ignorance of one's own position in society is the exception rather than the rule, the legitimizing role of ideology might be substantial. On the other hand, Tajfel (1984) argues that the greater the discrepancy in power the less the need to justify self-serving actions by the powerful. Much more needs to be learned about the degree to which justice beliefs reflect ideologies promoted by the powerful in a given society and how much they are determined by other factors such as consistency of fulfilled expectations, and/or humanitarian standards.

Both Kidder and Fine (1986) and Beit-Hallahmi (1981) suggest that psychologists can shape what people think about justice and how they interpret the injustices around them. This view recognizes that the research questions asked, the concepts used to define them, and the methods used to study them all make at least implicit assumptions about the causes and consequences of injustice (see also Rytina, Chapter 5, this volume).

Kidder and Fine distinguish two major approaches to thinking about injustice, one that assumes it is inherent in societal conflicts of interest, the other that views its sources as located in missed opportunities. The "conflicts of interests" view holds that it is *social structures* that create unequal opportunities and outcomes, whereas the "missed opportunities" view focuses on the *disadvantaged indi-*

vidual. The former emphasizes social justice (i.e., intergroup contexts) and often advocates group struggle to change the system as the solution to injustice. The latter emphasizes intra- and interpersonal justice and tends to view societal benevolence and remedial aid for disadvantaged individuals as the solution. Kidder and Fine argue that persons with power in a society are more likely to promote the missed opportunities view than are those with little power and that the powerful often have the necessary resources to have their view adopted as the truth. Part of a psychologist's responsibility has traditionally been to bring to people's attention diagnoses that tend to be excluded from consciousness or from public discourse. The social context and institutional determinants of injustice are issues that need much more attention by psychologists (Tajfel, 1984).[25]

Future work on the psychology of justice should pay greater attention to (a) the degree to which it merely reflects historically specific circumstances and their accompanying ideologies, and (b) how it interprets and demystifies injustice for laypeople. Although generally resistant to addressing these issues, psychology will be forced to examine them, thanks to recent challenges from within its own ranks (Gergen, 1973; Sampson, 1980; Wexler, 1983).

ACKNOWLEDGMENTS

The following colleagues generously read and commented on a previous draft of this chapter: Joan Acker, Wanda Bronson, Robyn Dawes, Morton Deutsch, Julian Edney, Baruch Fischhoff, Robert Folger, Robin Gregory, Richard Hersch, Martin Hoffman, Karen John, Mimi Johnson, Louise Kidder, Linda Kintz, Gerold Mikula, Mary Rothbart, Judith Smetana, Jean Stockard, and Tom Tyler.

More than anyone else, Ronald Cohen has been responsible for nurturing my thinking about justice and for helping me with the interminable task of trying to "get it right."

The research for and writing of this chapter would not have been possible without the constant support and understanding of Baruch Fischhoff, colleague, friend,—and sometimes-neglected collaborator.

[25]North American social psychology has been criticized for its pervasive individualistic bias (e.g., Furby, 1979; Sampson, 1980; Tajfel, 1984; Wexler, 1983). However, it would be equally mistaken to focus solely on group phenomena. Martin (1981) has shown, for example, how the failure of relative deprivation theorists (who were primarily sociologists) to examine individual-level phenomena undermined the utility of their framework.

References

Adams, J. S. (1963). Toward an understanding of inequity. *Journal of Abnormal and Social Psychology, 67*, 422–436.

Adams, J. S. (1965). Inequity in social exchange. In L. Berkowitz (Ed.), *Advances in experimental social psychology* (Vol. 2, pp. 267–299). New York: Academic Press.

Adams, J. S., & Freedman, S. (1976). Equity theory revisited: Comments and annotated bibliography. In L. Berkowitz & E. Walster (Eds.), *Advances in experimental social psychology* (Vol. 9, pp. 43–90). New York: Academic Press.

Adler, M. J. (1981). *Six great ideas.* New York: Macmillan.

Anderson, N. H., & Butzin, C. A. (1978). Integration theory applied to children's judgments of equity. *Developmental Psychology, 14*, 593–606.

Austin, W., & Hatfield, E. (1980). Equity theory, power and social justice. In G. Mikula (Ed.), *Justice and social interaction: Experimental and theoretical contributions from psychological research* (pp. 25–61). New York: Springer-Verlag.

Austin, W., & McGinn, N. C. (1977). Sex differences in choice of distribution rules. *Journal of Personality, 45*, 379–394.

Austin, W., & Tobiasen, J. M. (1984). Legal justice and the psychology of conflict resolution. In R. Folger (Ed.), *The sense of injustice* (pp. 227–274). New York: Plenum Press.

Bakeman, R., & Brownlee, J. R. (1982). Social rules governing object conflicts in toddlers and preschoolers. In K. H. Rubin & H. S. Ross (Eds.), *Peer relations and social skills in childhood* (pp. 99–111). New York: Springer.

Bandura, A. (1977). *Social learning theory.* Englewood Cliffs, NJ: Prentice-Hall.

Barry, B. (1973). *The liberal theory of justice: A critical examination of the principal doctrines in a theory of justice by John Rawls.* Oxford: Clarendon Press.

Barton, S. E. (1985). *Property rights and democracy.* Unpublished doctoral dissertation, University of California, Berkeley.

Baumrind, D. (1978). A dialectical materialist's perspective on knowing social reality. In W. Damon (Ed.), *New directions for child development* (Vol. 2, pp. 61–82). San Francisco: Jossey-Bass.

Baumrind, D. (1986). Sex differences in moral judgment: Critique of Walker's conclusion that there are none. *Child Development, 57*, 511–521.

Beit-Hallahmi, B. (1981). Ideology in psychology: How psychologists explain inequality. In R. Solo & C. W. Anderson (Eds.), *Value judgments and income distribution* (pp. 70–106). New York: Praeger.

Berger, J., Zelditch, M., Anderson, B., & Cohen, B. P. (1972). Structural aspects of distributive justice: A status value formulation. In J. Berger, M. Zelditch, & B. Anderson (Eds.), *Sociological theories in progress* (Vol. 2, pp. 119–146). Boston: Houghton Mifflin.

Blau, P. M. (1964). *Exchange and power in social life.* New York: Wiley.

Bloom, L. (1977). Two dimensions of moral reasoning: Social principledness and social humanism in cross-cultural perspectives. *Journal of Social Psychology, 101*, 29–44.

Blum, L. A. (1982). Kant's and Hegel's moral rationalism: A feminist perspective. *Canadian Journal of Philosophy, 12*, 287–302.

Brabeck, M. (1983). Moral judgment: Theory and research on differences between males and females. *Developmental Review, 3*, 274–291.

Brickman, P. (1977). Preference for inequality. *Sociometry, 40*, 303–310.

Brickman, P., Folger, R., Goode, E., & Schul, Y. (1981). Microjustice and macrojustice.

In M. J. Lerner & S. C. Lerner (Eds.), *The justice motive in social behavior: Adapting to times of scarcity and change* (pp. 173–202). New York: Plenum Press.

Brigham, J., & Brown, D. W. (1980). *Policy implementation: Penalties or incentives?* Beverly Hills: Sage Publications.

Broughton, J. M. (1983). Women's rationality and men's virtues: A critique of gender dualism in Gilligan's theory of moral development. *Social Research, 50,* 597–642.

Buchanan, A. (1975). Distributive justice and legitimate expectations. *Philosophical Studies, 28,* 419–425.

Buck-Morss, S. (1975). Socio-economic bias in Piaget's theory and its implications for cross-cultural studies. *Human Development, 18,* 35–49.

Buss, A. R. (1979). Causes and reasons in attribution theory: A conceptual critique. *Journal of Personality and Social Psychology, 37,* 1458–1461.

Chodorow, N. (1978). *The reproduction of mothering.* Berkeley: University of California Press.

Cohen, R. L. (1982). Perceiving justice: An attributional perspective. In J. Greenberg & R. L. Cohen (Eds.), *Equity and justice in social behavior* (pp. 119–160). New York: Academic Press.

Cohen, R. L. (1983, September). *A critique of the "contribution rule" in studies of distributive justice.* Paper presented at the University of Mannheim.

Cohen, R. L. (1985). Procedural justice and participation. *Human Relations, 38,* 643–663.

Cohen, R. L. (1986). Power and justice in intergroup relations. In H. W. Bierhoff, R. L. Cohen, & J. Greenberg (Eds.), *Justice in social relations* (pp. 65–84). New York: Plenum Press.

Colby, A., & Damon, W. (1983). Listening to a different voice: A review of Gilligan's *In a different voice. Merrill-Palmer Quarterly, 29,* 473–481.

Colby, A., Kohlberg, L., Gibbs, J. C., Candee, D., Hewer, R., Kaufman, K., Lieberman, M., Power, C., & Speicher-Dubin, B. (in press). *Assessing moral stages: A manual.* New York: Cambridge University Press.

Cook, K. S., & Hegtvedt, K. A. (1983). Distributive justice, equity, and equality. *Annual Review of Sociology, 9,* 217–241.

Cook, K. S., & Hegtvedt, K. A. (1986). Justice and power: An exchange analysis. In H. W. Bieroff, R. L. Cohen, & J. Greenberg (Eds.), *Justice in social relations* (pp. 19–41). New York: Plenum Press.

Cook, K. S., & Yamagishi, T. (1983). Social determinants of equity judgments: The problem of multidimensional input. In D. M. Messick & K. S. Cook (Eds.), *Equity theory: Psychological and sociological perspectives* (pp. 95–126). New York: Praeger.

Cortese, A. J. (1984a). Moral judgment in Chicano, black, and white young adults. *Sociological Focus, 17,* 189–199.

Cortese, A. J. (1984b). Standard issue scoring of moral reasoning: A critique. *Merrill-Palmer Quarterly, 30,* 227–246.

Crosby, F. (1976). A model of egoistical relative deprivation. *Psychological Review, 83,* 85–113.

Crosby, F., Muehrer, P., & Loewenstein, G. (1984). *Relative deprivation and explanation: Models and concepts.* Unpublished manuscript.

Daly, M. (1978). *Gyn/Ecology.* Boston: Beacon Press.

Damon, W. (1975). Early conceptions of positive justice as related in the development of logical operations. *Child Development, 46,* 301–312.

Damon, W. (1977). The social world of the child. San Francisco: Jossey-Bass.

Davies, J. C. (1969). The J-curve of rising and declining satisfaction as a cause of some great revolutions and a contained rebellion. In H. D. Graham & T. R. Gurr (Eds.), The history of violence in America (pp. 690–730). New York: Bantam Books.

Deaux, K. (1976). The behavior of men and women. Belmont, CA: Brooks/Cole.

Deaux, K. (1984). From individual differences to social categories: Analysis of a decade's research on gender. American Psychologist, 39, 105–116.

Deutsch, M. (1974). Awakening the sense of injustice. In M. Lerner & M. Ross (Eds.), The quest for justice: Myth, reality, ideal (pp. 19–41). New York: Holt, Rinehart & Winston.

Deutsch, M. (1975). Equity, equality and need: What determines which value will be used as a basis of distributive justice? Journal of Social Issues, 31, 137–149.

Deutsch, M. (1985). Distributive justice: A social psychological perspective. New Haven: Yale University Press.

Dien, D. S. (1982). A Chinese perspective on Kohlberg's theory of moral development. Developmental Review, 2, 331–341.

Edelman, M. (1964). The symbolic uses of politics. Urbana: University of Illinois Press.

Edney, J. (1984). Rationality and social justice. Human Relations, 37, 163–180.

Edwards, C. P. (1975). Societal complexity and moral development: A Kenyan study. Ethos, 3, 505–527.

Edwards, C. P. (1981a). The comparative study of the development of moral judgement and reasoning. In R. H. Munroe, R. L. Munroe, & B. B. Whiting (Eds.), Handbook of cross cultural human development (pp. 501–527). New York: Garland STPM Press.

Edwards, C. P. (1981b). Moral development in comparative cultural perspective. In D. A. Wagner & H. W. Stevenson (Eds.), Cultural perspectives on child development (pp. 248–279). San Francisco: Freeman.

Emler, N. (1983). Moral character. In H. Weinreich-Haste & D. Locke (Eds.), Morality in the making (pp. 47–71). New York: Wiley.

Emler, N., Renwick, S., & Malone, B. (1983). The relationship between moral reasoning and political orientation. Journal of Personality and Social Psychology, 45(5), 1073–1080.

Farkas, A. J., & Anderson, N. H. (1979). Multidimensional input in equity theory. Journal of Personality and Social Psychology 37, 879–896.

Fine, M. (1979). Options to injustice: Seeing other lights. Representative Research in Social Psychology, 10, 61–76.

Fine, M. (1983). The social context and a sense of injustice: The option to challenge. Representative Research in Social Psychology, 13, 15–33.

Fishkin, J., Keniston, K., & MacKinnon, C. (1973). Moral reasoning and political ideology. Journal of Personality and Social Psychology, 27, 109–119.

Flanagan, O. J., & Adler, J. E. (1983). Impartiality and particularity. Social Research, 50, 576–596.

Folger, R. (1977). Distributive and procedural justice: Combined impact of "voice" and improvement on experienced inequity. Journal of Personality and Social Psychology, 35, 108–119.

Folger, R. (1984a). Emerging issues in the social psychology of justice. In R. Folger (Ed.), The sense of injustice (pp. 3–24). New York: Plenum Press.

Folger, R. (Ed.). (1984b). The sense of injustice. New York: Plenum Press.

Folger, R. (In press). A referent cognitions theory of relative deprivation. In J. M.

Olson, C. P. Herman, & M. P. Zanna (Eds.), *Relative deprivation and social comparison: The Ontario Symposium* (Vol. 4). Hillsdale, NJ: Erlbaum.

Folger, R., Rosenfield, D., Grove, J., & Corkran, L. (1979). Effects of "voice" and peer opinions on responses to inequity. *Journal of Personality and Social Psychology, 35*, 108–119.

Folger, R., Rosenfield, D., Rheaume, K., & Martin, C. (1983). Relative deprivation and referent cognitions. *Journal of Experimental Social Psychology, 19*, 172–184.

Folger, R., Rosenfield, D., & Robinson, T. (1983). Relative deprivation and procedural justifications. *Journal of Personality and Social Psychology, 45*, 268–273.

Fox, D. R. (1985). Psychology, ideology, utopia, and the commons. *American Psychologist, 40*, 48–58.

Friedman, L. M. (1971). The idea of right as a social and legal concept. *Journal of Social Issues, 27*, 189–198.

Friedman, M. (1962). *Capitalism and freedom*. Chicago: University of Chicago Press.

Furby, L. (1979). Individualistic bias in studies of locus of control. In A. R. Buss (Ed.), *Psychology in social context* (pp. 169–190). New York: Irvington.

Furby, L. (1981). Satisfaction with outcome distributions in two small communities. *Personality and Social Psychology Bulletin, 7*, 206–211.

Furby, L. (1985a). *Justice and gender*. Unpublished manuscript.

Furby, L. (1985b). *Expectations, entitlement, and justice*. Unpublished manuscript.

Garside-Allen, C. (1971). Can a woman be good in the same way as a man? *Dialogue, 10*, 534–544.

Gergen, K. J. (1973). Social psychology as history. *Journal of Personality and Social Psychology, 26*, 309–320.

Gilligan, C. (1977). In a different voice: Women's conceptions of self and morality. *Harvard Educational Review, 47*, 481–517.

Gilligan, C. (1982). *In a different voice: Psychological theory and women's development*. Cambridge: Harvard University Press.

Gilligan, C. (1983). Do the social sciences have an adequate theory of moral development? In N. Haan, R. N. Bellah, P. Rabinow, & W. M. Sullivan (Eds.), *Social science as moral inquiry* (pp. 33–51). New York: Columbia University Press.

Gilligan, C. (In press). Remapping development: The power of divergent data. In L. Cirillo & S. Wapner (Eds.), *Value presuppositions in theories of human development*. Hillsdale, NJ: Erlbaum.

Gilligan, C., Kohlberg, L., Lerner, J., & Belenky, M. (1971). Moral reasoning about sexual dilemmas: The development of an interview and scoring system. In *Technical report of the president's commission on obscenity and pornography* (Vol. 1). Washington, DC: U.S. Government Printing Office.

Gorsuch, R. L., & Barnes, M. L. (1973). Stages of ethical reasoning and moral norms of Carib youths. *Journal of Cross-Cultural Psychology, 4*, 283–301.

Greenberg, J. (1982). Approaching equity and avoiding inequity in groups and organizations. In J. Greenberg & R. L. Cohen (Eds.), *Equity and justice in social behavior* (pp. 389–435). New York: Academic Press.

Greenberg, J. (1983). Effects of reward value and retaliative power on allocation decisions: Justice, generosity, or greed? *Journal of Personality and Social Psychology, 36*, 367–379.

Greenberg, J., & Cohen, R. L. (Eds.). (1982a). *Equity and justice in social behavior*. New York: Academic Press.

Greenberg, J., & Cohen, R. L. (1982b). Why justice? Normative and instrumental interpretations. In J. Greenberg & R. L. Cohen (Eds.), *Equity and justice in social behavior* (pp. 437–469). New York: Academic Press.

Gross, M., & Averill, M. B. (1983). Evolution and patriarchal myths of scarcity and competition. In S. Harding & M. B. Hintikka (Eds.), *Discovering reality* (pp. 71–95). Dordrecht, The Netherlands: D. Reidel Publishing.

Gurr, T. (1970). *Why men rebel.* Princeton: Princeton University Press.

Haan, N. (1978). Two moralities in action contexts: Relationships to thought, ego regulation, and development. *Journal of Personality and Social Psychology, 36,* 286–305.

Haan, N. (1983). An interactional morality of everyday life. In N. Haan, R. N. Bellah, P. Rabinow, & W. M. Sullivan (Eds.), *Social science as moral inquiry* (pp. 218–250). New York: Columbia University Press.

Haan, N. (1985). *With regard to Walker (1984) on sex "differences" in moral reasoning.* Manuscript submitted for publication.

Haan, N., Block, J., & Smith, B. (1968). Moral reasoning of young adults. *Journal of Personality and Social Psychology, 10,* 183–201.

Habermas, J. (1971). *Knowledge and human interests.* Boston: Beacon Press.

Hamilton, V. L. (1978). Who is responsible? Toward a social psychology of responsibility attribution. *Social Psychology, 41,* 316–328.

Hamilton, V. L., & Rytina, S. (1980). Social consensus on norms of justice: Should the punishment fit the crime? *American Journal of Sociology, 85,* 1117–1144.

Hardin, G. (1972). *Exploring new ethics for survival: The voyage of the Spaceship Beagle.* New York: Penguin.

Harkness, S., Edwards, C. P., & Super, C. M. (1981). Social roles and moral reasoning: A case study in a rural African community. *Developmental Psychology, 17,* 595–603.

Harris, R. J. (1983). Pinning down the equity formula. In D. M. Messick & K. S. Cook (Eds.), *Equity theory: Psychological and sociological perspectives* (pp. 207–242). New York: Praeger.

Harris, R. J., & Joyce, M. A. (198). What's fair? It depends on how you phrase the question. *Journal of Personality and Social Psychology, 38,* 165–179.

Heath, A. (1976). *Rational choice and social exchange: A critique of social exchange theory.* Cambridge: Cambridge University Press.

Held, V. (1979). Property rights and interests. *Social Research, 46,* 550–579.

Hirschman, A. O. (1970). *Exit, voice, and loyalty.* Cambridge: Harvard University Press.

Hoffman, M. L. (1975). Sex differences in moral internalization and values. *Journal of Personality and Social Psychology, 32,* 720–729.

Hoffman, M. L. (1977a). Empathy, its development and prosocial implications. In C. B. Keasey (Ed.), *Nebraska symposium on motivation* (Vol. 25, pp. 116–217). Lincoln: University of Nebraska.

Hoffman, M. L. (1977b). Sex differences in empathy and related behaviors. *Psychological Bulletin, 84,* 712–722.

Hoffman, M. L. (1982). Development of prosocial motivation: Empathy and guilt. In N. Eisenberg (Ed.), *The development of prosocial behavior* (pp. 281–313). New York: Academic.

Hogan, R. (1975). Theoretical egocentrism and the problem of compliance. *American Psychologist, 30,* 533–540.

Hogan, R., & Emler, N. P. (1978). The biases in contemporary social psychology. *Social Research, 45,* 478–534.

Hogan, R., & Emler, N. P. (1981). Retributive justice. In M. J. Lerner & S. C. Lerner (Eds.), *The justice motive in social behavior: Adapting to times of scarcity and change* (pp. 125–144). New York: Plenum Press.

Holstein, C. B. (1976). Irreversible, stepwise sequence in the development of moral judgment: A longitudinal study of males and females. *Child Development, 47*, 51–61.

Homans, G. C. (1961). *Social behavior: Its elementary forms.* New York: Harcourt, Brace & World.

Hook, J. G., & Cook, T. D. (1979). Equity theory and the cognitive ability of children. *Psychological Bulletin, 86*, 429–445.

Jasso, G., & Rossi, P. H. (1977). Distributive justice and earned income. *American Sociological Review, 42*, 639–651.

Johnson, M. M., Stockard, J., Acker, J., & Naffziger, C. (1975). Expressiveness re-evaluated. *School Review, 83*, 617–644.

Jones, E. E., & Nisbett, R. E. (1972). The actor and the observer: Divergent perceptions of the cause of behavior. In E. E. Jones, D. E. Kanouse, H. H. Kelley, R. E. Nisbett, S. Valins, & B. Weiner (Eds.), *Attribution: Perceiving the causes of behavior* (pp. 79–94). Morristown, NJ: General Learning Press.

Kahn, A. S., & Gaeddert, W. P. (1985). From theories of equity to theories of justice: The liberating consequences of studying women. In V. E. O'Leary, R. K. Unger, & B. S. Wallston (Eds.), *Women, gender, and social psychology* (pp. 129–148). Hillsdale, NJ: Erlbaum.

Kahneman, D., & Tversky, A. (1984). Choices, values, and frames. *American Psychologist, 39*, 341–350.

Kant, I. (1959). *Foundations of the metaphysics of morals.* Indianapolis: Bobbs-Merrills. (Original work published 1785).

Keil, L. J., & McClintock, C. G. (1983). A developmental perspective on distributive justice. In D. M. Messick & K. S. Cook (Eds.), *Equity theory: Psychological and sociological perspectives* (pp. 13–46). New York: Praeger.

Kidder, L. H., Bellettirie, G., & Cohn, E. S. (1977). Secret ambitions and public performances. *Journal of Experimental Social Psychology, 13*, 70–80.

Kidder, L. H., Fagan, M. A., & Cohn, E. S. (1981). Giving and receiving: Social justice in close relationships. In M. J. Lerner & S. C. Lerner (Eds.), *The justice motive in social behavior: Adapting to times of scarcity and change* (pp. 235–260). New York: Plenum Press.

Kidder, L. H., & Fine, M. (1986). Making sense of injustice: Social explanations, social action, and the role of the social scientist. In E. Seidman & J. Rappaport (Eds.), *Redefining social problems* (pp. 49–63). New York: Plenum Press.

Kilham, W., & Mann, L. (1974). Level of destructive obedience as a function of transmitter and executant roles in the Milgram obedience paradigm. *Journal of Personality and Social Psychology, 29*, 696–702.

Kohlberg, L. (1981). From is to ought: How to commit the naturalistic fallacy and get away with it in the study of moral development. In T. Mischel (Ed.), *Cognitive development and epistemology* (pp. 151–236). New York: Academic Press.

Kohlberg, L., & Kramer, R. (1969). Continuities and discontinuities in childhood and adult moral development. *Human Development, 12*, 93–120.

Kohlberg, L., Levine, C., & Hewer, A. (1983). *Moral stages: A current formulation and a response to critics.* Basel, Switzerland: S. Karger.

Kohler, I. (1962, May). Experiments with goggles. *Scientific American, 206(5)*, 62–72.

Kuhn, D., Langer, J., Kohlberg, L., & Haan, N. S. (1977). The development of formal operations in logical and moral judgment. *Genetic Psychology Monographs, 95,* 97–188.

Kurtines, W. M., & Gewirtz, J. L. (Eds.). (1984). *Morality, moral behavior, and moral development.* New York: Wiley.

Lambert, R., & Curtis, J. (1979). Notes on a sociology for bad times. *Alternatives, 8(2),* 32–53.

Lamm, H., Kayser, E., & Schanz, V. (1983). An attributional analysis of interpersonal justice: Ability and effort as inputs in the allocation of gain and losses. *The Journal of Social Psychology, 119,* 269–281.

Lange, L. (1983). Woman is not a rational animal: On Aristotle's biology of reproduction. In S. Harding & M. B. Hintikka (Eds.), *Discovering reality* (pp. 1–15). Dordrecht, The Netherlands: D. Reidel Publishing.

LaTour, S. (1978). Determinants of participant and observer satisfaction with adversary and inquisitorial modes of adjudication. *Journal of Personal and Social Psychology, 36,* 1531–1545.

Lerner, M. J. (1975). The justice motive in social behavior: Introduction. *Journal of Social Issues, 31,* 1–19.

Lerner, M. J. (1980). *The belief in a just world: A fundamental delusion.* New York: Plenum Press.

Lerner, M. J., & Lerner, S. C. (Eds.). (1981). *The justice motive in social behavior: Adapting to times of scarcity and change.* New York: Plenum Press.

Leventhal, G. S. (1976a). The distribution of rewards and resources in groups and organizations. In E. Walster & L. Berkowitz (Eds.), *Advances in experimental social psychology* (Vol. 9, pp. 91–131). New York: Academic Press.

Leventhal, G. S. (1976b). Fairness in social relationships. In J. Thibaut, J. Spence, & R. Carson (Eds.), *Contemporary topics in social psychology* (pp. 211–239). Morristown, NJ: General Learning Press.

Leventhal, G. S. (1980). What should be done with equity theory? In K. Gergen, M. Greenberg, & R. Willis (Eds.), *Social exchange theory* (pp. 27–55). New York: Plenum Press.

Lind, E. A., Lissak, R. I., & Conlon, D. E. (1983). Decision control and process control effects on procedural fairness judgments. *Journal of Applied Social Psychology, 13,* 338–350.

Loomis, L. R. (1943). (Ed.). *Aristotle: On man and the universe (Nichomachean Ethics,* pp. 84–242). Roslyn, NY: Walter J. Black.

Lyons, N. P. (1983). Two perspectives: On self, relationships, and morality. *Harvard Educational Review, 53,* 125–145.

MacIntyre, A. (1982). *After virtue.* Notre Dame: University of Notre Dame Press.

Major, B., & Deaux, K. (1982). Individual differences in justice behavior. In J. Greenberg & R. L. Cohen (Eds.), *Equity and justice in social behavior* (pp. 43–76). New York: Academic Press.

Martin, J. (1981). Relative deprivation: A theory of distributive injustice for an era of shrinking resources. In L. Cummings & B. Staw (Eds.), *Research in organizational behavior* (Vol. 3, pp. 53–107). Greenwich, CT: JAI Press.

Martin, J., & Murray, A. (1984). Catalysts for collective violence: The importance of a psychological approach. In R. Folger (Ed.), *The sense of injustice: Social psychological perspectives* (pp. 95–139). New York: Plenum Press.

McClintock, C. G., & Keil, L. J. (1982). Equity and social exchange. In J. Greenberg & R. L. Cohen (Eds.), *Equity and justice in social behavior* (pp. 337–388). New York: Academic Press.

Mikula, G. (1980a). On the role of justice in allocation decisions. In G. Mikula (Ed.),

Justice and social interaction: Experimental and theoretical contributions from psychological research (pp. 127–166). New York: Springer-Verlag.

Mikula, G. (1980b). *Justice and social interaction: Experimental and theoretical contributions from psychological research.* New York: Springer-Verlag.

Mikula, G. (1984). Justice and fairness in interpersonal relations: Thoughts and suggestions. In H. Tajfel (Ed.), *The social dimension: European developments in social psychology* (Vol. 1, pp. 204–249). New York: Cambridge University Press.

Mikula, G., & Schlamberger, K. (1986). What people think about an unjust event: Toward a better understanding of the phenomenology of experiences in justice. *European Journal of Social Psychology, 15,* 37–49.

Milgram, S. (1974). *Obedience to authority: An experimental view.* New York: Harper & Row.

Mill, J. S. (1957). *Utilitarianism.* New York: Liberal Arts Press. (Original work published 1861)

Miller, D. (1976). *Social justice.* Oxford: Clarendon Press.

Montada, L. (1980). Developmental changes in concepts of justice. In G. Mikula (Ed.), *Justice and social interaction: Experimental and theoretical contributions from psychological research* (pp. 257–284). New York: Springer-Verlag.

Moore, B. (1978). *Injustice: The social bases of obedience and revolt.* White Plains, NY: M. E. Sharpe.

Murphy-Berman, V., Berman, J. J., Singh, P., Pachauri, A., & Kumar, P. (1984). Factors affecting allocation to needy and meritorious recipients: A cross-cultural comparison. *Journal of Personality and Social Psychology, 46(6),* 1267–1272.

Nelson, S., & Dweck, C. (1977). Motivation and competence as determinants of young children's reward allocation. *Developmental Psychology, 13,* 192–197.

Newman, D., Riel, M., & Martin, L. M. W. (1983). Cultural practices and Piagetian theory: The impact of a cross-cultural research program. *Human Development, 8,* 135–154.

Nicholson, L. J. (1983). Women, morality, and history. *Social Research, 50,* 514–536.

Nisan, M. (1984). Distributive justice and social norms. *Child Development, 55,* 1020–1029.

Nozick, R. (1974). *Anarchy, state, and utopia.* New York: Basic Books.

O'Malley, M. N. (1983). Interpersonal and intrapersonal justice: The effect of subject and confederate outcomes on evaluations of fairness. *European Journal of Social Psychology, 13,* 121–128.

Ophuls, W. (1977). *Ecology and the politics of scarcity.* San Francisco: Freeman.

Parlee, M. B. (1981). Appropriate control groups in feminist research. *Psychology of Women Quarterly, 5,* 637–644.

Parsons, T., Bales, R. F., & Shils, E. (1954). *Working papers in the theory of action.* Glencoe, IL: Free Press.

Phillips, D. C., & Nicolayev, J. (1978). Kohlbergian moral development: A progressing or degenerating research program. *Education Theory, 28,* 286–301.

Piaget, J. (1965). *The moral judgment of the child* (M. Gabain, Trans.). New York: Free Press. (Original work published 1932)

Prakash, M. S. (1984, Summer). [Review of *In a different voice.*] *Educational Studies, 15(2),* 190–200.

Rabinowitz, V. C., Karuza, J., & Zevon, M. A. (1984). Fairness and effectiveness in premeditated helping. In R. Folger (Ed.), *The sense of injustice* (pp. 63–92). New York: Plenum Press.

Rawls, J. (1971). *A theory of justice.* Cambridge, MA: Belknap Press.

Reid, B. V. (1984). An anthropological reinterpretation of Kohlberg's stages of moral development. *Human Development, 27,* 57–64.

Reis, H. T. (1981). Self-presentation and distributive justice. In J. T. Tedeschi (Ed.), *Impression management theory and social psychological research* (pp. 269–291). New York: Academic Press.

Reis, H. T. (1984). The multidimensionality of justice. In R. Folger (Ed.), *The sense of injustice: Social psychological perspectives* (pp. 25–61). New York: Plenum Press.

Reis, H. T., & Jackson, L. A. (1981). Sex differences in reward allocation: Subjects, partners, and tasks. *Journal of Personality and Social Psychology, 40,* 465–478.

Rest, J. R. (1983). Morality. In P. H. Mussen (Ed.), *Handbook of Child Psychology* (Vol. 3, 556–629). New York: Wiley.

Rubin, Z., & Peplau, A. (1975). Who believes in a just world? *Journal of Social Issues, 31,* 65–89.

Sampson, E. E. (1969). Studies of status congruence. In L. Berkowitz (Ed.), *Advances in experimental social psychology* (Vol. 4, pp. 225–270). New York: Academic Press.

Sampson, E. E. (1975). On justice as equality. *Journal of Social Issues, 31,* 45–64.

Sampson, E. E. (1978). Scientific paradigms and social values: Wanted—A scientific revolution. *Journal of Personality and Social Psychology, 36,* 1332–1343.

Sampson, E. E. (1980). Justice and social character. In G. Mikula (Ed.), *Justice and social interaction: Experimental and theoretical contributions from psychological research* (pp. 285–312). New York: Springer-Verlag.

Sampson, E. E. (1981a). Cognitive psychology as ideology. *American Psychologist, 36,* 730–743.

Sampson, E. E. (1981b). Social change and the contents of justice motivation. In M. J. Lerner & S. C. Lerner (Eds.), *Justice motive in social behavior: Adapting to times of scarcity and change* (pp. 91–124). New York: Plenum Press.

Sampson, E. E. (1983). *Justice and the critique of pure psychology.* New York: Plenum Press.

Saxe, G. B. (1982). Culture and the development of numerical cognition studies among the Oksapmin of Papua New Guinea. In C. Brainerd (Ed.), *Children's logical and mathematical cognition* (pp. 157–176). New York: Springer.

Schwinger, T. (1980). Just allocation of goods: Decisions among three principles. In Mikula, G. (Ed.), *Justice and social interaction: Experimental and theoretical contributions from psychological research* (pp. 95–126). New York: Springer-Verlag.

Seligman, M. E. P. (1975). *Learned helplessness.* San Francisco: W. H. Freeman.

Shapiro, M. J. (1969). Rational political man: A synthesis of economic and social psychological perspectives. *American Political Science Review, 63,* 1106.

Shweder, R. A. (1982). Liberalism as destiny [Review of *The philosophy of moral development* (Vol. 1)]. *Contemporary Psychology, 27,* 421–424.

Simon, H. (1983). *Reason in human affairs.* Stanford, CA: Stanford University Press.

Simpson, E. L. (1974). Moral development research. *Human Development, 17,* 81–106.

Smetana, J. G. (1983). Social-cognitive development: Domain distinctions and coordinations. *Developmental Review, 3,* 131–147.

Smetana, J. G. (1984a). Toddlers' social interactions regarding moral and conventional transgressions. *Child Development, 55,* 1767–1776.

Smetana, J. G. (1984b). Morality and gender: A commentary on Pratt, Golding, and Hunter. *Merrill-Palmer Quarterly, 30,* 341–348.

Smetana, J. G. (1985). Preschool children's conceptions of transgressions: The effects of varying moral and conventional domain-related attributes. *Developmental Psychology, 21,* 18–29.

Smetana, J. G., Bridgeman, D. L., & Turiel, E. (1983). Differentiation of domains and prosocial behavior. In D. L. Bridgeman (Ed.), *The nature of prosocial development* (pp. 163–183). New York: Academic Press.

Smetana, J. G., Kelly, M., & Twentyman, C. T. (1984). Abused, neglected, and non-maltreated children's conceptions of moral and social transgressions. *Child Development, 55,* 277–287.

Stake, J. E. (1983). Factors in reward distribution: Allocation motive, gender, and Protestant ethic endorsement. *Journal of Personality and Social Psychology, 44,* 410–418.

Sullivan, E. V. (1977). A study of Kohlberg's structural theory of moral development: A critique of liberal social science ideology. *Human Development, 20,* 352–376.

Tajfel, H. (1984). Intergroup relations, social myths and social justice in social psychology. In H. Tajfel (Ed.), *The social dimension: European developments in social psychology* (Vol. 2, pp. 695–715). Cambridge: Cambridge University Press.

Thibaut, J., & Walker, L. (1975). *Procedural justice: A psychological analysis.* Hillsdale, NJ: Erlbaum.

Thibaut, J., & Walker, L. (1978). A theory of procedure. *California Law Review, 66,* 541–566.

Turiel, E. (1983). *The development of social knowledge: Morality and convention.* Cambridge: Cambridge University Press.

Turiel, E., Edwards, C. P., & Kohlberg, L. (1978). Moral development in Turkish children, adolescents, and young adults. *Journal of Cross-cultural Psychology, 9,* 75–86.

Tyler, T. R. (1984). Justice in the political arena. In R. Folger (Ed.), *The sense of injustice: Social psychological perspectives* (pp. 189–225). New York: Plenum Press.

Tyler, T. R., & Caine, A. (1981). The influence of outcomes and procedures on satisfaction with formal leaders. *Journal of Personality and Social Psychology, 41,* 643–655.

United Nations. (1980). *Program of action for the second half of the United Nations decade for women: Equality, development, and peace.* New York: United Nations.

Utne, M. K., & Kidd, R. F. (1980). Attribution and equity. In G. Mikula (Ed.), *Justice and social interaction* (pp. 63–94). New York: Springer-Verlag.

Walker, L. (1984). Sex differences in the development of moral reasoning: A critical review of the literature. *Child Development, 55,* 677–691.

Walster, E., Walster, G. W., & Berscheid, E. (1978). *Equity: Theory and research.* Boston: Allyn & Bacon.

Weber, M. (1930). *The protestant ethic and the spirit of capitalism.* London: Unwin University Books. (Original work published 1904–1905)

Wexler, P. (1983). *Critical social psychology.* Boston: Routledge & Kegan Paul.

Worland, S. T. (1977). Social economy and the theory of justice: Two new directions. *Review of Social Economy, 35,* 345–359.

Young, I. M. (1981). Toward a critical theory of justice. *Social Theory and Practice, 7,* 279–302.

Yussen, S. R. (1976). Moral reasoning from the perspective of others. *Child Development, 42,* 551–555.

Zuckerman, M., & Gerbasi, K. (1977). Belief in internal control or belief in a just world: The use and misuse of the I-E scale in prediction of attitudes and behavior. *Journal of Personality, 45,* 356–378.

CHAPTER 7

Anthropology and Justice

Laura Nader and Andrée Sursock

Introduction

Justice is so familiar a feature of daily life that we seldom pause to examine it. Anthropologists have only rarely been interested in cross-cultural conceptions of justice (Cohn, 1959; Gluckman, 1965a, 1965b; Lowie, 1925; Nader, 1975; Nader & Todd, 1978; Nduka, 1977; Pospisil, 1971; Williams, 1941) and almost never concerned with comparative conceptions of injustice.[1] The truth is, however, that anthropologists have provided the data for a comparative understanding of justice without often using the concept itself.

In this chapter, we will use these anthropological data to examine the way indigenous people and anthropologists alike deal with justice. We will also attempt to demonstrate that (a) justice beliefs and behaviors and the justice motive are universal phenomena; (b) the meaning of justice will vary with different social and cultural settings; and (c) different forms of justice may exist within one sociocultural setting and often in societies with ranked or stratified social structures. These points need to be examined empirically. It is

[1]Discussions of the idea of social justice often include mention of injustice, and people who write about inequality frequently make mention of injustice (see Rytina, Chapter 5, this volume). The work of Gerald D. Berreman has consistently worked in and around the concept of injustice, in particular as it relates to caste and class (Berreman, 1960). In connection with his research on India, he argues against the notion that the deprived and subject status in India can be justified by religion and philosophy and questions whether individuals in an inferior position would not change their lot if given the opportunity (see also Berreman 1966, 1971, 1981).

LAURA NADER and ANDRÉE SURSOCK • Department of Anthropology, University of California, Berkeley, California 94720.

the psychologists who have argued on the basis of child developmental data that the justice motive is a basic human motive found in all human societies and part of many, if not all, human interactions (see Furby, Chapter 6, this volume). Lerner and Whitehead (1980), for example, generalized that "considerations of justice shape the way people interact with one another in every encounter, especially where there is a common endeavor or resources to be allocated" (p. 242). Their statement is a reasonable beginning for us, and at the outset we will operate with the idea of justice that encompasses what people's expectations are in relation to the mechanisms of justice, what they feel they deserve, and the decision-making processes that are used in arriving at outcomes. In this sense of justice as idea and justice as action leading to outcome, the concern with justice would be well within what anthropologists might consider to be a guiding theme in all societies and thus to be found universally.

In another context, Pitkin (1972, p. 187) reminds us that as with any ideological concept, a tension exists between ideal standards of justice and its institutionalization. We can also describe the subject matter in terms of injustice: What do people do when they feel they have been wronged and why? Robert Seidman (n.d.) puts it more generally:

> Justice is not a static state of affairs. It is not a prizing—a blueprint of how things ought to be. Rather, it is a set of propositions instructing people how to act to solve the troubles that plague the human condition. (unpublished manuscript)

If we assume that all societies have an idea of justice stemming from human interaction that serves to motivate behavior and decision making, then we must also recognize that this idea of justice will vary with differing societies and cultures and, at times, within these units. In addition, the idea that there is more than one kind of justice in a society is certainly not new. It was elaborated in Western philosophy by Plato and Aristotle.

In *The Republic,* Plato viewed justice as an ordered universe where every person's position was due to his or her skills and talents. Aristotle shared Plato's view. He distinguished between two kinds of justice: distributive and rectificatory. He viewed the first as proportionate equity and the second as restoration of the status quo. For instance, a theft is rectified by the restitution of what was stolen. Thus, fairness and order were central components of the Greek conception of justice, and, as we will see, elsewhere in the Mediterranean world still today (e.g., Mayer, n.d.). But in addition to distribution and rectification, there are other concepts that enter discussions of justice regularly—equity, equality, parity, need, reciprocity, social ranking, competition, to mention only a few. However, not all kinds of justice are elaborated in each culture or indeed in each human encounter.

Greek conceptions of justice stressed equality and harmony and may seem universal and "natural," but we need only move to the other end of the world, to Korea for example, to realize that others might disagree. For people who live in a society where differences rather than sameness or universal qualities are the basis of organization, where social life is vertically structured because of a denial of the intrinsic equality of all people, the Greek concepts of justice may be anathema. A leading Korean scholar, the late Hahm Pyong-Choon (1967), expressed Korean differences with the Greeks in the following observations:

> The Western concept of justice is not an easy one to grasp. The Greeks had a concept of justice that was much less legalistic and individualistic than that of the Romans. They conceived justice as a harmonious life among the citizens rather than as freedom of an individual or his private rights. They nonetheless believed that this justice was to be secured through law. Freedom and the role of the law were thought to be the two supplemental aspects of good government, and justice also meant some kind of equality. In its broadest sense justice may be synonymous with virtue or good life, and in this sense it constituted an ideal in the Korean political tradition also. But our concept of justice never included elements of freedom, equality and the sovereignty of law as its constitutive parts. If we use Aristotle's scheme of distinguishing the two aspects of justice, the Koreans conceived justice only in its distributive aspect. The other aspect of justice, commutative or rectificatory, which should govern contract and should place all men on an equal term was singularly lacking in our tradition. This aspect of justice takes little account of the personal worth or merit of the men involved. Although the Legalists of China strongly advocated absolute equality in meting out punishment, taking no account of man's status, past good deeds or personal merits, the Koreans rather followed the Confucian way of taking a man's status and merits into account. (p. 40)

It is possible that what Hahm Pyong-Choon observed for Koreans may be more widely characteristic of societies where hierarchy is a central feature of social structure. In her work on Fijian society, Letitia Hickson (1979) described a kind of justice ideology equivalent to the reaffirmation of norms governing existing rank relations. The aim of the disputing process in Fijian society is to repair the structure of rank ordering that the conflict has disrupted. Safeguarding a hierarchical order might seem unjust to Westerners who equate justice ideology with equality principles. The question as to whether members of hierarchical societies see them as unjust has been discussed (Berreman, 1981), whereas the further question as to whether everyone recognizes universal human rights is still unanswered.

Hahm Pyong-Choon (1967) himself realized that with the growth of state power and state law the question of justice becomes one less concerned with the maintenance of traditional hierarchical structures, less rectificatory, and more concerned with distributive matters:

> In the field of law, the "distributive" aspects of justice, if we may employ the Aristotelian expression, is to be more emphasized than in the past. The traditional concept of the state as an entity to enforce only "corrective justice" is said to be insufficient. Law has come to be more concerned with each individual getting a fair share of life in the first place than in preventing him from upsetting the established social order. (p. 148)

It is with the development and spread of nation states that the demand for social justice is heard, and Hahm saw modernization as a series of endeavors to realize an ever-increasing degree of social justice. In these societies, distributive justice based on the ideology of egalitarianism (see Dumont, 1977) therefore becomes more prevalant.

In this chapter, we will address the two ideas of universality and variety by discussing justice as ideological value, by elaborating upon a model of legal procedure for describing the varieties of procedural justice, and by focusing attention on structural principles associated with justice ideas, such as harmony, balance, or reciprocity. Finally, we will discuss institutions other than law (e.g., religious, political, economic) in which justice operates as a means of identifying those variables essential to revealing the significance of both universality and variety in developing social science theories of justice.

Justice as an Ideological Value

In order to make some sense of the variety of cultures around the world, anthropologists have often presented polar types whose usefulness lies not so much in their accuracy as in their illumination of salient ideological values or social features. This section examines what we can learn about justice from Louis Dumont's contrast between individualistic and holistic societies.

In his comparative study of ideologies, Dumont (e.g., 1970, 1977) opposes societies that value equality and individualism to those that value hierarchy and holism. This is a powerful contrast that provides an adequate framework for analyzing notions of justice around the world. For example, seating arrangements in moots in Africa, or in court procedure among the Zapotec Mexican Indians, are characterized by crowdedness. This spatial arrangement is linked to the consensual mode of dispute resolution, and it stands in marked contrast to procedures in Western courts where the parties are in two distinct areas and the judge, standing slightly raised above the proceedings, represents and embodies justice and the law (Nader, 1969).

In addition, one of the important duties of the Western judge is the search for truth and evidence. It is only when all details of the case are uncovered that the judge will render a decision based on precedents and existing laws. But truth is not often a matter of great concern in non-Western societies. In Tivland, for instance, "truth . . . is an elusive matter because smooth social relationships are deemed of higher value than mere precision of facts" (Bohannan, 1957, p. 51). This is applicable to many other people, among which are the Koreans, who prefer "peace to justice, harmony to truth" (Hahm, 1969, p. 44).

Settlements of intracommunity disputes also express the stress on community ties. Among the Ndendeuli, for instance, the outcome of disputes is typically a compromise between conflicting claims. Even if one party has a much stronger claim, the community will try to give some credit to the opponent because the goal of dispute settlements is to preserve the cooperative spirit of the community (Gulliver, 1969).

The stress on community ties can be expressed in an emphasis on distributive justice, as among the Ibo of Nigeria, where distributive justice is the most articulated form of justice.

> This is hardly surprising since the communal life which is characteristic of Ibo society demands that resources of the community be distributed as widely and as equitably as possible. (Nduka, 1977, p. 95)

Justice may also focus on the individual in a social context. Rosen (1980–1981) reports that Moroccan society focuses on "the individual as the locus of a series of distinctive ties of obligation" (p. 228). In formulating his judgment, the judge takes into account the particulars of a case (e.g., education of litigants) and the implicit obligations that underlie a particular relation. As an example, Rosen reports the case of an old and sick woman who claimed that she sold, to her son, the land she inherited from her late husband (the man's father) with the understanding that a share of the income would be given to her as support.

There were no witnesses or documents to support her claim. The woman
kept interrupting her son as he denied that any support agreement was
attached to the land sale. The woman kept trying to swear that what she
said was true, but the qadi cut her off and summarily ordered the man to
pay eight dollars per month for support. Turning to the clerk, the qadi
said that the father would certainly not have wanted his wife to be
dispossessed by the son. (p. 228)

Thus it seems that justice, in its application and procedures, reflects
the importance of community ties in non-Western societies.

   In opposition to justice in non-Western societies, Western jurisprudence is characterized by a stress on individualism, and the concept of law is perhaps its best illustration. Central to Western law is
the idea that all people are equal and that no special circumstance
must be taken into account when applying the law. Yet in practice,
the principle of equality before the law has often been violated. The
idea of equality before the law was brilliantly developed by Kant
(Schneewind, 1984, p. 2) who argued that we respect the laws that
we ourselves make. Schneewind (1984) traces the history of this idea
back to the Christian scriptures and to St. Paul's Epistle to the Ro-
mans (2:14): "For when the Gentiles, which have not the law, do by
nature the things contained in the law, they, having not the law, are a
law unto themselves." This is a crucial text because it expresses one
of the most important ideas in Western ethics: The individual is a
bounded, reasonable entity, and the law is a natural extension of
individual reason.

   Now, because we are all reasonable human beings who embody
the law, why do we need the law at all? Simply put, because we are
weak. The law represents what is best in us and protects us against
what is worst. Law as an extension of individual reason implies that
justice in an individualistic ideology tends to be universal and
abstract.

   By contrast, with holism, justice tends to be particular, contextual, situational, and relativistic. Indeed, it has often been noted
that morality in primitive societies applies only to the narrow
bounds of the community. What would be considered theft if directed toward a member of one's community will be considered
daring when directed toward outsiders.

Navaho morality is . . . contextual rather than absolute. . . . The rules
vary with the situation. To deceive when trading with foreign tribes is a
morally accepted practice. Acts are not in themselves bad or good. . . . In
a large society like modern America, where people come and go and
business and other dealings must be carried on by people who never see
each other, it is functionally necessary to have abstract standards that
transcend an immediate concrete situation in which two or more persons are interacting. (Kluckhohn, 1959, p. 434)

Thus, justice in individualistic societies stresses abstraction. Each individual is seen as equal to everyone else. Equality implies that everyone should be treated the same. From the idea of equality derives a universal notion of laws embedded in the philosophy of natural law. Laws are just when they closely reflect natural laws. In turn, natural laws are universal. On the other hand, justice in holistic societies stresses concreteness because the individual is seen as a social being, a member of a group, be it a family, a clan, a religious sect, or a caste. Concreteness implies equity instead of equality. Because individuals are not abstract entities, because laws are not universal and are not rooted in the essence of human beings, justice is met when it takes into account the particulars of each case. In sum, equality is the central component of justice in individualistic societies, whereas equity is central to justice in holistic societies.

Furthermore, justice in individualistic societies tends to be universalistic, whereas it is particularistic in holistic societies. Writing about the Kapauku Papuans, Pospisil (1971) notes their relativistic *Weltanschauung*. They "certainly do not assume that their own concept of justice (*uta-uta*) is an expression of a universal and absolute truth" (p. 252).

If carried to its extreme, however, too particularistic a view of justice can undermine justice itself. Hahm wrote, about Korea, that such an extreme view led to a disrespect for the law: "An extreme form of 'particularistic justice' that obtained in Korea resulted in ultimate negation of justice itself" (1967, pp. 40–41). But, whether particularistic or not, procedures of justice are always carried out systematically in all societies.

Procedural Justice and Dispute Resolution

What one does about an injustice or felt injustice is directly related to what forums are available and how they operate (Nader, 1975). This in turn is related to the distribution of power. The procedures used by such forums are equated with procedural justice, and procedural justice is directly related to the evaluation of a just outcome. In this section, we will deal with procedures and outcomes that form a unitary complex that is, for our purposes, equivalent to procedural justice.

In his book *The Behavior of Law* (1976), Donald Black elaborates on earlier work (Nader, 1969) by formulating four ideal styles of law and by describing how these four styles conform to a style of social control. One could also look at these four styles as describing four mechanisms of procedural justice by linking procedural means with procedural goals.

Black (1976) distinguishes these four styles by function as penal, compensatory, therapeutic, and conciliatory.

> Penal control prohibits certain conduct, and it enforces its prohibitions with punishment. In case of violation, the group as a whole takes the initiative against an alleged offender, the question being his guilt or innocence. (p. 4)

Justice under this penal control style is retributive, and most usually is depicted from the group's point of view. *Penal* most readily describes the former system of group justice used among the Zuni Indians of the southwestern United States to handle witchcraft cases:

> A middle-aged man used to wander about and rarely stayed at home. His wife's family suspected him of something and asked him what he was doing. He replied that since it was a year of drought, there was not enough to eat at home, and he was looking for yucca seed pods. He did, in fact, bring back a few. This went on day after day.
>
> One day he went out again, on foot, and a sheep herder saw him go in the direction of the Zuni Mountains. The herder followed his tracks for about 50 yards. . . . He saw two footprints side by side, and then about six yards ahead two more, as if the man had jumped; but beyond that there were no more. It appeared to the herder that the man had flown away.
>
> The herder returned at once to Zuni and reported the story to the War Chief . . . (the elder brother Bow priest). Four members of the Bow Priest Society accompanied him to the end of the tracks, where they searched again but could find no more. The War Chief agreed that this was sufficient evidence that the man had flown. . . . [When the man returned] that evening he was arrested by the War Chief and questioned.
>
> Forest fires had recently occurred in the mountains, and under questioning the suspect confessed that he had set the fires and was responsible for the drought. He gave as his reason that he was jealous of other people who had better crops than he, and added that what he had done was only half of what he intended to do. He said that his wife's family knew nothing about his activities, but that his own family knew where he went and were partly responsible, and that some other people had helped him set fires but were not responsible for the drought. . . . He refused to name the "others". . . . They clubbed him to death. Then the Bow priests went to his house and clubbed to death the members of his family, seven in all. It was decided not to bury the bodies in the cemetery, but to drag them away from the village and let them rot in the open. (Smith & Roberts, 1954, pp. 41–42)

For the Bow priests, the focus of the process is determination of guilt, and the consequence is punishment.

In Black's (1976) second type, compensatory control, the initiative is taken by the victims. They allege that someone is their debtor, with an unfulfilled obligation. They demand payment. Compensatory justice can be seen as operating among the Jalé (Koch, 1969) where guilt is not the focus, but responsibility for debt is the concern. Intention is disregarded, and payment or restitution is required and expected of the person(s) held responsible for a grievance. The compensatory style has been given much attention by anthropologists (e.g., Nader & Combs-Schilling, 1976) because it is commonly found among people where liability is collective, that is, where it is the responsibility of the disputing parties' kin groups. Among the Berbers of the Middle Atlas Mountains of Morocco, Ernest Gellner (1969) describes the operation of compensatory justice. After the breaking of the rule, as for example by a murder, there is a cooling-off period and then a period of negotiation between the parties to the dispute to arrive at a mutually acceptable compensation agreement. Similar forms of compensatory justice are found among the Nuer (Evans-Pritchard, 1940), the Ifugao of the Philippines (Barton, 1919), or among the California Yurok (Kroeber, 1925). In these societies, compensation or restitution schemes are usually a part of the culture that is exactly detailed. Among the Yurok, for example, every possession, privilege, injury, and offense could be valued in terms of property, both wealth and service (Kroeber, 1925).

However, even though we might characterize a society as predominantly compensatory, both penal and compensatory justice are often found in the same society and maybe even in the same case. Again, the Zuni provide an example:

> Two young men who are friends were drinking during a dance and got into an argument, which soon developed into a fist fight. The one who had started the fight received no injuries but the other one was hurt. . . . The injured man wanted compensation and the families of the two antagonists "argued and argued" but could come to no settlement. Finally they decided to present the case to the Council.
>
> At the trial all councilmen were present as well as the antagonists and their families. Both sides said that they had been unable to "outargue" each other and that they wanted the Council to settle the dispute. The judge asked how the fight developed; neither man could remember how it began, but they agreed that one had attacked the other and that the peaceable one had been beaten up.
>
> The judge decided that the man who had been injured should receive compensation in the form of a turquoise shell necklace, one buckskin and a big rug. Payment was made by the family of the aggressor and given to the injured man personally. The trial was held in the plaza. (Smith & Roberts, 1954, p. 54)

This compensatory form of justice is victim oriented, and justice is compensatory to the plaintiff.

Although both penal and compensatory justice are, as Black states, accusatory, they are more than social control from the point of view of the initiator. They are the means whereby the parties get their "just deserts." In the case of penal justice, it is an impositional justice, at least in comparison with compensatory justice, that is often negotiated between differing parties. The implication of compensatory justice is that the parties actually involved in the conflict have the right to negotiate the terms of their own settlement, a right that they do not have with impositional justice. In addition, the duties and obligations of the disputing parties are set forth during the process of settlement. Durkheim (1893/1964) put this another way when he distinguished between the penal law of segmental societies and the restitutive law of organic societies. He wrote that in the case of restitutive law, which involves compensation and negotiation, the duties and obligations of both sides are precisely spelled out, and then the penalty or judgment is handed down.

> Penal law, on the contrary, sets forth only sanctions, but says nothing of the obligations to which they correspond. . . . It does not say to begin with . . . Here is the duty; but rather, Here is the punishment. (p. 75)

Therapeutic and conciliatory styles are next in Black's scheme. They are remedial styles, methods of social repair and maintenance, or assistance for people in trouble (Black, 1976, p. 4). In his study of the Kpelle of Liberia, Gibbs (1963) described the moot as the most representative form of disputes, which is based on an idea of therapy. Gibbs describes a situation where conflict is viewed as a need for help, especially within the context of the family. The aggrieved is responsible for initiating the moot. Gifts as well as apologies are given in the process, and the strengths as well as the weaknesses of each case are brought to light by the mediators. The procedures are therapeutic in that they "reeducate the parties" to the others' perception of the situation. In the therapeutic style, justice involves helping and needing. By a process of clarification, the disputants are led to a consensual outcome that is neither accusatory nor adversarial. The success of this process depends on the willingness of the parties to cooperate with the mediators in reaching satisfactory settlement of the dispute (Gibbs, 1963).

Among the mountain Zapotec of Oaxaca, Mexico, we find the conciliatory style of justice predominating (Nader, 1969). Black (1976) describes the conciliatory style as aiming toward social harmony with the desired outcome a resolution. The Zapotec town official is not so much interested in establishing guilt or debt; he is interested in resolving the conflict at hand, and restitution or punishment are means by which the resolution is achieved, but they in themselves are not the ends. However, as with the penal style of justice, conciliatory justice is impositional.

It should be made clear that the use of types for analytical purposes usually distorts the ethnographic reality. In her monograph on Zinacantecan law, Jane Collier (1973) compares the meaning of conciliation at the hamlet or neighborhood level with that of the town center. In her description, she points out that hamlet procedures are

> based on the assumption that the litigants want to settle their quarrel and become reconciled; ceremonial center proceedings assume that each litigant is out for what he can get but will agree on a compromise when all strategies are exhausted. (Collier, 1973, pp. 61–62)

She points out that as officials work toward compromise the tone is sometimes one of "compromise or else" that may be, as she suggests, a way of face-saving for the litigants. The aim is still to produce an outcome that is lasting. Collier does state, however, that Zinacantecos recognize that some outcomes are unjust:

> A defendant forced into a compromise by being threatened or jailed may be deeply resentful of the mediator and the plaintiff who put him in such a position. In Zinacanteco ideology these decisions do not produce a lasting solution. The defendant is seen as having been left with anger in his heart, which cries out to the gods for vengeance on those who committed the injustice. (1973, p. 99)

Conciliatory procedures are also used for other important goals in face-to-face societies. For example, among the Zapotec (Nader, 1969), the purpose of finding a just outcome in some cases is also related to factors that, from a Western point of view, may be seen as health related; disputing that stems from anger causes sickness. Some face-to-face societies, such as the Tiruray of the Philippines, specifically distinguish between issues that arise from a sense of injustice and those that arise from the need to arrive at agreements about new relations (Schlegel, 1970). The first has to do with norm violation and the need to repair relations by payment of damages. The other deals with creation of new contractual agreements regarding property transfer.

In describing systems of reconciliation in widely separated geographical areas, similar words are used by observers, suggesting that reconciliation as a process may be culture free:

> The aim of Burmese justice was to satisfy the two contending parties as much as possible, and thus restore goodwill and harmony between them. (Aung, 1962, p. 21)

In Korea, Hahm (1967) informed us:

> A judge did not "judge" his case. Since he did not adjudicate according to formal rules but wanted to take all the particular qualities of the parties into account, the best he could do was to arbitrate or mediate rather than judge. He tried his best to avoid holding one party "right" and the other "wrong." (p. 4)

In discussing disputing processes, we must be careful to identify to whom the particular justice value (in this case, penal, compensatory, conciliatory, or therapeutic) belongs and whether it is imposed or arrived at in a consensual manner—a result of negotiated agreement between parties. Within impositional frameworks of justice, disputing processes may have nothing to do with justice from the point of view of the defendant or victim. The composition of the justice model will depend on the weight given to different aspects of the disputing process in relation to a participant's goals (e.g., litigants or third parties). Thus, in assigning meaning to the different perceptions of procedural justice, one can compare the advantage of impositional and adversarial processes, or each with situations where litigants cooperate. The use of one or another justice mode by participants is often dependent on their relative status and rank (Black, 1976).

We wish to make clear here that the concept of procedural justice should refer to the methods employed in deciding about disputes and the outcome or goals of such methods. The control of procedures is of central importance in procedural justice. But there is more to justice than disputing processes, more than the legal process involving disputing and judicial decision making. Notions of justice are implicit in every culture and usually operate at the unconscious or semiconscious levels. These notions of justice often become explicit only when confronted by other contradictory notions of justice, grounded in another culture.

The types of procedural justice that we have discussed here are often found contrasted to each other when the situation of legal pluralism within a society forces comparison. And it is under conditions of pluralism that this comparison is made between legal and just outcome. In her comparison of Turkish village law to state district court law, June Starr (1978) distinguished two forms of "justice": paternalistic and bureaucratic. Paternalistic justice refers to a situation where the district court judge finds for the litigants what he expects they wish him to find. In bureaucratic justice, the situation is quite the opposite—where the district court judge is universalistic rather than particularistic, where he applies the law without regard to particulars such as the status relations between the litigants:

> The most striking characteristic of judges' decisions in rural Turkey is the effort these judges make to fit commonsense labels and issues in disputes (i.e., he took my cow, I want my motor back, he entered my house-yard at night) into Turkish categories. (Starr, 1978, p. 275)

Paternalistic judging may be more conciliatory, the bureaucratic form more punitive, or at least more "'rational legal.'"

In dealing with legal pluralism, Collier (1973) describes in some detail the difference between Zinacantecan ideologies and those of the Mexican legal system. The Zinacantecan ideology provides the rationale for compromise solutions and litigant praticipation:

> The final solution to a conflict may bear little relation to the "wrong" that initiated the settlement procedure, but it is considered satisfactory if plaintiff and defendant are reconciled. (p. 60)

If the ultimate reason given for settling conflicts or righting wrongs is to restore social and cosmic orders, for Zincantecans these orders are disturbed when a wrong is committed, not because of the wrong itself, but because the victims of the wrong have anger in their hearts and will seek vengeance. The rationale for settlement procedures, then, is to placate the victims and remove the anger from their hearts. Mexican legal procedures, on the other hand,

> are directed toward restoring social and cosmic order by righting the wrong. The focus is on the offender, who disturbed the order by breaking the rules, and not on his victim, who is seen simply as an unfortunate who happened to get in the way. Even when a victim receives compensation for injuries he has sustained, the compensation is justified as righting the original wrong, and not as a means of placating his anger. Given this ideology, the facts of the case are crucial, for how can a wrong be righted unless the specifics of the wrong are known? And the wishes of the litigants are completely irrelevant. Justice is blind to persons involved, and her scales balance only when the punishment is directly equal to the wrong committed, as determined by abstract rules. In Mexican ideology there is a "right" way of doing things, apart from the wishes of the individuals involved, whereas in Zinacanteco ideology the two are inseparable. Zinacanteco litigants speak for themselves, are cavalier about the facts, and expect and receive a compromise solution. Litigants before the Mexican authorities speak only when spoken to, and then answer questions designed by the officials to uncover the "facts" of the case. Solutions follow from these "facts" and tend to place all the blame on one side, producing a zero-sum decision. (Collier, 1973, pp. 60–61)

When the interaction between two systems with inherently irreconcilable values is suddenly stepped up, as in situations of legal reform, the differences in ideologies of procedural justice may result in the extinction or subordination of one or the other system. Under colonial law there are such examples, as with the British in India

(Cohn, 1959) or the French in Tunisia (Mayer, n.d.), A more recent example is the Iranian case (Craig, 1979). Under the Shah's White Revolution, a new legal administration was set up in the rural areas to bring the village justice system in line with the national system. Craig attributes the failure of these reforms to the incompatibility of the new system's egalitarian ideology with the values of the traditional feudal system: The dissonance between traditional ideals of justice as related to a community where everyone was a known quantity and the reform ideals related to nationalism proved to be too great.

In many societies, the goal of the litigants and the system being used will determine whether the mode of dispute processing and outcome are zero-sum or distributive. For instance, Michael Lowy (1971) observed in the Ghanian town of Kofourdua (population over 40,000) that the choice of remedy or outcome is often expressed in proverbial form: (a) You should not achieve 10 before your neighbor achieves 9; (b) if you pull a string too hard it will break; (c) if you pursue your own sweet case you do bad; and (d) a good name is worth more than money. The first proverb is used in rationalizing a distributive decision, as is the second. The third proverb reflects a moral ranking system—he or she who employs a zero-sum agent is least moral. In this town, zero-sum is used by supernatural agents in catching thieves or witches. At the other end of the continuum, we find moots because they are distributive in style and outcome. The courts are in between in that they use either zero-sum or distributive decisions.

Many such examples around the world also confirm the notion that balance is highly valued in small-scale societies, and many ethnographers have documented native perceptions that justice is done when the two parties to the dispute agree on a compromise. If it is substantiated that balance is a crucial element of justice around the world, one must keep in mind that, as a universal, balance is an abstract notion—an algebraic equation. Each society then fills in the terms of the equation and specifies how balance should be achieved, whether by penal, compensatory, therapeutic, or conciliatory means. Balance is also an essential feature in social or economic transactions involving reciprocity.

Justice as Reciprocity

Reciprocity is a pivotal mechanism of justice and of social solidarity. Marcel Mauss was the first anthropologist to offer a substantial treatment of the concept in *The Gift* (1925/1967). Building on

Durkheim's discussion of social solidarity in *The Division of Labor in Society* (1893/1964), Mauss developed the idea that reciprocity in gift exchange was the most important mechanism for forging ties of solidarity within a community and between communities.

The Gift is a comparative study of exchange that aims to answer two questions:

> In primitive or archaic societies what is the principle whereby the gift received has to be repaid? What force is there in the thing given which compels the recipient to make a return? (p. 1)

Mauss's answer is that the gift is compelling. It forces its acceptance and its repayment. Mauss sees the principle of reciprocity operating in all primitive exchange transactions. The process of exchange is in fact the social and economic basis of primitive life. Further, according to Mauss, primitive gift exchange has a moral aspect, and preliterate persons as gift givers are moral persons—bound and defined by the rules of their kin and community ties.

Since Mauss's work, the concept of reciprocity has had a rich and interesting history in anthropology. Lévi-Strauss's (1949) stress on alliance and sister exchange is but one stage in the development of a theory of reciprocity. On the American side of the Atlantic, Marshall Sahlins (1972) contributed significantly to the study of reciprocity by distinguishing three forms of exchange: generalized, balanced, and negative. Generalized exchange refers to long-term gift exchange where participants do not attempt to exchange objects of equal value. Such exchange is typical of kinship relations and is predominant in societies where kinship constitutes the major principle of social organization.

Balanced reciprocity takes place between people who do not necessarily want to establish a long-term relationship. In this case, they exchange objects of equal value, and the time in which exchange takes place is usually short. Balanced exchange is predominant in peasant societies that are linked to cultural and political centers by petty market trade and political dominance. The peasants provide cities with cash crops (e.g., rice) in exchange for tools, prestige goods, and cash (Sahlins, 1972, p. 224).

> The implication of an external trade in rice is not merely an internal ban on sharing it. . . but departure from ordinary characteristics of primitive distribution in virtually all respects. (p. 224)

Sharing within the village is virtually nonexistent, and reciprocity is generally balanced. The family becomes a distinct unit with weak ties to the larger community.

Negative reciprocity refers to a situation in which the two parties try to take advantage of each other; market exchange is one such instance. Such exchange generally takes place between strangers and becomes predominant in large-scale, mobile societies characterized by weak kin ties and a strong stress on individualism. Negative reciprocal exchange has been the focus of some anthropological studies, especially those that have to do with instances of economic exploitation and political rebellions. James C. Scott (1976) has argued that beyond differences and variations among agricultural societies around the world,

> the analogous problems of subsistence, rents, and taxes for cultivators who occupy similar positions in the social structure are likely to foster a body of shared sentiments about justice and exploitation. (p. 157)

His careful examination of agriculturalists' ideology in Southeast Asia shows that reciprocal arrangements between landlord and tenant are usually unequal—the landlord has the better end of the deal. Yet farmers do not feel exploited as long as landlords fulfill their obligations toward them and as long as tenants can insure their subsistence.

> We must begin, not with the balance of exchange alone, but with its effects on the life of the peasant household. If the balance of exchange is deteriorating but the material situation of the cultivator's family is stable or even improving, discontent may be evident but it is unlikely to provoke massive unrest. It is when the worsening balance of exchange menaces crucial elements of subsistence routines, when it stretches existing subsistence patterns to the breaking point, that we may expect explosions of rage and anger. (p. 178)

In other words, the question of justice is posed not only in terms of equity but also in terms of needs—of how exchange affects livelihood. What seems to be an unequal exchange is considered fair and just perhaps because imponderables—landlord obligations—are exchanged for goods and services that can be measured and counted or perhaps because the "image of limited good" (Foster, 1965, 1972a) is operative in reducing feelings of injustice because peasants think that the "good things" exist in finite quantities and "there is no way directly within peasant power to increase the available quantities" (Foster, 1965, p. 296). Or again, perhaps because, as Sahlins (1976) and Dumont (1977) have argued, in precapitalist societies the economy is embedded within the society and precapitalists do not distinguish, as we do, economic relations from other types of social ties. Labor, wages, rent, and profit are not the yardsticks by which relations are measured in such holistic societies.

> To be sure, exotic wealth objects may be measured by people, yet they are themselves pure integers, pure graph on the wall, the "bottom line," for the profit concept does not everywhere mediate between production

and consumption. Rather, the meaning of the surplus may be embedded in its concrete specifications, the conception in the sensibility. (Gudeman, 1979, pp. 369–370)

The "substantivist" argument does not imply that precapitalists, everywhere and at all times, accept their situation, however bad, without revolt and rebellions. Historical records are filled with accounts of uprisings, even in holistic societies (e.g., Hobsbawm, 1959; Rudé, 1980). Such uprisings occur when principles of reciprocity are violated to the point of endangering subsistence, or more generally, when rulers fail in their obligations to the ruled. These obligations include maintaining peace and order (i.e., settling quarrels fairly) and contributing to the material security of the subjects. According to Moore (1978), anger is aroused when "the authority obtains an advantage, causes harm to the aggrieved individual, without any real justification in terms of gains for the society as a whole" (p. 26).

Notions of equity and fairness, justice, and injustice are an integral part of reciprocal relations, but each type of reciprocity emphasizes one of these values. In societies where generalized reciprocity is predominant, equity and need will be the two dominant values. In societies where balanced reciprocity is predominant, equality will be stressed, and in those where negative reciprocity is practiced, we might assume that the goal is to achieve an unfair advantage rather than a just one.[2]

Different forms of exchange are associated with different types of political systems. Some time ago, Morton Fried (1967) developed an evolutionary perspective of societies that he divided into three

---

[2]Here Deutsch's (1975) framework can be useful. Deutsch argues that equity, equality, and need are the central values that underlie a given system of justice. He suggests that in relations where economic productivity is the primary goal, equity is the dominant value; in relations where "enjoyable social relations" are the primary goals, equality is the dominant value; and in relations where "personal development and personal welfare" are the primary goals, need is the dominant value.

Following Miller (1974), Heath (1976) suggests an alternative set of hypotheses adapted to societies rather than group behavior (social psychology) as in Deutsch's case: "A concern with rights will be greatest in a traditional or feudal society, and where there is little possibility of social mobility and little concern with individual autonomy or independence. . . . Criteria of deserts, on the other hand, will tend to flourish in a 'liberal society.' . . . Finally, if the maintenance of existing rights is the most conservative form of justice, distribution according to need is the most radical. If the criterion of desert serves to justify inequalities of outcome, the criterion of need is equally redistributive in its implications. We would not, accordingly, expect it to flourish in inegalitarian or even in market societies" (Heath, 1976, pp. 144–145). Need, according to Heath, flourishes in places like the family or working-class communities.

types: egalitarian, ranked, and stratified.[3] He detailed the economic, social, and political systems that characterize each type. For our purposes, it is interesting to note that he associated each one of these types with a kind of exchange system.

In egalitarian societies (e.g., those composed of hunters and gatherers), the economic system is based on generalized reciprocal relations and on equal access to resources. Equity and need are the dominant values.

Redistribution is the major economic mechanism for the exchange of goods in ranked societies, and equality and need are the dominant values. In these societies, conflicts are often solved by appealing to third parties. Ranking is reflected in the way justice is carried out, and the justice system is used to maintain the hierarchical structure of the society. Barton (1919) found that for the Ifugao the relative rank of the litigants was crucial for the determination of damages. There was a sliding-fee scale: The richest payed more for a given crime. This feature of the Ifugao justice system can be conceived as a case of redistributive justice; however, in practice, this was true only when a dispute occurred within a class. When a dispute occurred across class boundaries and the plaintiff was of superior standing, the defendant had to pay the maximum fine, but if class positions were reversed and the plaintiff was socially inferior to a defendant, then the latter had to pay the minimum fine. Thus those in power used the justice system to maintain the hierarchical structure of the society.

In stratified societies, ones in which members of the same sex and equivalent age status do not have equal access to basic resources:

> Whole sectors of the population have precarious relations to subsistence while other sectors are not only free to accumulate surpluses of both productive and consumption goods, but are encouraged to do so. (Fried, 1967, p. 215)

With the rise of stratification, Fried argues, there are structures in place that may promote greater injustices: slavery and the caste sys-

---

[3]Although there has been valid criticism of this and other similar typologies which tend to romanticize the "simpler" societies, we include Fried's scheme to underscore the relation between social structure, culture and the exercise of the justice motive. Undoubtedly the political and economic variables he discusses are of a constraining nature rather than deterministic, a one-to-one fit, but certainly part of what we need to consider in defining the role of power in the area of justice. In fact, although there are exceptions (e.g., Colson, 1974; Shapiro, 1981), too little attention has been paid in the cross-cultural literature to political organization and justice as they relate to order.

tem are two examples. The Indian caste system offers a rich and complex picture with regard to the administration of justice (Dumont, 1970). Each caste dominates the castes below it, but the lower castes are not without recourse (e.g., Epstein, 1967). In addition, Moore (1978) reminds us that rulers and ruled are bound by mutual obligations. This often implicit contract contains many ambiguities and gray areas; so,

> what takes place . . . is a continual probing on the part of the rulers and subjects to find out what they can get away with, to test and *discover* the limits of obedience and disobedience. (p. 18)

In addition, given an unequal power structure, there is the ever-present danger that leaders will confuse their personal interests with the "true common interest." They need then to "justify" their actions even when they are unjust. There are several legitimizing mechanisms at their disposal. Among such mechanisms, religion and the sacred have been used to justify a legal judgment, or more globally, a social order. Writing about daily life in China in the 13th century, Jacques Grenet (1970) notes that beyond the diversity of religious practices, "religious life seems to have been dominated by a sort of latent and unexpressed obsession: that of the possibility of cosmic disorder" (p. 197). The aim of the official cult, Confucianism, in the eyes of the bureaucrats was "to ensure the preservation of a universal order which was nothing other than the counterpart, on the supernatural level, of the political order imposed upon the world by the Emperor and his officials" (p. 203).

The stress on order was also manifest in the justice system of the time. Grenet reports that the Chinese administrative system was based on one principle: that order must reign.

> The people administered were hesitant about referring to the public authorities for settling their differences, and it was only when all other solutions (compromise or arbitration) had failed that they presented themselves before the court of justice held by the sub-prefect. An accused person was immediately thrown into prison: Even an innocent person wrongfully accused was guilty of having disturbed the peace of the locality and the tranquility of the judge. . . . In short, it was a system of justice apparently designed to discourage people from acquiring a taste for legal proceedings. (1970, p. 107)

In order to ensure that the moral order reflects the political order, rulers have often entered into a tug-of-war with priests over the control of religious practices and the religious center. Nor is this phenomenon restricted to complex state societies such as China. In some hunting and gathering societies, the political leader is at the same time a religious leader. Lowie, (1967) reviewing the literature on this topic, writes:

> In a not inconsiderable number of South American societies there is a personal union of temporal and spiritual functions. In Columbia, the Kagaba and Ica . . . do not dissociate the concepts of priest and chief. Among the Yaruro [Venezuela] each moiety recognizes a shaman as its head. In the Matto Grosso the Tupi-Kawahib chief is "first of all, a shaman, usually a psychotic addicted to dreams, visions, trances and impersonations." Another Brazilian group, the Botocudo, had as the leader of a band the "strongest" man, the epithet designating not muscular strength, but spiritual ascendency. (p. 85)

Such a consolidation of power easily leads to notions of god-given and natural justice, as well as to acceptance of the social and political orders whether they are just or not.

Islam, as any other religion, has struggled with the perceived injustices of the world. But because religious and state structure overlapped, the way Islam dealt with injustices had political implications. The Jabrite philosophical school of Islam believed that God is perfectly capable of committing injustices, whereas the Mu'tazilites argued that such a view would legitimize injustice with religious arguments. In fact, according to the Mu'tazilites, God is eminently equitable, and any injustice is the work of human beings (Hammond, 1972). Other religions posit the coexistence of benevolent and malevolent spirits (e.g., the Ibo of Nigeria) (Nduka, 1977, p. 98). Some ideologies, such as that of the Protestant ethic, place squarely on the individual the responsibility of his or her station in life, and still others are quite fatalist in their acceptance of injustices:

> According to Lao Tzu, the universe is neither kindly nor righteous. It goes its way regardless of human desires and human standards of conduct. The person who tries to reform morals or to right wrongs is wasting his efforts, for he is fighting the way of the universe. (MacNair, 1946, p. 268)

And finally, in his discussion of the social psychology of the world religions, Weber (1976) describes three basic systems of ideas that attempt to give "rationally satisfactory answers to the questioning between destiny and merit: the Indian doctrine of Kharma, Zoroastrian dualism, and the predestination decree of the deus abscondidus" (p. 275). The first "unites virtuosolike self-redemption by man's own effort with universal accessibility of salvation." The second "maintains that always the powers of light and truth, purity and goodness coexist and conflict with the powers of darkness and falsehood, impurity and evil (harmful) spirits." And the third "demands the assumption of a providential, and hence a somehow rational, destination of the condemned, not only to doom but to evil" (Weber, 1976, pp. 358–359). In other words, although different religions deal differently with the issue of injustices, all do address this question.

In this section, we have examined an important mechanism of justice—reciprocity. We have argued that different types of reciprocities are associated with different forms of social and political organizations. Because reciprocity is harder to achieve in stratified societies where a leader can abuse a leadership position, religion can be used to justify injustices. But religion is only one of the means used to justify events. The following section will examine other ways that people use to rationalize the world around them.

Justifying Events

Mainly on the basis of experimental psychological data, Melvin Lerner (1980) has argued that people must maintain the belief that they live in a just world. He sees this belief as fundamental, as an essential ingredient for dealing with life's inevitable tragedies, and he describes the mechanisms people use in defense of the belief in a just world (cf. Furby, Chapter 6, this volume). Although we are unable to validate the extent to which Lerner's observations are in fact fundamental to the human condition, there is reason to believe that his insights are important. Belief in a just world is expressed in sorcery and witchcraft. In Polynesia, every person is believed to have two spirits. The first is manifest in the shadow of the living person and dies with the person. The second, the kipua, is released at the death of the person and is responsible for the many events that happen in daily life. Sicknesses are believed to be caused by the second of these two spirits, as are other punishments (Hogbin, 1934).

Adultery and murder within the joint family, as well as cases of incest and usurpation of headmanship, are also situations where spirits are called upon to punish. Hogbin (1934) notes the importance of the belief in supernatural punishment to alleviate the burden of punishing close relatives. He writes:

> Belief in supernatural punishment is important not so much as a deterrent to crime but as a psychological mechanism, whereby persons who cannot execute justice without violating their strongest sentiments may nevertheless feel confident that justice will be done. (p. 154)

Although the kipua was in those cases an instrument of justice, sometimes it could be mean, unfair, and spiteful. For instance, the kipua of a husband could kill his widow when she remarried even though she had every right to do so.

For the Polynesian and for other people as well, it is important to understand the injustices and misfortunes that befall the innocent, the moral, or the complying person. In the first and most famous anthropological study of witchcraft, Evans-Pritchard (1937/1976) emphasizes the logical explanation that witchcraft offers.

> In Zandeland sometimes an old granary collapses. There is nothing remarkable in this. Every Zande knows that termites eat the supports in course of time and that even the hardest wood decays after years of service. . . . It may happen that there are people sitting beneath the granary when it collapses and they are injured. . . . Now why should these particular people have been sitting under this particular granary at the particular moment it collapsed? . . . It was due to the action of witchcraft. If there had been no witchcraft people would have been sitting under the granary and it would not have fallen on them, or it would have collapsed but the people would not have been sheltering under it at the time. Witchcraft explains the coincidence of these two happenings. (pp. 22–23)

Witchcraft for the Azande provides an explanation for misfortunes. It is also the idiom of moral rules. A person who harbors bad feelings (e.g., ill temper, greed, spite, envy) will become, perhaps inadvertently, a witch. Thus, belief in witchcraft is important in curbing ungenerous or unfair impulses.

> A householder who kills an animal sends presents of meat to the old men who occupy neighboring homesteads. For if an old witch receives no meat he will prevent the hunter from killing any more beasts, whereas if he receives his portions he will hope that more beasts are killed and will refrain from interference. Likewise a man will be careful not to anger his wives gratuitously, for if one of them is a witch she may bring misfortune on his head by a fit of bad temper. A man distributes meat fairly among his wives lest one of them, offended at receiving a smaller portion than the others should prevent him from killing more game. (p. 54)

In this instance, witchcraft seems to operate as a leveling mechanism. Yet, ironically, witchcraft accusations are seldom directed toward the richer and more powerful members of the community, "while those who make themselves a nuisance to their neighbours and those who are weak are most likely to be accused of witchcraft" (Evans-Pritchard, 1937/1976, p. 52). This contradiction, however, is only apparent. In normatively equal relations, the fear of witchcraft will ensure proper behavior; in unequal relations, the direction of witchcraft accusations expresses differences in power and wealth. Speaking about envy, Foster (1972b, pp. 170–171) presents a similar idea: Between nonequals envy

> is that of the "have-not" for the "have," and society's concern is to structure itself in such fashion that the disruptive effects of this envy will be minimized. This is commonly accomplished by means of age-grades, social classes, or a caste system, [although] no class or caste system, can of course, eliminate the basic envy of the have-nots for the haves.

Lerner (1980) showed that belief in a just world meant justifying even injustices. Rejecting injustices also expresses, albeit in a different way, belief in a just world. Millennial cults are mass movements that demand a redistribution of justice and order in this world. The Ghost Dance cult of the Indians of the western plains of the United states sought to return to prewhite-man time when hunting was good and quarreling and witchcraft were nonexistent. The Cargo Cult of the South Pacific sees the future as one where black people will have unrestricted access to white people's goods and when black will become superior to white. Although it may be argued that conventional religions legitimize a given social order—however unjust—millennial movements are essentially revolutionary in their desire to break with the present and look for a just society (e.g., Cohn, 1970; Wallace, 1970; Weber, 1976).

Central Themes

In summarizing, we would like to reiterate several points that we believe to be especially important in the development of justice theories. The first point concerns the presence of both universality and variety in relation to justice and action in all societies. An examination of the comparative literature certainly argues for the universality of the justice motive. It appears to be true in both the comparative cultural record (and the experimental materials) that

> the awareness of injustice elicits corrective activity with such regularity that it appears for all intents and purposes to have the characteristic of a biologically based reflex of tropism. And this reflexlike action to an injustice is often of sufficient strength that all other considerations are set aside. (Lerner, n.d., p. 1)

It also appears to be true that justice has two universal components that Malinowski described in another context (1926): balance (sometimes interchangeable with reciprocity) and order. Beyond these similarities, however, there are differences. And the varieties of expression of this "reflexlike action" demonstrate the ways in which culture molds the biological, if indeed the justice motive has a biological base.

Furthermore, close examination of the varied notions of justice indicates again that justice as concept and action, whether cultural, biological, or an interplay of both, is not limitless in its variety. The same categories are noted so regularly from culture to culture that the concept of just behavior seems to revolve everywhere around the choices that so many authors in this volume have isolated: harmony, need, equality, and equity (see also Lerner, 1975; Lerner & Lerner, 1981). As revealed in writings about revolutions, however, when translated into ideology, such gentle terms may often result in grotesque behaviors involving violence, albeit justified by ideas of fairness, equality, and the like; limited concepts of justice may lead to limitless consequences.

Our second point relates specifically to justification. Justification is especially necessary in societies where there are elaborate legal structures. There is, in such places, a tension between law and justice. A one-to-one fit is probably rare. The law, used here in Donald Black's (1976) sense of governmental social control, reflects the need to maintain a given social order, and the social order is not necessarily just. But the law must, at the same time, articulate the values of a society. In the West, as rationality became a predominant value, legal institutions became increasingly characterized by rationalization (Weber, 1954).

Weber (1954) saw rationalization as a major worldwide trend. In his view, the process of rationalization of law was fivefold. It included the predictability of outcomes, the explicit nature of decisions, the coherence of rules, institutionalization, and a reference to a scientific rather than a religious causality. In this context, Weber saw the process of rationalization that accompanied the development of the nation state and market economy as a positive means of furthering justice. Yet he also identified the link between power and the rationalization of the law:

> The decisive factors in this transformation. . . were, politically, the power needs of the rulers and officials of the state as it was growing in strength and, economically, the interests of those segments of society that were oriented towards power in the market, i.e., those individuals who are economically privileged in the formally free competitive struggle of the market by virtue of their class position as property owners. (Weber, 1954, p 146)

The fact that such a link exists does not necessarily mean that justice is not the end of the law—to reverse Roscoe Pound's formulation (1909). Rather, it means that in talking about justice in rational-legal societies, we must be aware that the law can be a tool for the dominance of the political and economic elite. Here, law and justice are not always necessarily congruent.

The distinction between law and morality (i.e., justice) is an important one for anthropologists who often study people without formal legal codes. Speaking to this question, Lucy Mair (1972) writes:

> Societies without courts, says Gluckman, have *rules of law* but not *legal rules*. He calls such societies *alegal*. The rules he refers to are those that Radcliffe-Brown called *jural*. The word comes from the Latin word *jus*, meaning a right, whereas "legal" comes from the Latin *lex*, meaning a law in the sense of something enacted ("the command of a sovereign"). So justice by derivation means giving people their rights rather than enforcing laws. (p. 144)

Llewellyn and Hoebel (1961) were the first to make the distinction between the justice of the fact and the justice of the law. The justice of the fact focuses on the veracity of the litigants' claims, whereas the justice of the law relates to the question of the morality of the law—whether the law itself is just (Pospisil, 1971). Preliterate people themselves make the distinction. For example, the Kapauku Papuans distinguish between the two as follows:

> The establishment of the factual evidence for a legal case (justice of the fact) they call *boko petai* (literally "to seek the vital substance"), while the dispensation of legal justice in the adjudication of a specific case they call *boko duwai* (literally "to cut the vital substance"). Both activities were, of course, part of litigation and the primary tasks of the *tonolui*, the Kapauku legal authority. (Pospisil, 1971, pp. 235–236)

When laws do not quite correspond to normative perceptions of justice, the process of rationalization justifies the social order and makes people believe that a particular social order is just. But not all do, and that is where the study of injustice enters the academy and in particular, the anthropological literature. For it is the realization that something is wrong, that something is unjust, that spurs ethnographic reports of cultural and personal genocide (e.g., Bodley, 1975; Davis, 1977; Heizer, 1974). Yet ethnographic (concrete) studies of injustice are even less tolerated in the American academic world than are ethnographic studies of justice, and for the same reason: Justice is seen as an ethnocentric concept that is not amenable to objective and analytical treatments.

We have argued a contrary position in this chapter—that the justice motive may be a need as basic as shelter, for example, and as such, an essential requirement for understanding the human condition.

References

Aung, M. H. (1962). Burmese law tales. London: Oxford University Press.

Barton, R. (1919). Ifugao law (Vol. 15). Berkeley: University of California Publications in Archeology and Ethnology.

Berreman, G. (1960). Caste in India and the United States. American Journal of Sociology, 66, 120–127.

Berreman, G. (1966). Structure and function of caste systems, In G. DeVos & H. Wagatsuma (Eds.), Japan's invisible race: Caste in culture and personality (pp. 277–324). Berkeley: University of California Press.

Berreman, G. (1971). The Brahmannical view of caste. Contribution to Indian Sociology, 5.

Berreman, G. (1981). Social inequality: A cross-cultural analysis. In G. Berreman (Ed.), Social inequality: Comparative and developmental approaches (pp. 3–40). New York: Academic Press.

Black, D. (1976). The behavior of law. New York: Academic Press.

Bodley, J. H. (1975). Victims of progress. Menlo Park, CA: Cummings Publishing.

Bohannan, P. (1957). Justice and judgment among the Tiv. London: Oxford University Press.

Cohn, B. S. (1959). Some notes on law and change in northern India. Economic Development and Cultural Change, 8, 79–93.

Cohn, N. (1970). The pursuit of the millennium. Oxford: Oxford University Press.

Collier, J. (1973). Law and social change in Zinacantan. Stanford: Stanford University Press.

Colson, E. (1974). Tradition and contract. Chicago: Aldine.

Craig, D. (1979). Tradition and legal reform in an Iranian village. In K. F. Koch (Ed.), Access to justice (pp. 147–170). Milan: Giuffré Editore.

Davis, S. (1977). Victims of the miracle: Development and the Indians of Brazil. New York: Cambridge University Press.

Deutsch, M. (1975). Equity, equality, and need: What determines which value will be used as the basis of distributive justice: Journal of Social Issues, 31, 137–149.

Dumont, L. (1970). Homo hierarchicus. Chicago: University of Chicago Press.

Dumont, L. (1977). From Mandeville to Marx. Chicago: University of Chicago Press.

Durkheim, E. (1964). The division of labor in society. New York: Macmillan. (Originally published 1893)

Epstein, S. (1967). Efficiency and systems of rewards in rural South India. In R. Firth (Ed.), Themes in economic anthropology (pp. 229–252). London: Tavistock.

Evans-Pritchard, E. E. (1940). The Nuer. London: Oxford University Press.

Evans-Pritchard, E. E. (1976). Witchcraft, oracles, and magic among the Azande (Abridged ed.). Oxford: Clarendon Press. (Originally published 1937)

Foster, G. M. (1965). Peasant society and the image of limited good. American Anthropologist, 67(2), 293–315.

Foster, G. M. (1972a). A second look at limited good. Anthropological Quarterly, 45(2), 57–64.

Foster, G. M. (1972b). The anatomy of envy: A study in symbolic behavior. Current Anthropology, 13(2), 165–186.

Fried, M. (1967). The evolution of political society: An essay in political anthropology. New York: Random House.

Gellner, E. (1969). Saints of the Atlas. Chicago: University of Chicago Press.

Gibbs, J. L. (1963). The Kpelle moot: A therapeutic model for the informal settlement of dispute. Africa, 33, 1–11.

Gluckman, M. (1965a). The ideas in Barotse jurisprudence. New Haven & London: Yale University Press.

Gluckman, M. (1965b). Reasonableness and responsibility in the law of segmentary societies. In H. Kuper & L. Kuper (Eds.), African law: Adaptation and development (pp. 120–146). Berkeley & Los Angeles: University of California Press.

Grenet, J. (1970). Daily life in China on the eve of the Mongol Invasion: 1250–1276. Stanford: Stanford University Press.

Gudeman, S. (1979). Anthropological economics: The question of distribution. Annual Review of Anthropology, 7, 347–377.

Gulliver, P. H. (1969). Case studies of law in non-Western societies. In L. Nader (Ed.), Law in culture and society (pp. 24–68). Chicago: Aldine.

Hahm, P.-C. (1967). The Korean legal tradition and law: Essays in Korean law and legal history. Seoul, Korea: Hollym.

Hahm, P.-C. (1969). Religion and law in Korea. Kroeber Anthropological Society Papers, 41, 8–53.

Hammond, K. (1972). The idea of justice in Islamic philosophy. Diogenes, 79, 81–108.

Heath, A. (1976). Rational choice and social exchange. Cambridge: Cambridge University Press.

Heizer, R. F. (1974). The destruction of California Indians: A collection of documents from the period 1847 to 1865. Santa Barbara, CA: Pregrine Smith.

Hickson, L. (1979). Hierarchy, conflict, and apology in Fiji. In K. F. Koch (Ed.), Access to justice (Vol. IV, pp. 17–40). Milan: Giuffré Editore.

Hobsbawm, E. J. (1959). Primitive rebels. Manchester: Manchester University Press.

Hogbin, I. (1934). Law and order in Polynesia. London: Christophers.

Kluckhohn, C. (1959). The philosophy of the Navaho Indians. In M. H. Fried (Ed.), Readings in anthropology (Vol. 2, pp. 424–449). New York: Crowell.

Koch, K. F. (1969). War and peace in Jalemo. Cambridge: Harvard University Press.

Kroeber, A. H. (1925). The Yurok: Law and custom. In Handbook of the Indians of California (pp. 20–52). Washington, DC: Government Printing Office.

Lerner, M. J. (n.d.). The justice motive in social behavior: Hypotheses as to its origins and forms, II. Unpublished manuscript, University of Waterloo.

Lerner, M. J. (Ed.). (1975). The justice motive in social behavior. Journal of Social Issues, 31 (3), pp. 1–19.

Lerner, M. J., (1980). The belief in a just world. New York: Plenum Press.

Lerner, M. J., & Lerner, S. C. (Eds.). (1981). The justice motive in social behavior. New York: Plenum Press.

Lerner, M. J., & Whitehead, L. A. (1980). Procedural justice viewed in the context of justice motive theory. In G. Mikula (Ed.), Justice and social interaction (pp. 219–256). New York: Springer-Verlag.

Lévi-Strauss, C. (1949). Les structures élémentaires de la parenté. Paris: Presses Universitaires de France.

Llewellyn, K. N., & Hoebel, E. A. (1961). The Cheyenne way. Norman: University of Oklahoma Press. (Originally published 1941)

Lowie, R. H. (1925). Primitive society. New York: Boni & Liveright.

Lowie, R. H. (1967). Some aspects of political organization among the American aboriginies. In R. Cohen & J. Middleton (Eds.), *Comparative political systems: Studies in the politics of pre-industrial societies* (pp. 63–87). Austin: University of Texas Press.

Lowy, M. J. (1971). *The ethnography of law in a changing Ghanian town.* Unpublished doctoral dissertation, University of California, Berkeley.

MacNair, H. F. (Ed.). (1946). *China.* Berkeley & Los Angeles: University of California Press.

Mair, L. (1972). *An introduction to social anthropology* (2nd ed.). New York: Oxford University Press.

Malinowski, B. (1926). *Crime and custom in savage society.* London: Routledge & Sons.

Mauss, M. (1967). *The gift.* New York: Norton. (Originally published 1925).

Mayer, A. (Ed.). (n.d.). *Property law and social structure in the Middle East.* Binghamton: State University of New York Press.

Miller, D. L. (1974). *Social justice.* Unpublished doctoral thesis, Oxford University.

Moore, B. M. Jr. (1978). *Injustice: The social bases of obedience and revolt.* White Plains, NY: M. E. Sharpe.

Nader, L. (1969). Styles of courtroom procedure: To make a balance. In L. Nader (Ed.), *Law in culture and society* (pp. 69–91). Chicago: Aldine.

Nader, L. (1975). Forums of justice: A cross-cultural perspective. *Journal of Social Issues, 31,* 151–170.

Nader, L., & Combs-Schilling, E. (1976). Restitution in cross-cultural perspective. In J. Hudson & B. Galaway (Eds.), *Restitution in criminal justice* (pp. 27–44). Lexington, MA: Heath Publishing Company.

Nader, L., & Todd, H. F. (1978). *The disputing process—Law in ten societies.* New York: Columbia University Press.

Nduka, O. (1977). The traditional concept of justice among the Ibo of South-Eastern Nigeria. *Odu, 15,* 91–103.

Pitkin, H. (1972). *Wittgenstein and justice.* Berkeley: University of California Press.

Pospisil, L. (1971). *Anthropology of law.* New Haven, CT: HRAF.

Pound, R. (1909). The causes of popular dissatisfaction with the administration of justice. *Report of the American Bar Association, 29* (Pt. 1), 295–417.

Rosen, L. (1980–1981). Equity and discretion in a modern Islamic legal system. *Law and Society, 15(2),* 215–245.

Rudé, G. (1980). *Ideology and popular protest.* New York: Pantheon Books.

Sahlins, M. (1972). On the sociology of primitive exchange. In *The relevance of models for social anthropology* (Association for Social Anthropologists, Monograph 1). New York: Praeger.

Sahlins, M. (1976). *Culture and practical reason.* Chicago: University of Chicago Press.

Schlegel, S. A. (1970). *Tiruray justice: Traditional Tiruray law and morality.* Berkeley: University of California Press.

Schneewind, J. B. (1984). *Autonomy in ethical theory.* Paper presented at a Symposium on Reconstructing Individualism, Stanford, CA.

Scott, J. C. (1976). *The moral economy of the peasant: Rebellion and subsistence in South East Asia.* New Haven, CT: Yale University Press.

Seidman, R. (n.d.). *The jural postulates of African law: An inquiry into the processes of determining what is just.* Unpublished manuscript.

Shapiro, M. (1981). *Courts.* Chicago: University of Chicago Press.

Smith, W., & Roberts, J. M. (1954). *Zuni law: A field of values.* Peabody Museum Papers, *43* (1), pp. 1–175.

Starr, J. (1978). *Dispute and settlement in rural Turkey.* London: E. J. Brill.

Wallace, A. F. C. (1970). *Death and rebirth of the Seneca.* New York: Knopf.

Weber, M. (1954). *Law in economy and society* (M. Rheinstein, Ed.). New York: Simon & Schuster.

Weber, M. (1976). *From Max Weber: Essays in sociology* (H.H. Gerth & C.W. Mills, Trans. and Eds.). Oxford: Oxford University Press.

Williams, F. E. (1941). Group sentiment and primitive justice. *American Anthropologist, 43* (4), 523–539.

CHAPTER 8

Public Policy and Justice

Karol Soltan

Introduction

Public policy analysis, together with management theory and legal theory, are areas in which intellectual work in the social sciences most directly impinges on practical questions. In all three of these areas the unity of theory and practice is not a slogan of a revolutionary party but the need of everyday (and quite unrevolutionary) experience. This determines the form that interest in justice takes in the policy sciences. There is little concern with metaethics or with philosophical assumptions. There is much concern, on the other hand, with concrete and precise normative recommendations and a reliance greater than in other fields on mathematics and on empirical evidence because of their superior capacity to convince.

The most prominent advocates of the unity of theory and practice have been Marxists. But in the Marxist tradition, the unity of theory and practice has been hard to come by. In a much-praised survey of Western Marxism written in the mid-1970s, Perry Anderson (1976) condemns its main exponents for a variety of sins, for example, preoccupation with method, predominant interest in culture (especially art) instead of political economy, and obscurity of language. All are by-products of the separation of theory and practice: Marxist intellectuals are now academics (and in the period Anderson describes they were predominantly philosophers) rather than activists. Revolutionary movements in Europe have either been

KAROL SOLTAN • Department of Government and, Politics, University of Maryland, College Park, Maryland 20742. Work on this chapter was supported in part by a research grant from the Graduate School of the University of Maryland.

bureaucratized, or defeated, or both. Unity of theory and practice in the Marxist style does seem to be an unlikely prospect.

But other intellectual traditions also offer a promise of some form of unity of theory and practice. The Aristotelians (see MacIntyre, 1981) have never abandoned the goal of practical wisdom based in part on empirical knowledge. Pragmatists, such as Dewey, have advocated their own version of unity of the descriptive and the practical. This tradition, too, is alive today in the jurisprudential sociology of Selznick (1969), for example. But in terms of analytical refinement, mathematical precision, and most importantly, practical effect, surely the most successful attempts to unify theory and practice have come from what can be broadly understood as the utilitarian tradition.

The original utilitarians, Bentham, James Mill, and others, provided the theoretical justification for one of the most successful sustained programs of reform ever—that of the British radicals in the early 19th century. Three claims seemed to be central to the success of the normative criterion they proposed. They claimed that this criterion expressed, in a more articulated and systematic form, a widely held morality. They claimed, further, that it reflected the nature of moral reasoning, in particular the central place within it of *impartial benevolence*. Finally they also claimed that the utilitarian test of rightness was an objective test relying on empirical evidence.

I believe that all three of these claims were mistaken when applied to utilitarianism in its classical form. But they do accurately reflect some of the considerations that make normative theories effective in practice. Such theories must have some determinate relations to the moral positions people hold. They must be based on an acceptable theory of moral reasoning. And they must allow for objective comparisons of policies and institutions.

Public policy analysis today, to the extent it relies on any normative criteria at all, relies heavily on criteria that are either straightforwardly utilitarian or derive from the utilitarian tradition in a clearly identifiable way. Critiques of utilitarianism have been the most fruitful source of normative criteria for the evaluation of policies. The present chapter will focus on these critiques. They reflect two main departures from the assumptions of the classical utilitarians. First, the human mind is seen as more limited in its capacities than the utilitarians assumed. Thus, for example, normative tests that are both objective and precise are far more difficult to construct than it seemed to the utilitarians. I discuss this in the second part of this chapter. It is also more difficult than the utilitarians thought to construct a unified normative theory that is morally acceptable. I discuss the normative pluralism that results in the third part of the chapter. The second departure is related to the first: The human mind is seen not only as more limited but also more complex. This leads to more complex models of moral reasoning and, more generally, of the formation of morality. I discuss some of these complexities in the fourth and fifth parts of the chapter. Throughout I assume the very broad definition of justice recently made current by the work of Rawls (1971), among others. A question of justice arises whenever we evaluate decisions allocating harms and/or benefits or whenever we evaluate rules governing those decisions. On this broad definition, utilitarianism is one important theory of justice. On narrower definitions of justice, definitions I do not adopt here, utilitarianism can be seen as an alternative to justice in the evaluation of policies and institutions.

Objectivity of Standards

The basic theme of this chapter is the contrast between the simplicity of utilitarianism, especially in its classical version, and the complexities introduced by various critiques of utilitarianism. But, in fact, the utilitarian tradition is quite diverse (see, for example, Miller & Williams, 1982; Sen & Williams, 1982; Smart, 1963; and Buchanan & Mathieu, Chapter 2 in this volume). Utilitarian standards can be used for the evaluation of actions as well as for the evaluation of rules (or institutions or policies). In the first of these tasks, we conventionally make the distinction between act utilitarianism and rule utilitarianism (e.g., Smart, 1973). I will be concerned only with evaluation of institutions, however; therefore this distinction will not be relevant. Another basic distinction is between two versions of the utilitarian rule. According to the first, a rule is right if it maximizes total happiness of the relevant population. According to the second, a rule is right if it maximizes average happiness. The difference between these two rules has a practical effect where different alternative policies are likely to produce populations of different size.

There are further distinctions, within the utilitarian tradition, depending on the choice of what is to be maximized: It can be happiness or welfare or satisfaction or good or utility defined in some other way. Buchanan and Mathieu (Chapter 2 in this volume) discuss this internal complexity of the utilitarian tradition in more detail. In this chapter, by contrast, we will look at departures from utilitarianism, especially those motivated by increased recognition of the intellectual and motivational limits of human beings and of the complexity both of human minds and of human institutions.

It was the recognition of the intellectual limits of human beings that led to the realization that a utilitarian standard that is both precise and objective will not be possible. There is a trade-off between precision and objectivity that cannot be avoided. In fact, much of the development of modern normative economics out of utilitarianism can be understood as an effort to trade precision for objectivity. The original utilitarian standard required the maximization of happiness. Happiness was the difference between the amount of pleasure and the amount of pain. And both pleasure and pain were thought to be measurable the way length is, using a ratio scale, the same scale for all persons, so that it made sense to add the pleasures and pains of different people.

In fact, of course, no methods of measurement of this kind ever existed; certainly none that were objective. Objectivity requires both the use of well-defined public procedures and reliable results, reliable in the sense that different observers would obtain identical results using the same procedures. To gain objectivity, trade-offs were necessary. These have been primarily of two kinds:

1. Loss of precision. The measures of happiness were now taken to be less precise than originally thought. The numbers assigned as such measures were held to be invariant under increasingly large classes of transformations. We moved from ratio scale to interval scale, and finally to ordinal scale measures of "happiness" or utility.
2. Indirect measurement. Because happiness (or utility, or intensity of preference) is not precisely and objectively measurable, an attempt was made to find indirect measures of happiness. If X is not precisely and objectively measurable but Y is, and Y is a known function of X, then measurements of Y can substitute for measurements of X.

Loss of Precision

Although pain and pleasure are hard to measure in an objective and precise way, it is not that difficult to measure ordinal preference. Every time a person acts, every time he or she chooses one alternative over another, we obtain objective evidence of that person's ordinal preferences. Furthermore, the same scale is applicable to all persons: For every person choice is an objective indication of preference. Although various methods have also been proposed to obtain at least interval scale measures of preferences (e.g., Von Neumann & Morgenstern, 1944), most have remained controversial. In any case, no objective interval-level measures of preference are available that would use the same scale on more than one person, thus making objective interpersonal comparisons of utility possible. Interpersonal comparisons of utility are, of course, possible and meaningful (we make them all the time); the difficulty is to make them objective.

With preferences of each person measured on an ordinal scale it makes no sense to add utilities of different persons, and thus the standard utilitarian criterion cannot be applied. A far weaker, but related, criterion (Pareto optimality) can be substituted. An alternative X is Pareto preferred to Y if no one prefers Y to X and at least some people prefer X to Y. An alternative X is Pareto efficient (or Pareto optimal) if there are no alternatives Pareto preferred to it. If an alternative X is Pareto preferred to Y, then X will also be preferred by the utilitarian criterion. So only Pareto efficient alternatives can be chosen on utilitarian grounds. But clearly many Pareto efficient alternatives will not be chosen by utilitarianism. In fact, Pareto efficient alternatives can be perfectly dreadful in hundreds of ways. Although Pareto efficiency is a virtue, it is compatible with much vice.

This weakness in the Pareto criterion has given rise to various attempts to extend it or strengthen it. One possible strategy of extension quickly runs into contradictions of the sort shown in Arrow's theorem. Another strategy has given us the Kaldor–Hicks criterion.

The first strategy attempts to construct a criterion that would combine Pareto efficiency with a few other considerations. Arrow (1951) proved that even if these other considerations are extremely weak, no such criterion can be constructed. And others have proved since that this holds for a variety of weak considerations and is relatively insensitive to the precise formulation of them (Sen, 1970). This strategy of going beyond strict Pareto efficiency does not seem, therefore, very promising.

The other strategy has been, by contrast, a great success, at least as far as the range of practical applications is concerned. The Kaldor–Hicks standard weakens the Pareto efficiency criterion as follows: X is a Kaldor–Hicks improvement over Y if it would be possible for winners to compensate losers in the move from Y to X in such a way that after compensation X would be Pareto preferred to Y. Such compensation need not actually take place; it only matters that it is possible. The Kaldor–Hicks criterion is the foundation of much work in normative economics and public policy analysis (see, for example, Mishan, 1976; Stokey & Zeckhauser, 1978).

When individual preference is assumed to be measured on the ordinal scale, the Pareto criterion, and its close relatives described previously, is perhaps the most obvious normative rule to adopt, at least within the "economic-utilitarian" tradition broadly conceived. Some writers have suggested, however, that we should assume an even simpler structure of preferences for each individual—a structure we might call *dichotomous ordinal*. Each person on this view divides his or her alternatives into two, and only two, categories: the satisfactory ones and the unsatisfactory ones. This is the structure of preferences assumed in Simon's models of choice (March & Simon, 1958; Simon & Stedry, 1968) in which persons are taken as searching for a satisfactory alternative rather than maximizing utility. This is also the structure of preferences underlying behavior that distinguishes an "in favor of X" attitude from an "against X" attitude. An example is the decision whether or not to attempt to change some policy or institution (what Hirschman, 1970, has called *voice*). To decide to attempt a change is to decide the policy or institution has moved from the satisfactory to the unsatisfactory range. It is of course possible that people's preferences have a complex structure that includes both an ordinal hierarchy and a division into satisfactory and unsatisfactory ranges. But if we assume the simplest possible structure, that is, all preferences are dichotomous ordinal, then a simple version of utilitarianism can be suggested, a version, in fact, of *negative* utilitarianism.

For a negative utilitarian the appropriate standard for the comparison of policies and institutions is not the maximization of happiness but rather the minimization of suffering (Moore, 1970; Popper, 1945; Watkins, 1963). But one needs to be rather careful in formulating this rule. As it stands, for example, it appears to justify the advocacy of an unexpected and painless destruction of all life, thus eliminating all possibility of suffering (see Smart, 1963). A more satisfactory version of negative utilitarianism could be formulated on the assumption of a dichotomous ordinal preference structure. It would require us to minimize the proportion of people for whom an institution is unsatisfactory. Equivalently, it would require us to maximize the proportion for whom the institution or policy is satisfactory. If this were our normative ideal, the logical collective decision procedure to use would be approval voting (Brams & Fishburn, 1982). In approval voting, every voter can vote for as many alternatives as he or she wants (presumably all those he or she finds satisfactory). Voters are not limited to one vote. The alternative that receives the most votes wins, and that is the alternative found satisfactory by most voters.

The adoption of standards that rely on very limited information about human preferences, such as the version of negative utilitarianism previously discussed, is one way to achieve greater objectivity at the cost of a loss of precision and detail. But it is not the only way. Instead of relying on less information, we can try to rely on more indirect information. The cost is the same: We will know less, though we will find it easier to agree on what we know.

Indirect Measurement

We have no direct access to people's preferences, but we can use, as an indirect measure of a person's preferences with regard to X, his or her willingness to sacrifice other things of value in order to get or to keep X. The greater the willingness to sacrifice, the more highly valued is X. The most commonly used version of this criterion relies on the fact that money is a conveniently available measure of value and it uses the willingness to sacrifice money for X (or the willingness to pay) as an index of the value of X. On this view, we ought to choose those policies or institutions for which, in the aggregate, people are willing to pay the most. Using this index, we move from maximization of utility to the maximization of willingness to pay or (which is the same thing) the maximization of wealth. This is a criterion familiar in normative economics, but it has at least two serious limitations: willingness to pay is an imperfect indicator of utility, and it is only one form of the willingness to sacrifice.

Willingness to Pay as an Imperfect Indicator of Utility

It is true that the more you prefer something (or the more utility you derive from it), the more you are willing to pay for it. And so willingness to pay is indeed an indicator of utility. But unfortunately (from the point of view of the accuracy of this indicator) it is also true that the more money you have available the more you will be willing to pay for anything. Willingness to pay is a function of both intensity of preference and availability of money. It is a biased indicator of utility, and the bias is in favor of the wealthy. There are at least three possible responses to this problem. First, it can be ignored. This is perhaps the most common response. Second, the criterion can be used where the effects of differences in wealth or income are in some ways minimized. We can try to construct wealth-neutral markets, for example (a useful discussion is in Calabresi & Bobbitt, 1978). Finally, we can abandon utilitarianism and advocate the maximization of wealth criterion on its own merits, as an alternative to utilitarianism, not an imperfect indicator of the utilitarian criterion. This line has recently been tried by Posner (1981), but the results are not promising (see discussion in Coleman, 1982; Dworkin, 1980).

Willingness to Pay as Only One Form of Willingness to Sacrifice

If everything could be given a money price, then the willingness to sacrifice anything of value could be translated into a willingness to pay. But in fact many resources that might be sacrificed do not have an explicit money price and could not be given one without incurring substantial costs. The clearest and most notorious example of such a "priceless" resource is life. Most ordinary people, and even some economists, consider the explicit pricing of life to be a cost-imposing activity. They would be willing to pay to avoid it. Although an implicit price is given to life by all of us every day, an explicit price is rarely put on life; it is notoriously unreliable and arouses much objection. Because of these difficulties of making explicit the trade-offs between money and life, it may be useful to accept as an approximation the view that life is priceless and that therefore the willingness to sacrifice life is incommensurate with the willingness to sacrifice money. We have then two possible criteria for the evaluation of institutions and policies based on the utilitarian tradition. One is the criterion well known to normative economics: Institutions ought to maximize willingness to pay, or wealth. But the other will seem quite foreign to the calculating rationality of utilitarianism; it seems altogether too romantic: Institutions ought to maximize the willingness to risk death. Those institutions are most valued in the defense of which (or for the obtaining of which) people are most willing to risk their own death. The ultimate (utilitarian!) value of institutions is tested on barricades and battlegrounds, not in markets.

How are we to choose between these two substitute indexes of

the utilitarian criterion—between maximization of wealth and maximization of willingness to die? Most of the time in practice a choice
will not be necessary because the relevant information will be available only for one of these criteria. When the choice is between alternative ways to clean up the Chesapeake Bay, the willingness of
Americans to die in defense of their institutions is not likely to be
significantly affected. But when there is a choice, it seems clear that
all (or almost all) would give life a priority over money and would
therefore give the maximization of willingness to die a priority (a
lexical priority, in the currently popular language) over maximization of the willingness to pay. This poses a problem. Thanks to the
development of modern economics, we know something both about
what institutions and policies are likely to maximize wealth and
about how to find out which institutions and policies are likely to
maximize wealth. With the maximization of the willingness to die,
we are far more in the dark (but see Kellett, 1982).

All criteria in the "willingness-to-sacrifice" family, both the
ones discussed before (willingness to pay, willingness to risk death)
and others (e.g., willingness to sacrifice time and effort), share the
limitation I have discussed in the case of willingness to pay. Measures of willingness to sacrifice are likely to be distorted by differences in how valuable the object sacrificed is to those sacrificing
it. Thus the rich, on the average, will be willing to pay more because
each dollar means less to them (again, on the average). Similarly,
institutions will have a relatively easy time causing people to risk
lives in their defense in societies where it is widely believed that this
life is nothing compared to the bliss that awaits the martyr after
death. The situation will be different in societies in which this life is
valued more highly relative to the one after death (especially once
the latter is discounted by both the probability that it does not exist
and the probability that it will be spent in hell). Because of these
differences, one cannot simply count martyrs in order to compare
institutions.

Normative Pluralism

Utilitarianism proposes a single standard for the evaluation of
all institutions, policies, and actions. It relies on a claim that we can
summarize all our moral judgments (to the extent they are morally or
rationally justifiable) in one simple formula. Many have doubted
that we can do this. Against the monism of utilitarianism, they have

argued that human morality is too complex and our minds too limited to make it possible for a single coherent moral theory to summarize all our moral judgments. These theorists, in various ways more skeptical about the capacities of human reason, have proposed normative pluralism as an alternative. Normative pluralism holds that there are multiple standards of evaluation and that it is not possible to organize them into a single coherent normative theory in the way the utilitarians suggest.

The proponents of normative pluralism have tended to be people with a pronounced preference for inductive (rather than deductive) thinking. Instead of beginning with a few simple and precisely defined first principles and deducing multiple and complex conclusions in the manner of the utilitarian-economic tradition, they have been more inclined to immerse themselves (in various ways) in the moral and institutional complexities of the world. Description of that world has played a larger role in their thinking.

This tendency is of course present in an extreme form in those empirical social scientists whose only aim is to describe—those, that is, who do not aspire to derive any normative conclusions from their work. Almost all empirical descriptive research on justice (and on other aspects of morality) has accepted some form of normative pluralism. This is true both of experimental work in social psychology (e.g., Deutsch, 1975; Leventhal, 1976; see the review in Soltan, 1982), in survey research in sociology (Alves & Rossi, 1978; Jasso & Rossi, 1977), and in the detailed look at how ordinary people actually think about justice that Hochschild's *What's Fair?* (1981) provides through her in-depth interviews. The conclusion of all these studies is always that people use more than one standard of justice. The conclusion is frequently also that different standards are felt to be appropriate in different circumstances. Hochschild, for example, concludes that we distribute according to need within the family. In economic organizations, we distribute according to desert. In the political sphere, when allocating basic political rights and liberties, we use the rule of equality.

Empirical social scientists are not the only ones who defend some version of normative pluralism. A variety of normative theories of distributive justice are also pluralist. Among the empirical social scientists, the work of Nicholas Rescher (1966) is often cited. But Rescher's position, though it recognizes a variety of principles of distribution, is not in any deeper sense pluralist because he accounts for this variety on basically utilitarian grounds. Among more recent theorists, an analysis of the language of political and moral discourse leads David Miller (1976) to conclude that there are at least three criteria of distributive justice: rights, desert, and need. These three, according to Miller, cannot be reduced to a single normative standard, utilitarian or otherwise. They are necessarily distinct and will be appropriate in different types of circumstances. Lucas (1980) has also relied primarily on an analysis of the use of language, but he considered a broader range of material and arrived at a correspondingly more complex set of conclusions. A quite different, Aristotelian, form of pluralism has been recently defended by Galston (1980). Finally, Walzer (1983) has proposed a version of pluralism in distributive standards as the most attractive form of egalitarianism. If different standards are used in different spheres, no one group will be able to dominate all spheres, and the prevention of such domination is, according to Walzer, the primary goal of egalitarianism.

If normative pluralists are correct, then the effort of philosophers and social scientists should shift from attempts to construct and refine overall normative theories (theories like utilitarianism and Rawls's contractarianism) and from attempts to apply these theories to concrete policy problems. We should be concerned rather with a different set of problems. These would include the articulation and clarification of particular standards or principles, the elaboration of the ways in which these standards can be and are related to each other, and the study of what makes different standards appropriate to different situation types.

Clarification of Standards

It is reasonably obvious that standards need to be clear (i.e., objective) if they are to give effective guidance in the making and in the evaluating of policy decisions. In the previous section of this chapter, I have outlined some of the changes in the utilitarian-economic tradition introduced to accommodate this requirement. The task was simplified by the fact that there was only one standard to be made more objective, that is, the utilitarian standard. A serious pluralist by contrast must do the same for multiple standards. As far as I can see, this work has barely begun. We do, however, have one excellent model for how this work ought to be done. I have in mind the analysis of equality performed by Douglas Rae and his associates (1981). They show how, except under very special circumstances (absent in real life situations), the idea of equality is in fact a set of ideals that often conflict with each other. Each one of these equality ideals can be defined with some precision, but equality in general is simply too internally complex and self-contradictory an ideal to provide consistent guidance in evaluation.

Relations among Standards

Relations among standards can take a variety of forms, but it will be useful to consider two ideal types of such relations. I will call them the model of principles and the model of rules (cf. Dworkin, 1977). If we think of standards on the model of principles, we think of them as arguments with a certain weight. The influence of a standard on evaluations and on decisions depends on its weight. The relative weights of different standards also determine what trade-offs we would be willing to accept among them, how much freedom, for example, would we be willing to sacrifice for a given gain in equality. In the most simpleminded versions of the model of principles, we might assume that the weight attached to each standard is constant and does not change from situation to situation. But there is really no reason to be that simpleminded. How much freedom we are willing to sacrifice for a given gain in equality will surely depend on how much freedom and equality we have. The weight of these two standards (freedom and equality) will therefore vary, and it will vary in a systematic way that is best captured by that standard device of price theory—the indifference map. Each line on an indifference map, such as the one in Figure 1, connects all points representing combinations of goods (in this case equality and freedom) between which a person is indifferent. Indifference curves farther to the "northeast" in the diagram represent more preferred combinations of goods. If the indifference curves were straight lines in Figure 1, it would indicate that the weights attached to equality and freedom are constant and do not depend on how much equality and freedom we have. But in general we can safely assume that these weights will not be constant.

But even the indifference curve model seems too crude as an account of the relation among independent standards. In institutional design, we do not trade off equality and freedom (or need and desert) in a way we might trade off, say, quality and quantity when we buy wine. Perhaps the best analogy here is to the work of an architect. This may involve some quantitative trade-offs of the sort described by the indifference curve. But for the most part, it is more akin to solving a puzzle than to solving a maximization problem by choosing the optimal trade-offs. The main design problem is how to

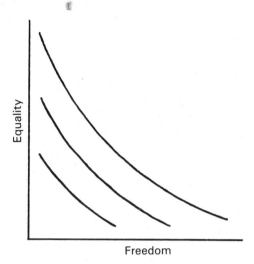

Figure 1. Trade-off between freedom and equality.

fit together different qualitative desiderata. The role a standard plays in any given design will depend on how, in the case of that particular design, its demands can be fit together with the demands of other standards. Weights or indifference curves will be of limited significance in this process.

If relations among standards take the form of the *model of rules*, no weights are given to these standards, and no trade-offs among them are possible. Instead, for each situation type that we define, we assign a unique standard as appropriate for use in that type of situation. Once we know in what type of situation we find ourselves, we know also which unique standard to use, and our decision is fully determined. So although we accept many standards, these standards never really conflict because they never apply simultaneously in the same situation. The standards therefore have no weights nor are indifference curves required to describe relations among them.

The model of rules is an extreme one, and it is unlikely to find broad application in practice. What we are likely to find instead is closer to the model of principles: a set of standards with different weights that vary from situation to situation. On the indifference curve model, the weight of one principle relative to another will depend exclusively on the extent to which the demands of the two principles are already satisfied. We find, however, that the weight of a standard depends on more than that. A few examples will be useful (in a different context these might be proposed as empirical hypotheses worthy of further investigation).

1. The requirements of *formal justice* (explicit rules impartially applied, treat equals equally) appear to increase in weight as a function of weakness of trust in a situation. The weaker the trust the greater the importance of formal justice, that is, of explicit and objective rules. In an organization that trusts its managers, for example, promotion on the basis of merit may be held to be fair even if merit cannot be defined with great precision or measured. In an organization with little trust, by contrast, no one will believe that promotions are really based on merit unless merit is made measurable. Failing that, something as objective as seniority may be held more equitable as a basis for promotion.

2. Some principles are applicable only where there is sufficient agreement on relevant issues. So, for example, distribution according to need will be more appropriate where there is agreement on the definition of need—where there is, in short, a shared altruism. Distribution according to desert (or merit) will be, by contrast, more appropriate where there is agreement on the relevant standards of evaluation, the standards that determine who deserves praise or criticism, reward or punishment.

3. In certain situations the choice of what would be easiest to agree on is more appropriate than the choice of what is right. In the terminology I develop in the next section, morality of compromise and convention is sometimes more appropriate than the morality of right. What is required by the morality of convention is furthermore itself dependent on circumstances. Sometimes it is the protection of legitimate expectations established by relevant precedent (Soltan, in press). At other times it is absolute equality in the allocation of resources. But there are many other possibilities as well.

The morality of convention, no matter what it requires, is appropriate whenever the benefit to be derived from agreeing rather than disagreeing far outweighs any differences between the alternatives to be agreed upon. It is appropriate, in short, in situations that approximate what Schelling (1963) has called coordination games (and the requirements of the morality of convention are closely related to choice in coordination games). Among examples of such situations are those where the cost of disagreement is very high and where agreements are fragile. Perhaps feudal society in Europe fits this description (this is Miller's [1976] view). A Hobbesian state of nature certainly does fit. Other examples include situations where the matter to be decided is relatively trivial. Splitting the difference or dividing a good (a pie) equally are most appropriate when no one wants to spend time on a decision because the resources at stake are too trivial. Splitting the difference and absolute equality are also characteristically conventional distributive decisions.

In the three examples just cited the weight of a standard is a function of what is clear or unclear in a situation, what is agreed upon or not agreed upon in a situation, and what costs and benefits various methods of conflict resolution carry in a situation. There is a fourth consideration, however, which is perhaps more important than any of these three. The appropriateness of a standard depends on institutional loyalties and traditions inherited from the past. We are neither entirely free to choose whatever standards we want, nor rational enough to choose them on the basis of the persuasiveness of rational and explicit arguments alone. For that reason, it is certainly true in fact that the weight we attach to various standards is influenced by institutional precedent and by tradition. But it is also arguably a good thing that this should be so. Certainly, many have deduced from the limited capacities of human reason the conclusion that most of the institutions we inherit are likely to contain much more wisdom than we could ever consciously understand. As they have evolved, they adapted piecemeal to their complex environment in a way intended or designed by no single person. And no single person is likely at any given moment to fully understand the institutional result. Such institutions then deserve our loyalty even if our understanding of why they are the way they are is limited. In evaluating policies we ought to rely on standards our institutional loyalties suggest. They represent both a collective wisdom (greater than anything an individual may possess) and a wisdom based on long experience (experience longer than the life span of any individual). In the history of political thought, this view and the severe assumptions about human limitations on which it rests have been associated with conservatism and the political right (e.g., Burke, 1790/1967; Hayek, 1973). I do not believe this is necessarily so, but the argument to the contrary is far too complex to develop here.

Complexity of Impartiality

One of the more pervasive controversies in the social sciences is the controversy between advocates of the use of complex models of the human mind and advocates of simple models. The simpler the model of the human mind, the more explanation of human behavior relies on environmental and situational variables. The complexity of human behavior is seen as a set of responses of a basically simple mind to a complex environment.This is, for example, the position of behaviorism in psychology and of someone like Gary Becker (1976) in economics. It is a position that has considerable successes to its credit. It turns out that one can explain much of human behavior based on the most rudimentary assumptions about the human mind, that is, with very little understanding of human minds. For some purposes, however, more complex models (and deeper understanding) are necessary. They are necessary, for one, just to make sense of utilitarianism. But they are even more necessary, I will suggest in the present section, to correct for the oversimplifications of utilitarianism.

According to a commonly accepted simple model of choice, all behavior is a product of the maximization of some utility function, a function that represents the values and preferences of the person whose behavior it is. The utility function of Person A is written

$$u_A = f(x_1, \ldots, x_i, \ldots, x_n)$$

where each x_i is some variable capable of affecting the well-being of Person A. For certain limited purposes, we can restrict what these variables are assumed to be. Thus, for example, some economic models assume that each x_i represents the quantity of some commodity consumed by Person A. But the more general model makes no such assumption. In fact, it makes no substantive assumptions about the content of the Function u and usually makes only the most minimal assumptions about its form. Complexity of decision-making models can be developed from this starting point in a number of ways. I consider two main ones in this chapter. In this section I discuss models that incorporate an impartial component into the simple utility function. It turns out that simple models of impartiality (which I consider first), such as those of Harsanyi, are inadequate. We have to recognize the diversity of impartial points of view. I suggest later three different pure types of impartiality (or morality). Then in the next section, I turn to a different kind of complexity due to the difference between treating institutions (or actions, or persons) as means and treating them as ends. I conclude that institutions and actions can be rational in two very different ways and that our evaluation of institutions and actions must be correspondingly complex.

Simple Models of Impartiality

Even the simplest utilitarianism appears to require a more differentiated model of choice than the simple utility-maximizing model sketched before. The appropriate model has been most fully elaborated by Harsanyi (1955, 1976, 1982). In it, each person has two utility functions. The first, a moral or impartial ordering, is used by a person only in those, possibly rare, occasions when he or she attempts an evaluation of a situation or institution not from his or her personal point of view but more impartially and objectively. The other ordering, personal (or subjective), is used at other times.

Given this model of choice, utilitarianism can be seen as a recommendation concerning how the impartial component of utility ought to be constructed or how morality ought to be formed. In Harsanyi's view, an impartial (or moral) choice in any situation is the choice one would make if one had an equal chance to be each person in that situation. This is proposed as an elaboration of a view that goes back at least to Adam Smith (1759/1976), according to which the standpoint of an impartial but sympathetic spectator defines what morality and justice require. The rational rule to adopt in such choice is to maximize the average of the utility functions of all the persons in that situation, and this is the utilitarian rule.

Harsanyi seems to assume that in computing our utilitarian impartial preferences each person takes into account only the self-interested, personal ("subjective") preferences of all the persons affected. But he does not make clear what is the justification for this strong assumption. In Harsanyi's view, my preference for X over Y will enter into the utilitarian calculation if it is due to my being better off under alternative X, but it will not enter if it is due to my belief that X is (objectively) better than Y or more perfect in the eyes of the Lord or in closer agreement with natural law. Morally based preferences of any kind are excluded in the determination of moral preferences according to this utilitarian criterion. Such a conclusion is in line with the utilitarian tradition but not with the simple idea that moral preferences ought to be determined by imagining how you would choose if you were equally likely to hold any position in a situation.

This should become clearer if we elaborate Harsanyi's still very simple model of human preferences slightly. We can distinguish three utility functions: the self-interested one, the impartial one, and a third, we might call it complete utility, that combines the elements of self-interest and impartiality. It is the complete utility function that is revealed in behavior. It will only rarely depend exclusively on self-interest and even more rarely exclusively on impartiality. Most often the two will be mixed in various proportions.

With this elaboration it should become clear that if we had an equal chance of holding any position in a situation, we would not choose a rule that resembles traditional utilitarianism all that closely. We would not choose to maximize the average self-interested utility of all the persons involved, which is (approximately) the utilitarian criterion. We would choose instead to maximize the average complete utility, and that is quite different. The utilitarian rule ignores each person's morality; the rule that maximizes complete utility does not. The latter rule also leads to paradoxes that make it unlikely that it would ever displace the traditional utilitarian rule.

If the maximization of average complete utility becomes the utilitarian rule, then there will be circumstances in which utilitarianism reduces to the relativist position according to which what is believed to be right in a given society is in fact right for that society. This will follow in the case of all societies in which moral indoctrination is strong enough. In such societies, a population's response to an institution or policy will be primarily a function of the degree of agreement between the institution or policy and moral standards widely held in the society. Self-interest will affect the response relatively less and will be therefore taken into account less by this form of the utilitarian criterion. The institutions that are believed to be right will be judged to be right on utilitarian grounds.

This consequence is avoided in most versions of utilitarianism by restricting what enters into the function to be maximized. Instead of maximizing average utility taking each individual's (complete) utility function as given, these rules allow only certain aspects of the individual's utility to count. One possibility is to maximize average self-interested utility, abstracting from the effect of morality on each individual's response. But why stop there? Other versions of utilitarianism have also required that only those self-interested orderings that are based on adequate information and are otherwise rational ought to enter into utilitarian calculations. Some have also required that we abstract from any "antisocial" desires (e.g., envy or sadomasochism) that might be found in the population (see, e.g., Harsanyi, 1982). These restrictions make the conclusions when applying a utilitarian criterion more palatable. But they also have at least two less desirable consequences. They make it all but impossible to have objective comparisons of institutions based, even approximately, on the utilitarian criterion. They also depart from Harsanyi's simple notion that utilitarianism can be thought of as a product of rational choice behind a certain kind of "veil of ignorance."

Perhaps the most famous alternative to utilitarianism is Rawls's (1971) theory of justice. In Rawls's theory, the principles of justice are the principles that would be agreed to in a situation designed to guarantee the fairness of agreements (hence "justice as fairness" is Rawls's slogan). Such a situation, according to Rawls, is one in which all parties to the agreement are kept ignorant about the position they would hold in the society in which the principles of justice will apply. They are also ignorant about their own moral beliefs (their sense of justice and their conception of the good). In such a situation all relevant differences among these parties are in practice eliminated; agreement is possible because all parties base their decision on the same knowledge about themselves and the world. Thus Rawls's model of contract among parties in what he calls the original position is very similar to Harsanyi's. Yet the normative conclusions of Rawls are different from Harsanyi's utilitarianism. Instead of the simplicity of a single utilitarian rule, the most elaborate version of Rawls's theory proposes three principles in a "lexical order." The first priority goes to the principle that maximum liberty be guaranteed to every individual compatible with like liberty for all. Only if we cannot choose among alternative institutions on the basis of this principle do we rely on the second that requires that positions be open to all in accordance with fair equality of opportunity. Only when institutions cannot be ranked relative to each other on the basis of both of these two principles will the third one be used: Inequalities are justified only when they improve the position of the least advantaged (for more details, see Buchanan & Mathieu, Chapter 2 and DiQuattro, Chapter 4, in this volume).

The immediate source of the difference between the conclusions of Harsanyi and Rawls is quite simple. For Harsanyi, the choice behind a veil of ignorance requires the assumption of an equal probability of holding any position in society. For Rawls, choice behind a veil of ignorance in the original position requires ignorance both about what position anyone will hold and about the probability of holding any position. For Harsanyi, impartiality means assuming one is equally likely to be in any position. For Rawls, it means assuming one does not know how likely one is to be in any position. In the impartiality-imposing situation on Harsanyi's model, rational choice clearly requires that we maximize expected utility. The utilitarian rule is the conclusion. In the impartiality-imposing situation on Rawls's model it is less clear what it would be rational to do. Rawls argues in favor of maximizing the minimum, that is, choosing that alternative in which the worst off are best off. If we accept this, then Rawls's third principle follows. But the argument for the other principles and for the strict priorities among them is far more complex and goes considerably beyond the sort of modeling that Harsanyi has done. A key, though often neglected, role in the argument is played by the criterion of stability. A theory of justice is preferred (according to this criterion) if institutions based on it are more stable (in the sense defined) than those based on alternative theories. An institution is stable to the extent it is voluntarily complied with or to the extent it can survive on the persuasive force of the arguments justifying it and does not require other kinds of force. Rawls claims institutions based on his theory would be more stable in this sense than institutions based on utilitarianism.

Rawls's stability criterion takes us away from the basic model of impartiality as choice by self-interested parties behind a "veil of ignorance." It moves us closer to some other alternatives to utilitarianism, which require more basic departures from the utilitarian view of the process through which the impartial aspect of utility functions ought to be constructed, and which introduce greater complexity into our understanding of impartiality.

Three Moral Points of View

We can begin the discussion by considering again the idea of impartial choice as the choice we would make if we had an equal chance of being in all positions in a situation. That idea leads to paradoxes in its general form, as I have argued before. The conclusion that we maximize average complete utility is not sensible in general (as I explained). But the conclusion may be more reasonable in special cases. For example, in situations where we can presume that most people are (almost) purely self-interested, the maximize-average-complete-utility rule reduces to the more familiar utilitarian rule: Maximize average self-interested utility. It so happens that human behavior in markets is in this way almost exclusively self-interested. So for market-related behavior, the Harsanyi model gives a reasonable solution. But in situations where behavior is heavily influenced by morality, the Harsanyi model is inadequate. This is clearest in the pure case. Consider a society in which all individuals act exclusively on impartial principle and are uninfluenced by self-interest. The maximize-complete-utility rule would require us to take an average of principled positions. This would be what utilitarianism demands (on this extended view, based on the Harsanyi model). But principled positions are not the sorts of things that ought to be averaged. The resolution of a conflict by splitting the difference (i.e., averaging) is usually a sign that the parties are willing to depart from principle (in order to avoid higher negotiation costs). To avoid such unsatisfactory conclusions, we need a more complex model of impartiality.

The tradition of normative political economy, a tradition whose elements I have been sketching in this chapter, characteristically establishes a close relation between its models of individual moral reasoning and its models of collective decision making. This is, I believe, a feature of the tradition that is worth preserving. At a sufficient level of abstraction, one can construct a single model with two interpretations. So, for example, Arrow's theorem can be taken to show both the impossibility of a certain type of criterion for the evaluation of institutions and the impossibility of a certain type of collective decision procedure.

Moral reasoning can be indeed usefully thought of as an internalized collective decision in an idealized form (cf. Kohlberg, 1979; Mead, 1934). We can, up to a point, develop jointly our understanding of these two processes, that is, collective decisions and the formation of the moral point of view. But taking this task seriously will force us rather quickly beyond the confines of the usual utilitarian model. The processes of collective decision can be divided into two aspects or stages. The first is a position-changing stage, such as a debate in a parliament. The second is a position aggregation stage, such as a vote in a parliament. The first stage is not at all represented in the models of contemporary political theory, whether in utilitarianism (Harsanyi), welfare economics (Arrow), or contractarianism (Rawls). Instead, a collective decision is obtained in these models in two ways: by position aggregation exclusively (as in Arrow's social welfare function) or by defining the situation of choice in such a way that collective decisions are reduced to individual decisions because all differences between individuals are eliminated by assumption (this is true both in Harsanyi's construction and in Rawls's original position). This misses, I believe, precisely the most important area of overlap between collective decisions and the process of formation of morality. I have in mind the various processes of position change. These can be studied, for example, as an aspect of n-person cooperative games (we could ask what contributes to the equilibrium properties of alternatives in such games) or under the heading of theories of preference formation, a subject explicitly and deliberately left open by economics (with some exceptions: Hirschman, 1982; McPherson, 1983; Michael & Becker, 1973; Stigler & Becker, 1977). But I think it will be good to start by distinguishing various types of position-changing processes.

We can distinguish at least three pure types of position-changing processes. They correspond to three different methods of collective decision making and to three different forms of morality. I call the three, bargaining, reconciliation, and argument on merits (cf. Barry, 1965). In bargaining, although each party's bargaining position changes, the underlying preferences and values are not expected to change. There is no right solution the parties could find; at best there may be solutions easy to agree on, thus saving on bargaining costs. If Schelling (1963) is right, it is the obviousness of a solution that makes it easy to agree on. In bargaining, therefore, it is obviousness, not rightness, that matters. In an argument on merits, by contrast, it is rightness that matters. The parties assume there may be a correct solution. They attempt to find it and to persuade others of its correctness. The goal of argument on merits is not simply to change the publicly stated positions of the other parties but to change something deeper—their underlying preferences and values. The means used are rational arguments. Reconciliation also aims to transform the preferences and values of others, but it uses different means. It attempts to enhance empathy and develop mutual comprehension through fuller communication, forgiveness, and the unconditional giving of trust. When these three processes are internalized, they give rise to three pure forms of morality. Bargaining gives rise to a morality of compromise and convention. Argument on merits gives rise to a morality of rightness and justice. Reconciliation gives rise to a morality of love. In reality, of course, these three forms will almost never appear in pure form. Most people, most of the time will exhibit various mixtures of the three.

In the discussion that follows, I abstract from some of the complexity in the model of choice these distinctions introduce. I consider the morality of compromise and the morality of right, but not the morality of love. Morality of love is, unfortunately, both less relevant to public policy and more difficult to understand. I will also not discuss further complications that seem related to the morality of love, such as the inclusion of an altruistic component as distinct from the impartial component in the utility functions. As Sen has argued (1977), this inclusion constitutes a less drastic departure from the assumption of self-interest that is usual in economic discussion. Impartiality (or what Sen has called *commitment*) constitutes a more serious and therefore more interesting departure.

If we thus exclude reconciliation (and the morality of love), two kinds of conflicts remain to consider: conflict of interest and conflict of principle. Bargaining to a compromise is a method appropriate for the resolution of only the first of these two. Argument on merits, based on the assumption that some solutions are better than others, is appropriate for both kinds of conflicts but in quite different ways.

The morality of convention simply picks that alternative that would be easiest to agree on. The morality of right picks the alternative backed by the most persuasive arguments. Morality of convention minimizes the costs of collective decision making; the morality of right does not. There will be times when the higher costs of the morality of right will be worth incurring, but this will not always happen. The relation between the morality of right and the morality of convention seems to me much like the relation between science and common sense. We know that science is better, but it cannot replace common sense. Without the latter we could not survive.

To determine what alternative would be chosen if we were choosing in accordance with the morality of convention, we must know which alternative would be chosen at the lowest cost (this would mean, primarily, in the shortest time). If we run collective decision experiments, we would not be interested to find out which alternative is chosen most often but rather which alternative is chosen when the choice is made most quickly and easily. If you were a judge trying to choose in accordance with the morality of convention, you would not ask, following Posner (1977), what alternative would the parties have agreed to, had they had a chance to agree in advance. You would ask instead what alternatives would be easiest to agree on.

Judges, however, will want—at least sometimes—to choose in accordance with the morality of right. The process of choice is then quite different. It can be thought of as an argument on merits. Those inclined to political philosophy may think of Socratic dialogue as the appropriate model. Those with an interest in law may think of it as an idealized form of legal debates in courts (cf. Ackerman, 1980, 1984). The question morality of justice asks is: What policies or institutions would be chosen in situations where the force of argument is the only force? These are what Habermas has called *ideal speech situations* (1970, 1973; see also McCarthy, 1981). The situations may involve either conflict of interest or conflict of principle (or both). If the conflict is a conflict of principles, then the persuasive arguments are applied to the preferences of the parties directly. The goal is to bring those preferences in closer agreement with each other. If the conflict is a conflict of interest, on the other hand, the preferences of the parties can be assumed to be immune from the effect of persuasive arguments. But persuasive arguments may still influence the collective decision: They may favor one or the other of the possible compromises among existing interests. Utilitarianism can best be seen as a moral theory appropriate to this sphere of morality, that is, to a morality of right applied to conflicts of interests. In other spheres, other theories will hold their own.

The main alternative is the situation in which conflicts of principle are resolved by arguments on merits. To find out what would be chosen in such situations, we must determine what arguments have the greatest persuasive force. This can be done empirically to the extent situations in which the force of argument is the only force can be approximated in reality. I believe they can be.

Such situations must be, first of all, ones in which the causal force of self-interest is controlled for (as much as possible). To the extent they are, they will impose impartiality on those choosing within them. They must be, further, situations in which the process of position change approximates as closely as possible a pure form of argument on merits. Elements of bargaining and reconciliation (and the forces associated with them) are relatively weak. Other forces and constraints that impinge on human evaluation and choice must also be relatively weak. The effect of biases, prejudices, irrational fears, and other such factors must be controlled for as much as possible.

In order to achieve this, we need first an operational criterion that would separate the rational factors that influence preferences and values (i.e., rational arguments) from irrational factors. And then, of course, we need some way to control for the latter. This is more complex than it may appear (see Soltan, in press), but it is not impossible. The result ought to be a wide range of studies both in natural settings and in experiments aiming to discover what gives force to moral arguments, and, therefore (indirectly) what alternatives would be chosen in situations in which the only force is the force of argument. A number of existing studies are either explicitly designed to do this (Soltan, 1983) or else can be interpreted as doing it even though the intention of the authors was different (e.g. Brickman, 1977; Frohlich & Oppenheimer, 1984). This seems a very fruitful line of research for the future.

Institutions as Ends and as Means

In the previous section, I sketched some aspects of a more complex view of human preferences and of the impartial aspect of those preferences in particular. In this section, I will introduce a further complexity into the model of preferences and a corresponding complexity in the standards of evaluation of institutions, a complexity that roughly corresponds to the traditional distinction in moral philosophy between teleological theories (with utilitarianism as an example) and deontological theories (with Kant as the example).

Based on two independent contrasts, between self-interest and impartiality and between ends and means, we can distinguish four ways to evaluate an action, a policy, or an institution. These four types of evaluation take the following forms:

1. "X in itself is better than Y in itself for me." This is an evaluation of X and Y as ends in themselves from the self-interested point of view. X is judged to be more intrinsically rewarding than Y.
2. "X is better than Y for me as a means to my set of ends E." This is an evaluation of X and Y as means to the ends I accept. The point of view is still self-interested, but X and Y are now seen as instruments to other ends.
3. "X in itself is better than Y in itself." This is an evaluation of X and Y as ends in themselves from an impartial point of view. The consequences of X and Y will not matter to this judgment. We might call it an impartial deontological evaluation.
4. "X is better than Y as a means to the set of collective ends E." This is an evaluation of X and Y as means to the set of ends E. This may be, as a special case, a single end, such as the end of maximizing average happiness. We have here, roughly, the form of an impartial teleological judgment.

Utilitarianism is a normative position that puts forward one form of the judgment of this fourth type—what I have called an *impartial teleological judgment*. It treats institutions and policies as instruments and nothing but instruments in the service of the ultimate goal of maximizing average happiness or average utility. Similarly, a common view in normative economics sees institutions and politics as nothing but (good or bad) instruments for the maximization of wealth. The view of institutions as nothing but instruments is common not just in normative theories such as these but also in explanatory theories in the social sciences. Perhaps the best examples are provided by some forms of functionalism (e.g., Merton, 1968; Stinchcombe, 1968; Sztompka, 1974). In functionalism, the institutional goal is taken to be survival, and features of the institution are explained by showing how their consequences favor the survival of the institution. An instrumental view is both more common and more reasonable for some institutions than for others. Both participants and outside observers tend toward an instrumental view of special purpose organizations such as a modern industrial corporation or a trade union. For other institutions, for example, families, the instrumental view will be less common, at least outside the social sciences.

In the case of formal organizations, the goals are publicly held by the organization itself and used to justify decisions within it. The goals may be to produce the best car in its class, to capture 30% of the market, or to land a man on the moon before the end of a decade. In other cases, the goals may be imputed to the institution by outside observers. The ends proposed by utilitarianism and normative economics can operate either way. In management and in public policy, the instrumental view of institutions is the dominant view. It is in fact dominant more generally, not only when applied to institutions but to anything that is (even in part) a product of human design. The instrumental view dominates what Simon has called the sciences of the artificial (1969).

Alternatives to the instrumental view are not nearly as clear nor as well developed. It is difficult to see how institutions can be rational except as effective instruments and how they can be justified if they are not rational. Yet the view that institutions are nothing but means to collective goals that are established independently is not the only view.

Public policy analysis and, more generally, normative theory within the social sciences inherit first of all from moral philosophy the distinction between deontological and teleological theories. Teleological theories evaluate actions and institutions by their consequences, their effect on the accepted goals or goal (the telos). Deontological theories evaluate actions and policies without regard to consequences, as right or wrong, good or bad, just or unjust in themselves. In the area of legal theory, which increasingly overlaps with policy analysis (Ackerman, 1984), perhaps the chief defender of this view has been Charles Fried (1978). But the difficulty of abandoning the instrumental view is illustrated by a number of recently developed alternatives to utilitarianism, which on closer inspection turn out to be simply different versions of instrumentalism. The work of Dworkin (1977) and MacIntyre (1981) will serve as examples.

In an extensive review of Rawls's book, Dworkin (1977) distinguishes three kinds of normative political theory: Goal-based theories take collective goals as fundamental; right-based theories take rights as fundamental; duty-based theories take duties as fundamental. Goal-based theories are, roughly, those that treat policies and institutions purely as means to collective goals. Duty-based theories are those that impose requirements on policies or institutions no matter what the consequences are for the collective goals. So far this is the traditional contrast between teleology and deontology. But it is rights-based theory that Dworkin himself elaborates in his jurisprudence, and it is as a rights-based theory that he praises Rawls's position. Rights-based theories treat policies and institutions as means to individual goals. They treat individual rights as fundamental, and an individual has a right to something according to a theory if the theory requires that the individual get it, if he or she wants it. The contrast between goal-based and rights-based theories can be made clearer by considering the institutions that constitute best models for each. A special purpose formal organization with well-defined collective goals is the best model for a goal-based theory. A contract requiring the agreement of all parties affected is the best model for a rights-based theory. For that reason, among others, Dworkin has no trouble identifying Rawls's contractarianism as a rights-based theory. The important thing to notice is that the rights-based theories Dworkin advocates are still instrumentalist. Institutions are seen as instruments, though instruments in the service of individual rather than collective goals. Such theories are in fact commonly accepted in the normative economics-public policy-public choice community in a way more purely deontological theories are not.

The fundamental contrast in MacIntyre's theory is that between goods internal to a practice and goods external to a practice. Virtues, according to MacIntyre, are those acquired human capacities that are indispensable for the provision of internal goods. And MacIntyre's central goal is to develop a virtue-centered moral theory. Much then turns on the identification of internal goods. If we take, as does MacIntyre, chess as an example of practice or institution (MacIntyre distinguishes these two, but the distinction is not relevant to my argument here), then a certain kind of mastery of a complex problem will count as a good internal to chess, whereas money or status will be an external good. Money and status will be external because, although it is possible to achieve them by playing chess, there are also other ways of achieving them (e.g., playing the New York lottery). A good is internal to a practice if it can be defined only in terms of the practice and if it can be recognized only through the experience of participating in the practice. Internal goods are distinctive in the essential connection they have to particular practices or institutions. The contrast between internal and external goods is thus, roughly, the contrast between goals that can be recognized only locally and those that, at least potentially, could be universally recognized.

Public policy based on MacIntyre's virtue-centered moral theory would be concerned with the development and protection of those institutions and practices within which we can pursue internal goods. These would be institutions that both require and promote the development of virtues. This moral theory is just as goal-based as utilitarianism; it only rejects the collective goal that the utilitarians propose. It rejects it on the ground that it could be universally recognized. The goal of maximizing average utility (or, for that matter, the goal of maximizing wealth) could be understood and accepted by anyone, whether or not the person is familiar with any given practice. Furthermore, it is a goal for which there are many alternative means. It is, in short, an external good. If these seem rather odd reasons for the rejection of utilitarianism (as they do to me), it is, I believe, because the distinction between internal and external goods, as MacIntyre formulates it, is not really relevant. The fundamental contrast is between treating institutions as means only (which utilitarianism does) and treating them as ends also. Institutions as ends need not be ends unique to those institutions; they can equally well be approximate and concrete expressions of more general ends. The fundamental contrast is not between internal and external goods but between two very different forms of rationality. On the one hand, we have the rationality characteristic of the process of choosing the best means to given ends. The instrumental-teleological view of institutions (represented by the dominant normative traditions in public policy analysis and management, such as utilitarianism and normative economics) is based on this view of rationality. On the other hand, however, we also have the rationality characteristic of the development of mathematics and science. *Generalization* is a key process in that development. A new theory X is a generalization of the old theory Y if it can be shown that Y is an approximation to a special case of X. This is, for example, the relation between Newton's and Einstein's theories. Aspects of policies and institutions can be seen not just as means to given ends but as approximate expressions of more general ends. We show them to be rational (explain them or justify them) when we explicitly formulate these more general ends. This alternative kind of institutional rationality has not been studied in the past and is little understood. But I believe it is the most promising path for those who would want to develop an evaluative position more complex than the simple instrumentalism of the utilitarians and the wealth maximizers.

This brief discussion of Dworkin's and MacIntyre's positions shows, I hope, how much of a simplification it is to think of human preferences as taking the four forms outlined at the beginning of this section. Let me end, however, by returning to this fourfold contrast. People will differ in the weight they give to each of the four types of judgments. Figure 2 gives illustrative labels to the prototypical value positions in four categories, each representing people who are extreme in the weight they give to one of the four forms of evaluation.

I believe we can go beyond a simple statement of human diversity in this matter. A more significant hypothesis can be suggested. In order to state it, I need to introduce the notion of a second-order preference that has been much discussed recently (Frankfurt, 1971; Hirschman 1982; Sen, 1977). A second-order preference is a preference among different preference orderings. Often people prefer to have preferences other than the ones they actually have. An alcoholic who wants to reform is an obvious example. More generally, people not only have preference orderings among different courses of action but also preference orderings among different preference orderings. And it is possible, though often difficult, to discover what these second-order preference orderings are.

My hypotheses are as follows. First, second-order preference orderings favor those first-order preferences for which institutions and actions are more nearly ends in themselves, rather than means

ACTION/ INSTITUTION AS	EVALUATION	
	Impartial	Self-interested
End	Deontological morality	Selfish self-actualization (cf. Maslow, 1954)
Means	Teleological morality	Selfish materialism

Figure 2. Four value positions.

only. Second, second-order preferences favor more nearly impartial first-order preferences over self-interested ones. If both of these hypotheses are correct, then second-order preferences impose a partial ranking on the four pure types of value positions identified before. The position that is both impartial and treats institutions and actions as ends in themselves, that is, deontological morality, is ranked highest. The position that is self-interested and instrumentalist, that is, "selfish materialism," ranks lowest. The other two positions are intermediate (and are not ranked relative to each other by the two hypotheses).

The obvious question about these hypotheses is: *Whose* second-order preference are we here talking about? The answer is not clear. Their precise limits are not known, so we might as well be daring (though tentative): These are universal second-order preferences. If this true, or even approximately true, or at least true in an important class of cases, then deontological theories of justice clearly have a special claim to our attention. Teleological theories, utility maximizing and wealth maximizing among them, have a weaker claim.

Conclusion: Research on Responses to Policies and Institutions

The study of the problem of evaluation of institutions and policies, as I have sketched it here, is part of a more general field of study concerned with the incidence of evaluative responses to policies and institutions. These evaluative responses can be divided into two types: those expressed in willingness to sacrifice and those expressed in consent and objection. The questions that can be raised about them range from the problem of institutional stability far removed from normative evaluation to various empirical problems closely integrated with a number of reasonable normative theories.

The most simpleminded question one can ask in this area is this: What will be the effect of a given change in policies or in institutions on the incidence of evaluative responses? The question is simpleminded because it ignores at least two kinds of complexity: the complexity of the consequences of responses and the complexity of the causes of responses. If we take account of these complexities, we are led to deeper and more interesting questions.

To take account of the complexity of the consequences of responses, we will have to consider at least two difficult questions.

First, what radicalizes objections? What transforms objections to a part of the system into objections to the whole system? Clearly, the consequence of objections will be quite different depending on how radical the objections are. The tendency to radicalization depends in large part on the extent to which a system is perceived as tightly causally connected (so that you cannot change one part without changing the whole). But it depends on other factors as well. The consequences of evaluative responses (and objections in particular) will depend also (obviously) on the strength of the resources available to those who object, compared to the strength of those willing to defend a system from objections. The availability of resources and the skill in their use is then the second question that needs to be considered. The stability of an institution or policy will depend not simply on the incidence of evaluative responses to it; it will depend also on how radical are these responses and how powerful are the resources backing them up.

When we take account of the complexity of the causes of responses to institutions or policies, we move in the direction of problems of normative evaluation. These responses are in part a product of self-interest and in part impartial. They are in part a consequence of treating the institution or policy as a means to some end and in part a consequence of treating it as an end in itself, thus differentiating questions of institutional effectiveness from those of institutional "legitimacy" (cf. Lipset, 1960). To the extent the responses are impartial, they can be influenced by the various kinds of impartialities: the morality of love, the morality of convention and compromise, and the morality of right. The morality of right will produce different results depending on whether the conflict to which it is applied is a conflict of interest or a conflict of principle. Only in the first case are we likely to obtain normative criteria of the utilitarian type. The more we try to disentangle this complexity and attempt to study some of these factors in abstraction from the others the closer we will come to questions of normative relevance. This seems to me one of the most promising paths to take if we want to develop empirical research and theory that matter to normative questions and that therefore can help to integrate theory and practice. It is also a path that allows for, and even requires, the recognition of the limits and of the complexity both of human minds and of human institutions. The future of research on justice relevant to public policy lies, I believe, in that direction. It will combine empirical research with formal modeling, as the utilitarians aimed to do. But it will also increasingly take account of both complexity and limits.

References

Ackerman, B. (1980). *Social justice and the liberal state*. New Haven: Yale University Press.

Ackerman, B. (1984). *Reconstructing American law*. Cambridge: Harvard University Press.

Alves, W., & Rossi, P. (1978). Who should get what? Fairness judgments of the distribution of earnings. *American Journal of Sociology, 84*, 541–564.

Anderson, P. (1976). *Considerations on Western Marxism*. London: Verso.

Arrow, K. (1951). *Social choice and individual values*. New Haven: Yale University Press.

Barry, B. (1965). *Political argument*. London: Routledge & Kegan Paul.

Becker, G. (1976). *Economic approach to human behavior*. Chicago: University of Chicago Press.

Brams, S., & Fishburn, P. (1982). *Approval voting*. Boston: Birkhauser.

Brickman, P. (1977). Preference for inequality. *Sociometry, 40*, 303–310.

Burke, E. (1967). *Reflections on the revolution in France*. London: Dent & Sons. (Originally published 1790)

Calabresi, G., & Bobbitt, P. (1978). *Tragic choices*. New York: Norton.

Coleman, J. (1982). The economic analysis of law. In J. R. Pennock & J. Chapman (Eds.), *Ethics, economics, and the law: Nomos XXIV* (pp. 83–103). New York: New York University Press. (Reprinted in M. Kuperberg & C. Beitz (Eds.). [1983]. *Law, economics, and philosophy* [pp. 102–121]. Totowa, NJ: Rowman & Allenheld).

Deutsch, M. (1975). Equity, equality, and need: What determines which value will be used as the basis of distributive justice? *Journal of Social Issues, 31*, 137–150.

Dworkin, R. (1977). *Taking rights seriously*. Cambridge: Harvard University Press.

Dworkin, R. (1980). Why efficiency? *Hofstra Law Review, 8*, 563–591. (Reprinted in M. Kuperberg & C. Beitz [Eds.]. [1983]. *Law, economics, and philosophy* [pp. 123–140]. Totowa, NJ: Rowman & Allenheld)

Frankfurt, H. (1971). Freedom of the will and the concept of a person. *The Journal of Philosophy, 68*, 5–20.

Fried, C. (1978). *Right and wrong*. Cambridge: Harvard University Press.

Frohlich, N., & Oppenheimer, J. (1984, March). *Tests of Rawls's distributive justice: An experimental first cut*. Paper delivered at the Stanford Conference on the Political Economy of Public Policy, Stanford, CA.

Galston, W. (1980). *Justice and the human good*. Chicago: University of Chicago Press.

Habermas, J. (1970). Towards a theory of communicative competence. *Inquiry, 13*, 360–376.

Habermas, J. (1973). Wahrheitstheorien. In H. Fahrenbach (Ed.), *Wirklichkeit und Reflexion: Walter Schulz zum 60. Geburtstag* (pp. 211–265). Pfullingen: Neske.

Harsanyi, J. (1955). Cardinal utility, individualistic ethics, and interpersonal comparisons of utility. *Journal of Political Economy, 63*, 309–321.

Harsanyi, J. (1976). *Essays on ethics, social behavior, and scientific explanation*. Dordrecht, Holland: Reidel.

Harsanyi, J. (1982). Morality and the theory of rational behavior. In A. Sen & B. Williams (Eds.), *Utilitarianism and beyond* (pp. 39–62). Cambridge: Cambridge University Press.

Hayek, F. (1973). *Rules and order: Vol. 1. Law, legislation, and liberty*. Chicago: University of Chicago Press.

Hirschman, A. O. (1970). *Exit, voice, and loyalty.* Cambridge: Harvard University Press.

Hirschman, A. O. (1982). *Shifting involvements.* Princeton: Princeton University Press.

Hochschild, J. (1981). *What's fair? American beliefs about distributive justice.* Cambridge: Harvard University Press.

Jasso, G., & Rossi, P. (1977). Distributive justice and earned income. *American Sociological Review, 47,* 639–651.

Kellet, A. (1982). *Combat motivation: The behavior of soldiers in battle.* Hingham, MA: Kluwer-Nijhoff.

Kohlberg, L. (1979). Justice as reversibility. In P. Laslett & J. Fishkin (Eds.), *Philosophy, politics, and society* (Fifth Series, pp. 257–272). New Haven: Yale University Press.

Kuperberg, M., & Beitz, C. (Eds.). (1983). *Law, economics, and philosophy.* Totowa, NJ: Rowman & Allenheld.

Leventhal, G. S. (1976). The distribution of rewards and resources in groups and organizations. In L. Berkowitz & E. Walster (Eds.), *Advances in experimental social psychology* (Vol. 9, pp. 91–131). New York: Academic Press.

Lipset, S. M. (1960). *Political man.* New York: Doubleday.

Lucas, J. R. (1980). *On justice.* Oxford: Clarendon Press.

MacIntyre, A. (1981). *After virtue.* Notre Dame: University of Notre Dame Press.

March, J., & Simon, H. (1958). *Organizations.* New York: Wiley.

Maslow, A. (1954). *Motivation and personality.* New York: Harper & Row.

McCarthy, T. (1981). *The critical theory of Jürgen Habermas.* Cambridge: MIT Press.

McPherson, M. (1983). Want formation, morality, and some interpretive aspects of economic inquiry. In N. Haan, R. N. Bellah, P. Rabinow, & W. M. Sullivan (Eds.), *Social science as moral inquiry* (pp. 96–124). New York: Columbia University Press.

Mead, G. H. (1934). *Mind, self, and society.* Chicago: University of Chicago Press.

Merton, R. (1968). *Social theory and social structure* (3rd ed.). New York: Free Press.

Michael, R., & Becker, G. (1973). On the new theory of consumer behavior. *Swedish Journal of Economics, 75,* 378–395.

Miller, D. (1976). *Social justice.* Oxford: Clarendon Press.

Miller, H., & Williams, W. (Eds.). (1982). *The limits of utilitarianism.* Minneapolis: University of Minnesota Press.

Mishan, E. J. (1976). *Cost-benefit analysis: An informal introduction* (3rd ed.). New York: Praeger.

Moore, B., Jr. (1970). *Reflections on the causes of human misery.* Boston: Beacon Press.

Neumann, J., Von, & Morgenstern, O. (1944). *Theory of games and economic behavior.* Princeton: Princeton University Press.

Popper, K. (1945). *The open society and its enemies.* London: Routledge & Kegan Paul.

Posner, R. (1977). *The economic analysis of law.* Boston: Little, Brown.

Posner, R. (1981). *The economics of justice.* Cambridge: Harvard University Press.

Rae, D., Yates, D., Hochschild, J., Morone, J., & Fessler, C. (1981). *Equalities.* Cambridge, MA: Harvard University Press.

Rawls, J. (1971). *A theory of justice.* Cambridge: Harvard University Press.

Rescher, N. (1966). *Distributive justice.* Indianapolis, IN: Bobbs-Merrill.

Schelling, T. (1963). *The strategy of conflict.* New York: Oxford University Press.

Selznick, P. (1969). *Law, society, and industrial justice.* New York: Russell Sage.

Sen, A. (1970). *Collective choice and social welfare.* San Francisco: Holden Day.

Sen, A. (1977). Rational fools. *Philosophy and Public Affairs, 6,* 317–344.

Sen, A., & Williams, B. (Eds.). (1982). *Utilitarianism and beyond.* Cambridge: Cambridge University Press.

Simon, H. (1969). *The sciences of the artificial.* Cambridge: MIT Press.

Simon, H., & Stedry, A. (1968). Psychology and economics. In G. Lindzey & E. Aronson (Eds.), *Handbook of social psychology* (Vol. 5, pp. 269–314). Reading, MA: Addison-Wesley.

Smart, J. J. C. (1973). An outline of a system of utilitarian ethics. In J. J. C. Smart & B. Williams (Eds.), *Utilitarianism: For and against* (pp. 1–74). Cambridge: Cambridge University Press.

Smith, A. (1976). *The theory of moral sentiments.* Indianapolis, IN: Liberty Classics Edition. (Originally published 1759)

Soltan, K. (1982). Empirical studies of distributive justice. *Ethics, 92,* 673–691.

Soltan, K. (in press). *Causal theory of justice.* Berkeley: University of California Press.

Stigler, G., & Becker, G. (1977). De gustibus non est disputandum. *American Economic Review, 67,* 76–90.

Stinchcombe, A. (1968). *Constructing social theories.* New York: Harcourt, Brace, and World.

Stokey, E., & Zeckhauser, R. (1978). *A primer for policy analysis.* New York: Norton.

Sztompka, P. (1974). *System and function.* New York: Academic Press.

Walzer, M. (1983). *Spheres of justice.* New York: Basic Books.

Watkins, J. W. N. (1963). Negative utilitarianism. *Proceedings of the Aristotelian Society* (Supplement), *37,* 95–114.

Author Index

Subject Index

A